How Did I Get Here?

BARBARA DE ANGELIS, PH.D.

How Did I Get Here?

*Finding Your Way
to Renewed Hope and Happiness When
Life and Love Take Unexpected Turns*

ST. MARTIN'S GRIFFIN

NEW YORK

The author gratefully acknowledges permission to use the following excerpts:

"American Tune" copyright © 1973 Paul Simon. Used by permission of the publisher: Paul Simon Music.

Excerpt from the poem *The Guest House*, by Jalad ud-Din Rumi, translated by Coleman Barks.

Excerpt from *I Will Not Die an Unlived Life*, by Dawna Markova, used with permission of Conari Press, an imprint of Red Wheeler/Weiser, Boston, Mass., and York Beach, Me.

From *I Heard God Laughing*, by Daniel Ladinsky. Copyright © 1996 by Daniel Ladinsky. Reprinted by permission of the author.

Excerpt from *Hush Don't Say Anything to God: Passionate Poems of Rumi*, translated by Shahram Shiva. Copyright © 1999 with permission by Jain Publishing Co.

www.stmartins.com

Library of Congress Cataloging-in-Publication Data

De Angelis, Barbara.
    How did I get here? : finding your way to renewed hope and happiness when life and love take unexpected turns / Barbara De Angelis.
        p. cm.
    ISBN 0-312-33015-4 (hc)
    ISBN 0-312-33016-2 (pbk)
    EAN 978-0-312-33016-3
    1. Self-actualization (Psychology) 2. Change (Psychology) I. Title.

BF637.S4
[D395 2005]
158.1—dc22

2004063287

First St. Martin's Griffin Edition: May 2006

10   9   8   7   6   5   4   3   2   1

In memory of

Luna

my moon goddess

my ancient friend

my love teacher

Contents

PART THREE

Roads to Awakening

How Did I Get Here?

Introduction

I don't know a soul who's not been battered
Don't have a friend who feels at ease
Don't know a dream that's not been shattered
Or driven to its knees.
—Paul Simon, "American Tune"

All of us find ourselves, at one time or another in our lives, facing the unexpected. We arrive at places we never planned to be, confronting obstacles we did not expect to encounter, feeling emotions we did not expect to feel. We don't recognize the destination at which we find ourselves as one we chose to travel to, yet, inexplicably, there we are. Somehow our plan for how we intended things to turn out seems to have been replaced by a set of circumstances we could never have imagined, let alone wished for:

- A relationship we thought would last forever ends, and we are suddenly and painfully alone.

- A job we counted on vanishes, and we feel lost, with no purpose or direction.

- Our health or that of a loved one, which has always been good, becomes threatened by illness or disease.

- Events beyond our control destroy our financial well-being.

Or perhaps a moment comes when we see our life as it really is instead of seeing it as we want it to be. To our great dismay, we realize that it is time for a change:

- Our relationship has become passionless, and sex is something we remember doing months or even years ago.

- Our job has turned into something we are utterly bored with or, worse, that we dread.

- We have the house, the family and the business for which we worked so hard, but somehow we feel a sense of deep dissatisfaction and disconnection.

What is happening? We are standing face to face with what amounts to a gap—*the gap between where we thought we'd be and where we actually are, between our expectations of what we hoped would happen and what has actually happened, between the life we planned and the life we inhabit.*

What makes these moments so difficult and disturbing is not simply that we are facing problems or emotionally rough times. Each of us has braved, battled and survived many challenges in our lives. What's different about these particular experiences is that along with the pain there is a sense of bewilderment, a sort of shock, a disconnect between what we thought we knew to be true and what is actually occurring. **We feel as if we are waking up as a stranger in our own lives.** We don't recognize the landscape, the emotions, the circumstances as anything vaguely resembling those things we had expected. And so we find ourselves asking: **"How did I get here?"** No immediate answer comes to us. It is the presence of this question and the absence of answers that plunges us headfirst into a spiritual and emotional crisis.

· · ·

"Last month my husband told me he wants a divorce. After fifteen years of marriage, it's over. I can't believe I am losing him, that our family is being torn apart. The house, our friends and the life we built—it's all going to vanish. I am so furious at him for destroying my dream. What am I supposed to do now? How can this be happening to me? How did I get here?"

. . .

"I've been dreading going to work for a while now, and I finally admitted the truth to myself: I'm miserable because I hate what I do for a living. I don't understand how this can be happening—I spent years in medical school studying to be a doctor, and I have a really successful practice. This is what I planned to do since I was a teenager, and I'm good at it. But I just don't want to do it anymore. I'm really frightened—I can't start over at fifty-six with two kids in college. **How did I get here?"**

. . .

"I just bought my first house, but it's thrown me into a deep depression—I'm forty-two years old and still single, and here I am living alone in this beautiful home. This is not the way things were supposed to turn out for me. I was supposed to be with the man of my dreams and have had children by now. **How did I get here?"**

. . .

"From the outside, my marriage looks perfect. I have a wonderful, successful husband and two terrific kids. But I feel like I have this awful secret—my husband and I haven't had sex in two years. Somewhere along the way, we lost our passion. Now we're living like two polite but celibate roommates. I'm too young to have no sex life. **How did I get here?"**

. . .

Perhaps as you read this now, the same question resonates with something inside you. Perhaps it is a question that has not yet been formed into words in your consciousness. Perhaps it is more of a feeling, an unnamed anxiety, an undefined restlessness, a confusing sense of discomfort with your life, your work or your relationship. Something doesn't feel quite right, but you don't know what it is.

Or perhaps there is no mystery about what is bothering you. Perhaps like the people quoted here, you, too, are facing an unexpected turn on your life journey. You remember starting out with a clear idea of where you wanted to go, but now you look around at where you've ended up, and it's nothing like what you'd expected. This is not the way you thought things would turn out. This is not the way you thought you'd feel about your husband or wife, your marriage, your job, your life. Whispered to you from the depths of your being, you hear the question:

"How did I get here?"

This book is about that question, and it is a guide to help you discover the answer.

It is a book about the power this question has to profoundly transform your life and your relationships.

It is a book about recognizing and understanding these significant transitions, turning points and crossroads on your path, so that you can move through them with less fear, confusion and guilt, and more grace, dignity and vision.

It is a book about the suffering you unknowingly create for yourself and the price you pay in work or relationships when that question calls to you from within and you ignore it. It is about how to find the courage to ask yourself that question and to pay attention to the answers you receive.

It is a book about how to avoid getting stuck in places and phases that are meant to be temporary and how to use those places as a springboard for regeneration and rebirth.

It is a book about how asking and answering this question will release you from the fear, confusion and grief that so often keep us trapped in the past or stagnating in the present and will free you to finally move forward into a life of more purpose, joy, true contentment and renewed passion.

What do you do when you realize that your old map has taken you in a direction you no longer wish to travel? What do you do if you come to a fork in the road and don't know which way to go? How do you map out the next part of your journey? How do you redesign the blueprint of your life? How do you begin again?

How Did I Get Here? is about finding your way to renewed

hope and happiness from wherever you are. It is about opening these doorways into personal transformation that often come disguised as dead ends. It offers you ways to take charge of your circumstances by first assessing where you are, how your map got you here, and dealing with all the issues that come with finding yourself at unexpected places, whether in your outer world or your inner world. It acts as a navigational handbook, guiding you through the thick jungle of thoughts and emotions that we must often pass through in order to emerge on the other side of a powerful rebirth. It will help you to understand the map you've been using, and invites you to craft a new one by moving beyond the question **"How did I get here?"** to **"What are my choices?" "What do I do now?" "How do I move forward?" "Where is it that I want to go?"** And it will support you in discovering the answers.

. . .

I've always said that my books don't come "from" me but "through" me, for that is my experience. I don't choose the topic I am going to write about; it chooses me. It is as if a book compels itself to be written, calling to me from wherever books come from, thrusting its way into my awareness, exclaiming: *"Here I am! Pay attention to everything I have to say, and write it down carefully."* For me, writing a book has always been my answer to that call.

How Did I Get Here? is just such a book, born of a powerful, insistent voice that demanded to be heard. Its message is for me, for you and for many of the people you know and love. It is a guide for all of us on the path of self-discovery in these changing, turbulent times. It is the most important book I believe I can write, and one to which I deeply relate, for it has emerged from my own very eventful journey, a journey characterized by frequent and revolutionary transformation, both personally and professionally.

I have not had an easy life. It has been riddled with disappointments and disillusionment, barraged by loss and betrayal, and besieged with far too many occasions for sadness and despair. I've been forced to learn how to navigate through the unexpected again and again . . . and again.

I know what it's like to have the person you love walk out on you with no explanation, never to return. I know what it's like to lie in bed next to someone who used to love you and feel him cringe when you try to touch him. I know what it's like to have shared a dream with someone and helplessly watch that dream shatter into pieces until there is nothing left. I know what it's like to work hard in your career to build something you believe in, only to have someone come along and try to destroy it all. I know what it's like to lose the comforts and abundance you waited so many years to enjoy, and wonder if you will ever have them again. I know what it's like to come face to face with circumstances and events that seem horribly unfair, as if you are being singled out for extra suffering by some Universal Power. I know what it's like to feel your heart sink as you realize that once again you are going to have to start over, and not be sure that you have the energy, the courage and the faith to begin one more time.

I have known all of these challenges and more. And so, you see, it was for my own emotional survival that I've had to become an expert at change, to define and understand the mechanics of personal transformation, to figure out how to go through profound transitions without falling apart or going crazy. Whenever I'm interviewed about my career and am asked who or what has had the most meaningful influence on my work, I always give the same answer, to the great surprise of the interviewer: "Painful experience— it turned me into a transformational specialist." In no way do I think of these hurts, heartbreaks and challenges as mistakes. After two decades helping hundreds of thousands of people, I've come to know with total certainty that the opposite is true: *My life has been "transformationally eventful" for a reason.*

. . .

L et me tell you a story:
     Many years ago, when I was just beginning to teach seminars to small groups of people in Los Angeles, a friend of mine invited me to meet someone he called "a very unusual man."

"This guy may seem eccentric," my friend explained, "but he has a real gift—he can look at you for just a minute, and tell you your purpose in life."

I was intrigued by this claim, and being a student of metaphysics and spiritual growth, I decided I had to pay a visit to this interesting fellow.

"You won't be sorry!" my friend promised.

The next evening he drove me to an apartment complex near the ocean where I was to wait with dozens of other curious seekers for my two-minute encounter.

The moment arrived, and I was ushered into a small room in which the mystical seer was seated on a couch. He was dressed in a dark and well-tailored suit ornamented by a shiny gold pocket watch. To be honest, he looked more like a dapper, well-fed English gentleman than someone who could see into a person's destiny. He asked me my name and welcomed me, all the while peering intently into my eyes.

Suddenly, in a deep booming voice, he blurted out, *"Rhinoceros!"*

"Rhinoceros—what does that have to do with my purpose in life?" I thought to myself. "What is he telling me—that I should become a zoologist or move to Africa?" I was completely perplexed and began to wonder if my friend had set me up for a practical joke.

"Excuse me?" I replied. Perhaps I hadn't heard him correctly. He did have an odd accent. Maybe he'd said "Philosopher," and I thought I'd heard "rhinoceros." I could relate to that answer. Now my mind was racing. *"Rhine"* something. Could he have said "rhinoplasty"? Wasn't that the term for a nose job? I'd always liked my nose. Did he think I needed plastic surgery?

"Rhinoceros!" he exclaimed again, interrupting my reverie, this time with a huge smile. I shook my head, trying to indicate that I had absolutely no idea what he was talking about, and got up to leave when he practically shouted, *"The horn! The horn of the rhinoceros! That is what you are, my dear."*

I sat back down. "Please explain what you mean," I asked.

"You are the horn of the rhinoceros, the part that boldly sticks out and precedes the body. The horn goes first, you see. The horn is strong, courageous, relentless. It explores the unknown and the

dangerous; it pierces the barriers; it removes all obstacles in the path of the rhinoceros so he can travel safely and with greater speed. The horn confronts the problems on the path, and lets the body of the rhinoceros know about them. It helps him change direction, protects him from harm. The horn is the teacher, the body the follower. The horn gets scarred so the body can be saved from calamity. The horn discovers the truth on the path so the body can move forward in freedom."

I listened with fascination to everything he was telling me. According to him, this was my purpose in life, to be the horn of the rhinoceros. I thought I understood part of what he was describing. Even in those early years of working with people, I had a sense that my own experiences were going to be the core of the knowledge I had to offer others. I remember thinking that what he said resonated with something I felt inside, but I wasn't sure exactly what that something was. Still, I was glad I had come to see him. As I thanked him and walked toward the door. He waved his finger at me with great emphasis, calling, *"Don't forget—you are the horn!"*

I didn't forget, but I didn't completely understand, either. Little did I know that my career as "the horn" was just beginning.

Over the next ten years, my destiny as a teacher unfolded in ways I couldn't have imagined. Along with writing, lecturing and creating television shows, I founded a large personal growth center in Los Angeles to which people from all over North America came to participate in transformational seminars. One evening just as a weekend seminar was coming to a close, I was approached by a man in the class.

"I want to give you something," he began. "It's to thank you for everything you did for me and all of us this weekend, but even more, to thank you for everything you've gone through in your own life. If you hadn't been brave enough to love so deeply, and to try again no matter how much you've been disappointed, you would never have learned all these lessons you've taught us. If you hadn't taken so many risks, and weren't willing to be so honest, I wouldn't be standing here right now feeling so inspired. I saw this in a gift shop and for some reason it reminded me of you—maybe because you had the guts to go through so much first so you could teach us about it."

He held out his hand, and in it was a small silver-gray object made out of pewter. **It was a rhinoceros.**

Shaking my head in amazement, I took the rhinoceros from him. All at once, the words of that unusual man flashed through my mind like lightning, words I hadn't thought of for years:

"The horn goes first."

Standing there in the seminar hall, looking back on the many years that had passed since my visit, I suddenly understood that the curious man I'd met had been a remarkable visionary after all. He had indeed seen my future and known my purpose. Everything he'd said about the rhinoceros horn accurately described the reality of my life. Time after time, I had undergone painful, often dramatic personal lessons and then, through my work, shared the wisdom I'd uncovered so that others wouldn't have to experience the same disappointments; I had lived boldly and courageously, and had many scars on my heart to show for it. I taught not *in spite of* the experiences in my own life, but *from* the experiences in my own life. Rather than disqualifying myself as a teacher because of the less-than-perfect scenarios in my personal history, I was deeply grateful for them, using the wisdom and clarity I gained to design emotional maps I could pass on to others, guiding them through the complex and challenging labyrinths of life's difficult times.

The pewter rhinoceros has been with me now for more than fifteen years. It sits on my computer stand, the strong little horn proudly turned upright. It has kept me company in my many solitary hours spent writing, contemplating, creating. It is looking at me right now, reminding me of who I am.

Some facts I've learned about the horn of a rhinoceros:
It is reported to have powerful medicinal, even magical properties, and because of this has been an object of great value for thousands of years.

*It was used to detect the presence of poison, and thus to pro-
tect the one who owned it from harm.*
  And if by chance it breaks off, it grows back as good as new.

. . .

Why have I shared this story with you? Because whether you
realize it or not, you, too, have a "rhinoceros horn." It is the
part of you that has started over even after you have failed. It's the
part of you that has loved even after you've been hurt. It's the part
of you that plunges ahead into change even though you may be terrified. It's the part of you that feels your way forward in the darkness even though you may not be sure exactly where you are going.
It's the part of you that is your courage—courage to question,
courage to be willing to hear the answers, courage to look within,
courage to pick up this book and hope that what you read will
teach you more about yourself.

I honor that courage in you. In the pages that follow, I offer
you everything I've learned about harnessing your own natural
courage and using it to navigate through whatever you are facing
on your journey. **Changing, transitioning and transforming in life
aren't things that just happen to you. They are skills you can actually learn and master.** Instead of feeling like a victim of circumstances, and wishing or praying that the challenges you're facing
will soon be over, you can actively participate in the process you're
going through and use it for tremendous growth, insight and awakening.

This knowledge is what has sustained and liberated me, and it is
the heart of the message that permeates this book:

**It is not how you deal with what is expected
and hoped for in your life
that ultimately defines and elevates you
as a human being.
Rather, it is how you interact with the unexpected,
how you brave the unanticipated,**

how you navigate through the unforeseen and emerge, transformed and reborn, on the other side.

At first it is disconcerting, even disturbing, to find yourself in circumstances you did not expect, let alone desire. However, once you get over the shock of being in an unexpected place in your life, you have a precious opportunity to explore all the new pathways that place has led you to. *Unexpected destinations hold the promise of unexpected experiences, unexpected wisdom, unexpected awakenings, and ultimately, unexpected blessings.* Finally, this is what this book is about—moving forward and seeing the future with new, hopeful eyes.

This is what will reveal your true strength, your true greatness. This is what will make you wise. This is what will give you the experience of true passion, true joy, and ultimately, true freedom.

Offered with love,

Barbara De Angelis
Santa Barbara, California

PART ONE

How Did You Get Here?

✒ 1 ✑

Digging Deep for Wisdom

*It may be that when we no longer know what to do,
we have come to our real work,
and when we no longer know which way to go,
we have begun our real journey.*
—Wendell Berry

We begin with a story:

A man who always considered himself clever and capable died at the end of a long life and found himself on The Other Side, waiting for an interview with God. Time seemed to be nonexistent as he sat alone in a light-filled room with no ceiling, no walls and no floor, trying to adjust to his new circumstances and anxiously anticipating his upcoming meeting.

"What will God ask me?" he wondered. "I was never much of a deep thinker. What if he asks me about the meaning of life? I won't know what to say. I could always tell the truth—I was too busy being successful to think about that kind of thing. After all, my accomplishments have been very impressive—even God should be able to see that!"

With intense concentration, he tried to recall all of the marvelous things he had achieved during his lifetime, so he'd be ready to talk to God.

Suddenly God appeared before him and sat down in the other empty chair. "It is good to see you," God began. "So tell me, how do you think you did?"

The man breathed an enormous sigh of relief to hear that this was the question God was asking the one question he was sure he could answer. Feeling confident, he began: "Well, I thought you might ask that, so I've made a short list of my accomplishments. I wanted to own my own business and become financially successful, and I did that. I wanted to have a good marriage, and I stayed married until my wife passed away—fifty-two years! I wanted to put my two children through college, and I did that. I wanted to own a luxurious home, and I did that. I wanted to learn to play golf and break ninety, and I did that. I wanted to buy a boat, and I did that. Oh, I can't forget this one—I wanted to donate money to worthy causes on a regular basis, and I did that." The man felt quite satisfied with himself, hearing his own list. Surely God was going to be impressed.

"So in conclusion," he declared, "I would say without wanting to sound immodest or anything, that I did very well, considering I accomplished most of the things I set out to do. But of course, since you're God, you knew all of this already."

God smiled kindly at the man. "Actually, you're mistaken."

"Mistaken?" the man asked. "I don't understand."

"You're mistaken," God repeated, "Because I wasn't paying much attention to the goals you achieved."

The man was taken aback. "You weren't? But I thought . . ."

"I know," God interrupted. "Everyone thinks the better their life went, the more successful their life was. But it doesn't work that way up here. I didn't pay attention to all the times you got what you expected and hoped for, for that wouldn't teach me much about what you were learning in your earthly existence. *I was watching you most closely during all those difficult times when you encountered the unexpected, the things you did not plan on or want to happen. You see, it is how you dealt with these that reflects the growth and wisdom of your soul."*

The man was stunned. He'd gotten it all wrong! He'd spent his whole life trying to do everything right. "How should I know what lessons I learned from life's difficult moments?" he wondered in a panic. "I never even liked to admit I had any problems. What am I supposed to tell God now?"

For a moment, he was speechless, but never one for enjoying defeat, he soon got a second wind of energy. 'Don't just sit here!!' he told himself sternly. 'You never lost a negotiation on earth. Try again!" Gathering up all of his confidence, he began once more:

"Well, to tell the truth, God, I was just being polite before. Actually—and don't take this personally—my life was hell! What hardships, what disappointments, what tests and trials! Let me tell you about the time my mother-in-law moved in with us for months. And then there was the time I passed two kidney stones—at once! And my youngest son, he was nothing but trouble. And my wife, don't get me started on my wife or I'll be here forever. . . ."

"Take your time," God replied. "I'm in no hurry . . ."

In one way or another, we are all like the man in my little fable. We do our best in life to get things right. We make lists, set goals, study, train, learn, commit to our relationships and our dreams, get organized, pray, affirm and problem-solve, hoping to experience the happiness and success we imagine for ourselves. Yet, inevitably, all of us arrive at times when, in spite of how steadfastly we have worked, how well we have prepared, how deeply we have loved, things still don't turn out the way we thought they would. *No matter how hard we try, we cannot plan for the unexpected.*

Whether these difficult surprises come in the form of small setbacks, horrible shocks, or gradual, painful awakenings, the result is the same: We end up face-to-face with jaw-dropping moments of unwelcome revelation when we realize to our great dismay that we are living a life that does not look like the one we wanted. And unlike the man in the story, we are usually not so quick with a snappy comeback to the unexpected. More often, we are left shaken, disoriented and desperate for answers.

After two decades of writing, researching and teaching about personal transformation, I've come to the conclusion that so much of the pain, confusion and unhappiness most people—including myself—struggle with comes from our encounters with the unexpected, in both our outer and our inner worlds. Try as we might, these encounters are inescapable, an inevitable part of being human. Even though each of us secretly suspects that we're the only one whose life is so off-course or inexplicably unsatisfying, and that everyone else is deliriously happy, the truth is something quite different: **All of us are lifetime warriors in a prolonged battle— with change, with reluctant endings and scary beginnings, with assessments and reassessments, with more moments of disappointment than we care to count.**

Recently I was going through some old notebooks I'd kept from college, and I discovered a page I'd written in my early twenties listing my personal goals and dreams. As I read the items on my life wish list, I was astonished by two things. The first was that I had indeed accomplished many of the goals I'd set for myself over thirty years ago: to become a published author, to move to California, to teach people about relationships and personal growth, to create a community of conscious people, to travel to exotic places around the world, to study with wise spiritual teachers, to fall in love and have a beautiful wedding, to own a home, to perform onstage, just to name a few.

The second realization I had as I read the items I'd included was more sobering. I became aware of how many unexpected things had happened to me that certainly were not on my original wish list. I had not written: *Get divorced . . . more than once; be cheated by dishonest business partners; lose lots of money in the stock market; create alliances with companies that go bankrupt; Battle unfair lawsuit; brave slanderous attacks by jealous colleague; lose dear friends to cancer.* I certainly didn't remember setting *these* events as goals, yet they had occurred just the same.

Then it dawned on me—like so many of us, like the clever man in the fable, I had always believed my challenges would lie in overcoming the obstacles to my goals. But I was wrong. My deepest turmoil has had nothing to do with the things I *didn't* get, but rather with *the things I did not expect,* and got anyway.

It is *not* the things we want and don't get
that are the source of our greatest tests and trials—
it is the things we *do get that we did* not *want*
and never expected.

. . .

"It's a dangerous business, Frodo, going out of your door,"
he used to say. "You step into the Road, and if you don't keep
your feet, there is no knowing where you might be swept off to."
—J. R. R. Tolkien

Here is how it happens—*you are going along with your life, minding your own business, when suddenly "it" hits you, and you are stopped dead in your tracks.* What is "it"? "It" may be an event that forces you to pay attention to the realities of your life that you've been avoiding: the passionless marriage you pretend is better than ever until one day your husband walks out; the distant daughter you tell everyone is really doing fine until you discover the stash of heavy drugs in her drawer; the sixty-hour-a-week job you claim to love in spite of how exhausted you always are, until you collapse with a heart attack one day.

Sometimes "it" is loss—loss of love, loss of money, loss of trust, loss of security, loss of job, loss of health, loss of opportunity, loss of hope. Sometimes "it" sneaks up on you quietly, like a thick fog slowly rolling in over your life, so that nothing seems clear to you anymore and you feel lost. And sometimes "it" isn't sneaky at all, but bold. You know "it" is coming—you can feel it breathing down your neck. Still, you tell yourself it will miss you, like those asteroids that hurtle toward the earth but never quite get a direct hit. But you are wrong. "It" does not miss.

"It" is whatever you didn't want to happen, whatever you didn't want to feel, whatever you didn't want to face, whatever you didn't want ever to have to experience. "It" is always unexpected, even when you've watched "it" approach every step of the way, because there is simply no way you can imagine that you will feel so scared or confused or miserable or disheartened or stuck or out of control—until you do.

I've concluded something else about the unexpected—it always seems to show up at the worst moment. Like a guest with horrific timing who, year after year, invariably chooses the most hectic weekend of your life to come stay with you, the unexpected has a knack for choosing just the wrong instant to arrive. Doesn't "it" always seem to happen when you are already the most stressed, overextended and under pressure, when you have just announced that you cannot take one more thing going wrong? *"I can't deal with this right now!"* you lament. *"This is not a good time."* But let's be honest—is there ever a "good" time for the arrival of unwelcome events, insights, or challenges? Of course there isn't.

The unexpected is always inconvenient.

The great statesman Henry Kissinger summed it up succinctly: "Next week there can't be any crisis. My schedule is already full."

. . .

The most precious opportunity presents itself when we come to a
place where we think we can't handle what is happening
It's too much. It's gone too far. . . . There's no way we can
manipulate the situation to make ourselves come out looking
good. No matter how hard we try, it just won't work.
Basically, life has just nailed us.
—Pema Chodron

When I was in elementary school, I had a teacher whom I will
call Mrs. Rhodes. She was one of those educators whose
choice of vocation was a mystery, for it was obvious, even to me at
the tender age of eight, that she possessed an intense dislike of children that she made no attempt to hide from us. Determined to re-
taliate, the little boys used to amuse themselves by tossing wads of
spit-covered chewing gum at her head when she wasn't looking,
hoping to implant their peppermint-scented weapons in her tight
mass of metallic-gray pin curls.

Mrs. Rhodes was a stickler for accuracy in all things, and one
of her favorite ways to torture us was to excoriate us for our mistakes in front of the entire class. I will never forget the time I became the "victim of the day." We were in the middle of a writing
exercise, and I raised my hand to make a request.

"Yes, Barbara?" Mrs. Rhodes said scowling at me.

"May I please be excused to go to the bathroom?" I said in as
soft a voice as possible.

"Don't mumble—I hate mumblers—what did you say?"

"I said, may I please be excused."

"Why?" Mrs. Rhodes barked.

"I can't believe she is going to make me say it," I thought to
myself. I took a deep breath. *"Because I want to go to the bath-*
room."

Everyone in the class began to giggle. "SILENCE!" Mrs.
Rhodes shouted, and then she turned back to me. "Barbara De Angelis," she said, "So you want to go to the bathroom. Well, we all

want lots of things, don't we, class? But we don't get them! No ma'am."

"Please, Mrs. Rhodes," I pleaded, "I just want to go to the bathroom."

Mrs. Rhodes walked up to the blackboard, picked up a piece of chalk, and in large letters wrote the word *W-A-N-T*. "Do you see this word, class?" she squawked. "To use it is to express a personal preference, as in 'I want to play on the swings', or 'I want to eat a candy bar.' It does NOT mean the same thing as this word—" and she spelled out *N-E-E-D*. "This word does not express a personal preference, it expresses what one considers a necessity, a requirement, an emergency, as in, 'Mrs. Rhodes, I need to go to the bathroom.'"

She turned back toward me. I had sunk down as low as I could in my metal chair, for even my little eight-year-old brain knew what was coming next. My classmates were giddy with anticipation, drunk with the joy of watching someone other than themselves be mortified.

"So, Barbara, would you like to rephrase your statement?" Her voice oozed with disdain.

Like a confession given to the enemy only under prolonged torture, the words came tumbling reluctantly out of my mouth: "I . . . I . . . nee . . . need to go to the bathroom!"

"Well, then," she said with a sick smile, "why didn't you say so? By all means, go. We wouldn't want you to have an *accident*, would we, class?"

I fled. The memory is so vivid, even decades later—my little legs speeding down the empty hallway toward the restroom, the sound of mocking laughter still echoing in the distance behind me. You will be relieved to know that I made it on time. Believe me, so was I.

I share this gruesome tale to make a point crucial to the premise of this book:

When we are uncomfortable enough in life, we will begin to ask questions in an attempt to relieve ourselves of our misery. We will do this regardless of how frightened we are of asking the questions

or hearing the answers. We will question because we can't *not* question anymore. We will question not simply because we want to, but because we need to.

And the question that rises up from deep within us will be:
"How did I get here?"

At times of confusion, crisis, frustration and bewilderment, in moments as Pema Chodron stated above, when "life has nailed us" and we can no longer pretend that things don't feel awful, "How did I get here?" is the most honest, and in fact the only response we can have. When you are squirming in your seat long enough, you have no choice but to finally raise your hand. As I learned from Mrs. Rhodes, when you have to go, you have to go.

. . .

If you get rid of the pain before you have answered its questions, you get rid of the self along with it.
—Carl Jung

The process of gaining wisdom begins with the asking of questions. The word "question" is derived from the Latin root *quaerere,* which translates as "to seek." This same root is the source of the word "quest," to go on a search or a pursuit. Ultimately, that is what a question is—the first step in a search for knowledge, for insight, for truth.

We spend our life looking for answers. This need to know is deeply human and starts in our earliest years. Any parent is aware of this from having listened to the constant inquiries of his son or daughter: "Why is the sky blue? Where do we go when we die? Why do you wear glasses? How does Grandma's voice get in the telephone? Where do babies come from?" As children, we turned to our elders with our questions, confident that they would have answers. After all, they were the grown-ups.

Now we are the adults, the ones who are supposed to have the answers for our own children or grandchildren, for our clients and employees, for our students and patients, for our customers and co-workers. So when we go through challenging times, when we stare into the unfriendly face of unexpected developments that have arrived uninvited into our world, it is hard to admit to others, and even to ourselves, that our minds are haunted by questions for which we have no answers, dilemmas for which we have no solution.

There are questions we formulate with our intellect when we want to solve a problem, for example, "How can I increase sales for my business?" or "How can I lose twenty pounds?" We ponder these questions when we have time or interest, and then when we're tired of considering them, we put the questions in the "To Do" pile in our brain. And then there are the other kinds of questions, the ones that insistently push their way into our awareness and refuse to leave until they are heard: *How did I get here? What's happening to me and my life?* These are questions that we cannot control. They haunt us like stubborn ghosts and will not be dismissed until we give them our attention.

Ingrid Bengis, a wonderful Russian-American writer, speaks eloquently about these moments in her book *Combat in the Erogenous Zone:*

> The real questions are the ones that obtrude upon your consciousness whether you like it or not, the ones that make your mind start vibrating like a jackhammer, the ones that you "come to terms with" only to discover that they are still there. The real questions refuse to be placated. They barge into your life at the times when it seems most important for them to stay away. They are the questions asked most frequently and answered most inadequately, the ones that reveal their true natures slowly, reluctantly, most often against your will.

As travelers on life's path, we are defined by both the questions we ask ourselves and by the ones we *avoid* asking. Just as when we were children, we encounter moments as adults when we need to ask, *"How did I get here?"* in order to become wiser about who we are.

Times of questioning are not moments of weakness, nor are they moments of failure. In truth, they are moments of clarity, of wakefulness, when our quest for wholeness demands that we live a more conscious, more authentic life.

How we deal with these crucial moments of self-inquiry determines the outcome of our journey. Embracing the question, we open ourselves to receiving insight, revelation, healing and the deep peace that can only be achieved when we are not running away from anything, especially from ourselves. Turning away from the voice that asks, "How did I get here?" we close off to growth, to change, to movement, and condemn ourselves to a pattern of resistance and denial. Why? Because the question doesn't disappear. It eats away at us, gnawing on our awareness in an attempt to get our attention.

.   .   .

There is a classic Zen Buddhist story, or koan, about a person who is receiving instruction on passing through the Gateless Gate—the barrier of ignorance—in an attempt to discover the Truth of Life and to achieve the Buddha Nature. The Zen Master warns the student that in contemplating the ultimate question of the nature of reality, he will feel as if he has swallowed a red-hot iron ball that is stuck in his throat—he cannot gulp it down, and he cannot spit it out. All the student can do is to concentrate his full attention and awareness on the question and not give up, and his attainment of truth will be such that it will illuminate the universe.

Of course, this is easier said than done. Most of us do not greet the arrival of burning questions with a Zen-like attitude of acceptance, but rather with the kind of dread we feel when we are about to have painful dental surgery. We get very good at stubbornly ignoring the arrival of crises even while we're in the midst of them. We become experts in negation—*"What red-hot iron ball . . . ?"*—as we reach for our tenth glass of ice water.

Denial is no easy task. It takes a tremendous amount of energy to drown out the insistent voice of *"How did I get here?"* Some people turn to addictions to anesthetize themselves from the constant discomfort caused by the invisible presence of the question. Others distract themselves with everything from work to exercise to caretaking those around them—anything to avoid dealing with the issues they know on some level they must face. And there are those who lapse into "magical thinking," convincing themselves that if they just act as if everything is going to be fine, some mysterious shift will happen and everything will be wonderful again—their estranged husband will suddenly fall back in love with them, their alcoholic wife will miraculously stop drinking, they will wake up one day and all the things they thought were wrong with their life will magically have vanished.

But this is not how it turns out. Instead, when we ignore the questions our inner voice is asking us, we suffer. We become irritable, angry, depressed or simply exhausted. We disconnect from ourselves, our dreams and our own passion. We disconnect from our mate and our sexuality. **We turn off in every sense of the word.**

It takes great courage to allow ourselves to arrive at the place at which we are finally willing to hear burning questions and begin to seek answers. It takes great courage to not freeze up in the face of our fear, to allow these difficult questions and painful realities to pierce our illusions, to shake up our picture of how we want our life to appear and confront it as it really is.

True transformation requires great acts of courage: the courage to ask ourselves the difficult questions that seem, at first, to have no answers; the courage to hold these questions firmly in our awareness while they burn away our illusions, our sense of comfort, sometimes our very sense of self.

When the Questions Outnumber the Answers

For a long time it seemed to me that life was about to begin—
real life—but there was always some obstacle in the way,
something to be gotten through first, some unfinished business,
time still to be served, a debt to be paid. At last it dawned on me
that these obstacles were my life.
—Alfred D'Souza

I used to believe if I did everything perfectly, nothing unexpected would happen to me. I grew into a young adult in the 1960s and began my career in the 1970s. Like many baby boomers, I was fed a sociological diet of confidence, optimism and unlimited possibilities. "Discover your dream, create a plan, work hard to meet your goals, and you will live happily and successfully ever after." This was the prevailing conventional wisdom, and I eagerly put it into practice. By my mid-thirties, I had achieved more than I could have ever imagined for myself. During the next ten years, every area of my life continued to expand in success and personal fulfillment. It seemed that all my efforts, determination and hard work had paid off a thousandfold.

And then things changed. One after another, a series of unpredictable and unwelcome events marched into my life like a rowdy invading army, trampling disrespectfully over my carefully planned and impeccably executed picture of how things were supposed to turn out. Within a few years, several of my long-term personal and professional relationships came to end, some gracefully, others awkwardly, but all very painfully. A number of projects on which I'd worked for quite a while unexpectedly developed into situations that were much less satisfying to me. Some opportunities that I had been excited about turned into complicated ordeals that were uninspiring and unappealing.

Suddenly nothing seemed clear anymore. So many things I had been certain about in my life now appeared murky and confused. People and situations I'd counted on to always be there as my anchors had vanished. Accomplishments that had always given me joy felt flat and tedious. The most frightening thing of all was that I found myself beginning to reevaluate the very success and lifestyle I'd worked so hard to achieve. *Was this really what I wanted to be doing? Was this where and how I wanted to live? Was this who I really was?*

I'd thought I'd been traveling on a well-marked and very straight path, but here I was, standing at an intersection containing so many crossroads that I became dizzy just looking at all of them. I felt disoriented, bewildered and unsure of how to proceed or which turn to take next. How had this happened? Everything had seemed to be on track. And I knew I had tried my hardest and done my best. **So how, then, did I arrive at a time and place in my life where I had more questions than answers?** *How did I get here?*

I was certain about one thing—I desperately needed to get away from my daily routine, to try to sort through the jumble of thoughts and feelings I was struggling to untangle and to find my way back to some kind of inner peace and clarity. I decided to attend a month-long meditation retreat with a spiritual teacher with whom I'd recently begun studying. I knew the answers I sought weren't going to come from anything I did on the outside but rather, as they always had in the past, from turning deep within.

From the moment I arrived at the retreat, I threw myself into the daily routine with my usual determination and firm intention. I followed the schedule diligently, listened to my teacher's lectures with total concentration, and dove into my meditation practice with renewed enthusiasm. I was going to figure all of this out. I was going to get things under control again. I was going to get back to my old self. "You've always been great at fixing things," I reminded myself. "You can do this!"

One day while I was sitting alone having my lunch, a woman on the ashram staff approached me and introduced herself. "My name is Catherine," she said with a warm smile. "I have a message for you."

My heart raced with excitement. This was the moment I'd been waiting for! I had been praying for guidance, asking for direction, and even though I hadn't met privately with my teacher on this particular visit, I secretly hoped that she would know I was struggling, tune in to my agitated state, and point me in the right direction "This is amazing," I thought with tremendous relief. "At last I will know what to do."

"Yes, Catherine," I replied. "I would love to hear the message from our teacher."

"The message she told me to give you is: *It would be good for you to be a nothing and a nobody for a while. You won't learn anything if you keep doing what you are already good at.*'"

I was stunned. This was the message? I was supposed to be "a nothing and a nobody"? I didn't understand. I had worked my whole life to be the opposite: a something and a somebody! All my efforts, all my dreams, all my contributions were about doing whatever I could to make a difference in the world. And she was right—I *was* good at it. I had struggled to become good at it.

I prided myself on being able to juggle ten projects or activities at once, like many women I know. I had always been inspired by the sacred goddess figures in Eastern religions, female deities depicted with multiple arms representing their many spiritual powers and gifts: the Hindu goddesses Durga wielding various weapons of protection to fight off evil, Lakshmi grasping symbols that bestow beauty, wealth and liberation, and Saraswati holding knowledge and self-realization; and the Buddhist goddess Quan Yin doling out mercy, compassion and healing.

My own life reflected this same attempt at superwoman multitasking. I had just recently ended a year during which I had been writing, producing and appearing in my own national television show; writing and promoting a new book; running a full-time seminar business; traveling around the country giving workshops; appearing regularly on other TV programs; and working on developing several new projects. I was, indeed, a many-armed wonder.

Ever since I can remember, I have always had a dread of coming to the end of my life and feeling disappointed in myself that I hadn't done the things I believed I was meant to do. I'd been driven to achieve, not only for the reasons we all set goals—the desire to accomplish something significant and meaningful—but also because I was terrified of not doing enough, not making enough of a contribution, not using enough of my talents. Now I was being told to do the opposite—to be "a nothing and a nobody for a while," to focus on something I had feared and fled from.

There are moments in our lives when someone speaks the truth in a way that finally compels us to hear it. For years people close to me had said: "You should slow down" or "You should take some time off—you're working much too hard." I knew that these were healthy suggestions, but the inner voice that had always pushed me to achieve and excel warned, "You can't stop, even for a moment. You will lose momentum, you will lose ground, and then what will happen to your career, your dreams, your vision for yourself? If you slow down, you won't get enough done, and you will feel like a failure." This time I had been softened up by the onslaught of so many unexpected challenges one after the other—by loss, by disappointment, by heartache, by my own dissatisfaction and disillusionment. And so when I heard my teacher's words that day, finally I listened.

I returned home and immediately began looking at my life through the revealing lens of the message I had received. *Who was I without all of my achievements and roles, without my hectic schedule and important meetings, without my to-do lists and my interviews? Who was I without an audience, without students, without clients? Who was I when I didn't have to be wise or inspiring, when I didn't always have to have answers for everyone, including myself? What did it mean for me to be a nothing and a nobody for a while? What would that look like?*

Since I was eighteen years old, I had been on a conscious path of growth. In my twenties, long before I began my career, I spent many years immersed in spiritual studies and meditation retreats that lasted for months at a time. From this platform of inner awakening, I launched myself as a teacher and a writer, and it catapulted me into several decades of success, accomplishment and profound fulfillment. Now I found myself at the summit of that success. It was as if I had been climbing a very challenging mountain, thinking that if I reached the highest peaks, I would have accomplished my goal.

So here I stood, having finally made it to the top, and as I gazed around in amazement, my new vantage point brought into perspective another alluring horizon I never knew existed, a horizon I instantly knew I had to explore. I would never have seen this new vista if I hadn't climbed this far and this high. But there it was, glittering in the distance, beckoning to me to come and stand on its majestic peaks, which would offer me yet another enlightening view, and I knew I had to answer its call.

The only way to get there, however, was to do the opposite of what I'd been doing in my long and arduous climb—I needed to descend, to leave this sunny spot from where I could see everything and go back down the other side of the mountain into the cold gray shadows of the waiting valley. Once again, it was time for me to pull back and journey deep within myself. I had come full circle.

In order to do this, I needed time—time to question, time to contemplate, time to find myself outside of my successes and the constant attention and demands that came with them. In order to find that time, I decided to pull back—not to abandon my life and my work totally, but to walk a few steps away from it for a while. I had a very successful personal growth center in Los Angeles where thousands of people a month would come to participate in seminars and trainings, and I closed it down. I had a television show in development, and I decided not to go forward with it. I said no to people and opportunities that had been waiting for my energy and attention.

None of this was easy. It went against all of my deepest instincts, which were to hold on tightly to everything I had and to the promise of more. Instead, I had to let go of my attachment to writing and publishing one new book every year like clockwork, my attachment to never going for more than a few months without being on television, my attachment to giving enough seminars to make a certain amount of money, my attachment to being the biggest something and somebody I could be. Even though I knew I was doing the right thing, I still wasn't completely sure why. I secretly dreaded that rather than coming together in a new way, I was falling apart. *"You're going through a rebirth,"* the courageous part of me whispered reassuringly, but the truth was, I felt as if I were dying.

Digging Deep for Wisdom

One night soon after I began the process of making these dramatic changes, I had a very powerful and vivid dream. In this dream, I was using a large, heavy shovel to dig a deep hole in the middle of a beautifully landscaped garden. The garden was filled with lovely, cheerful flowers, perfectly planted in orderly designs, but I wasn't paying attention to them. I just kept vigorously digging away, dirt flying everywhere, ripping up the flowers with each thrust of my shovel, crushing the delicate petals under piles of stones and debris.

At this point in the dream, a woman came along, and when she saw me digging, she became very upset.

"What are you doing?" she yelled. "You're destroying the garden. It was perfect. Now you've ruined it. What's wrong with you? Why are you doing this?"

I turned to the woman and calmly answered: "I'm digging deep for wisdom." Then I went back to my digging.

The next morning when I woke up and remembered the dream, I realized what an important message it contained from my inner self to me. The garden represented the life I'd known that had looked perfect on the outside, orderly and attractive in every way. There I was digging an enormous hole right in the middle of all that beauty, uprooting the plants and flowers, throwing dirt on top of what had once been so carefully designed and cultivated. This was just what I'd been doing in my waking world—questioning every aspect of my life; uprooting old beliefs, goals and ideas I'd never had the courage to challenge; making some radical changes.

Who was the woman screaming at me? One interpretation was that she represented many people in my life who disapproved of the intense transformational process I was undergoing. To them, I was just making a mess. They preferred the orderly version of Barbara and Barbara's life, the one they recognized and understood. Many people who worked for me or with me had been watching in thinly veiled horror as I chose to do less and less. Some were frightened about what would happen to them if I made too many changes. Would they lose their jobs? Some were angry as I downsized my life—would they miss out on opportunities or income because I was no longer willing to overextend myself or to do things that weren't fulfilling to me? Others, including several friends, were threatened by my very act of questioning, afraid that somehow it would rub off on them, and they would suddenly find themselves wildly digging up their own orderly gardens.

Of course, I knew the deeper meaning of the woman screaming at me: she was a piece of my own self, horribly alarmed at my process of radical questioning that was turning my life upside down. *"What are you doing?"* that part of Barbara was yelling at me. *"You're destroying everything you worked so hard to build. It was perfect. Now you're ruining it. Why are you doing this?"*

Why *was* I doing this? How did I get here with a shovel in my hand, unearthing all the goals and dreams I'd spent so much time planting and protecting? It was a good question with no simple answer. I was reexamining everything because events I couldn't have predicted were forcing me to travel down roads for which I had no map. I was searching for clarity, for revelation, called by something I could not yet define, something compelling me to reassess everything about myself and my life. I was digging because somehow I knew it was time to dig.

Did I know *where* all of this was leading? No, and that was indeed terrifying. I had never liked proceeding without a carefully structured plan, and to do so in my late forties felt foolhardy and even dangerous. But my illuminating dream had reminded me that although I didn't know where I would end up, I did know what I was doing—*I was digging deep for wisdom, allowing the process of questioning and contemplation to penetrate me to my very core, so I could emerge transformed and more in touch with my true self than ever before.*

Living in the Questions

Be patient with all that is unresolved in your heart
And try to love the questions themselves.
Do not seek for the answers that cannot be given
For you would not be able to live them.
And the point is to live everything.
Live the questions now,
And perhaps without knowing it
You will live along, someday into the answers.
—Rainer Maria Rilke

So how do we dig deep for wisdom? Where do we begin? **The first step is simply to admit to yourself that you are where you are—in a place of uncertainty or confusion or doubt, in a time of reevaluation and reassessment, in a process of transformation and rebirth.** Digging deep for wisdom means:

- Being honest about the fact that at least for the moment, your reality is comprised more of questions than answers.

- Allowing these questions to exist, acknowledging that they are piled up around you like mysterious boxes waiting to be opened.

- Not fleeing from the questions anymore, but embracing them, entering into them, and in turn inviting them to take root inside you.

This is not an easy task—facing your questions can be a painful, unnerving process. **Most of us are much more comfortable with answers than with questions, much more at ease with certainty than with doubt.** Too often we flee from our uncertainties, desperate to get back to hard facts, to emotional and intellectual solid ground, to things we are sure of. We do not like to linger too long in the land of "I don't know."

This reluctance is understandable. *We live in a society where absolute certainty, even if it is biased, narrow-minded, or just plain incorrect, is rewarded*—just turn on the television or radio and you will be barraged with countless examples of this: opinion-ated commentators who never waver from their rigid points of view; talk show experts who harshly preach black and white and nothing in between; reality TV contestants who win the prize, the date, the proposal or the job, often because they display the most un-wavering, arrogant assuredness. *Doubt, hesitation, introspection— these don't sell. Certainty does.* Is it any wonder, then, that we learn to bury our uncertainties beneath a thick covering of avoid-ance and denial?

Imagine going to a party and seeing an acquaintance you haven't been in touch with for some time. "How have you been?" your friend asks. Most likely, you wouldn't answer, "Actually, I'm confused. You see, I am in a period of deep questioning." To con-fess that you are unsure or disoriented would make you feel vul-nerable, insecure, exposed. To admit, even to yourself, that you are feeling lost can cause you to feel that somehow you have failed.

This is precisely what will happen when you begin to dig deep—at least in the privacy of your own heart. You will begin to question. You will begin to ask yourself, "How did I get here?" You will feel disoriented, vulnerable, even lost.

But you are *not* lost.

"How did I get here?" has a "here" in it.
You *are* somewhere.
Just because you may not yet understand where
that somewhere is does not mean you are in the
wrong place, or even necessarily off course.
To arrive at a place we don't recognize is indeed
a legitimate destination in life.

· · ·

A few weeks ago I met my friend Molly for coffee. I hadn't seen her for a while, and Molly, who is a single parent with a rebellious fifteen-year-old daughter, proceeded to tell me about her latest crisis. Molly's daughter had been lying to her, hanging out with some very troubled kids, and neglecting her schoolwork. "I am so stressed out," Molly confessed. "After all I have done for Jenna, how can she treat me like this? It makes me feel like I am a bad mother and that I haven't done a good job. And of all times— I am so swamped at work. I've decided I'm giving myself two days to process all of this, and then I'm putting it behind me."

As Molly finished her story, she noticed that in spite of my best efforts to disguise it, I was smiling. "What?" she said. "I know you, Barbara, and when you get that look on your face, it means you're about to tell me something you are seeing about my situation that I haven't figured out yet! Come on, I can take it."

"You're right," I admitted. "Actually, I was just thinking how much you remind me of myself. Throughout my life, I have always been in a rush to find the answers, to have the realizations, to get to certainty about everything. When you said that you were giving yourself two days to process your problems with Jenna, and no more, it cracked me up! It's like insisting, 'I will extract the lesson from this now even if it kills me!' Whenever I have done this, it's my way of trying to get things back under control. I am in a hurry to find solutions because I feel so uncomfortable lingering in the problems."

Molly laughed. "You're right. Part of me just wants to get this whole thing over with. But I know it is going to take a lot longer than two days to deal with how I am feeling. I just can't help wishing there was a way to speed it up."

We all know how Molly feels. After all, we live in a society defined by our hunger for instant gratification. When I enter the word "instant" into my computer's search engine, I get **25,700,000** references, instantly, of course! From instant soup to instant replay, instant Internet connections, instant messaging, instant credit, instant face-lifts, instant erections—we want what we want *now*. We are impatient, not very good at waiting for long-term results and possessing little tolerance of things that take time.

Wouldn't it be wonderful if we could set a time limit on our trials and challenges, like those speed-dating services that offer meetings with twenty people in one evening? This would be "speed-growing"—go through your issues and learn your lessons in one day! Unfortunately, as you already know too well, this isn't how it works.

Digging deep for wisdom isn't something that goes quickly or can be rushed through. It is more a state of mind than a set time period during which we decide to examine our lives. The process of digging deep can last for months, even years. It requires that we stay with the questions, and that we not be in a hurry to answer them.

Digging deep for wisdom takes time because it is not simply a search for some facts or answers, but a search for the truth. Our usual skills of problem-solving, finding answers and figuring things out will not do. Digging deep requires authentic and prolonged contemplation.

Contemplation has been an integral part of the path of all great philosophers and spiritual seekers since the beginning of recorded history. The word *contemplation* contains the Latin root *templum,* meaning a piece of consecrated ground, a building (temple) of worship, a place devoted to a special and lofty purpose. The dictionary defines contemplation as "to view with continued attention." In traditional religious understanding, contemplation is an inner communion with God, as opposed to prayer, which might be called a conversation with God.

For our purposes, we can think of contemplation as **the act of paying continued attention to that special place within us from which truth, insight, revelation and enlightenment spring forth. When you dig deep for wisdom, you contemplate your questions, your unexpected challenges and your turning points, and you wait**

for answers. As Rilke put it in his beautiful poem, you "live the questions."

Have you ever gazed at the night sky, hoping to see a shooting star? You stare for a long time at the twinkling constellations, the distant galaxies, and they are beautiful, but no shooting stars appear. Suddenly, just when you think your search has been in vain, you see it—a brilliant flash of light arching across the heavens. It is spectacular, and something worth waiting for.

Contemplation is slow. It takes time. It can be uncomfortable, exasperating, even painful. But if you are patient, your wait will be worth it.

· · ·

Several months ago, I decided to replant a portion of my garden. I'd tried to get flowers to grow in this part of the yard, but for some reason they always died. I thought perhaps the soil needed to be weeded and turned over, and that this would help the new flowers to thrive, and so I hired a man to dig up all of the weeds and prepare the soil for planting.

The gardener began his work early one morning, but within minutes he came to the front door and asked me to look at something he'd found while digging. "See this?" he said pointing into the freshly dug hole. "These are the old roots of a tree that must have been here at one time. It was a big tree, because these roots go very deep and spread out for ten feet in each direction. No wonder you had a hard time getting things to grow."

There is an old saying: *"Dig deep enough and you will hit something."* Usually we hit something we didn't know was there, something unexpected. There are many things within you waiting to be discovered like the old roots buried beneath the soil in my garden. Perhaps some are roots of old emotional issues that you did not know existed, ones that have been keeping you blocked that you can now dig out and remove. Others are rare, important treasures, excavated from the depths of your being, priceless gems of understanding and clarity that, once revealed, will change you forever.

**Digging deep for wisdom means being
willing to unearth anything and everything
you find inside yourself. It means digging
until you discover precious treasures of insight,
revelation and awakening, that which
transforms you, that which you could
have never known was there unless you
were forced to dig.**

. . .

I n my first year of college, I began practicing daily meditation,
and soon after I attended a six-month meditation intensive with
a renowned spiritual master in order to become a meditation
teacher myself. The course consisted of some lectures, studies and
yoga, but the core of the process was meditating for up to twelve
hours a day. I'd always had profound experiences meditating for
twenty minutes at a time and never found it challenging, but this
was different. Sitting in meditation for this many hours was like
taking the biggest shovel in existence and digging deep, deep, deep
within myself. I would be fine for the first half-hour, but then I
would hit a roadblock of thoughts and emotions that seemed to
prevent me from going deeper. "I must be doing this wrong," I would
think to myself in a panic. "Maybe I should get up for a while,
and then start over when I am more relaxed." The truth was that I
was terrified to go deeper. What if I found out something about
myself I didn't like? What if I didn't have a core of peace and happiness inside?

My teacher was a wonderful storyteller with a compassionate,
joyful presence. He took great delight in the tales he told us, as if
he himself had never heard them before. Every evening after our
long day of meditation and study, he would gather us together to
sit with him, and for several hours he would share his wisdom, answer questions, and of course tell marvelous stories.

One night a young man stood up and complained that he had
been feeling restless and distracted during meditation, as I had,

and he confessed that whenever this happened, he would get up, walk to the store in the nearby village, read through some magazines, and then when he felt less agitated, he would walk back and sit down again to meditate. When my teacher heard this, he laughed and laughed as if he'd never heard anything so amusing in his life. When he finally stopped laughing, he shared this story with us, his version of a classic ancient parable. Here it is as I remember it:

Once there was a farmer who was in desperate need of water to save his crops from dying. The drought had lasted for several years, and so with no hope of rain, he decided to dig a well. He began digging, and hour by hour the hole got deeper and deeper, but still no there was no water to be found. "I must be digging in the wrong spot," he concluded at the end of the day, "for all I've discovered in this hole are rocks and tree roots." Exhausted and discouraged, he returned home.

The next morning, shovel in hand, the farmer began digging again, this time in a different spot. As the sun blazed overhead and he dug deeper, again he found no water. "This second hole is as bad as the first," he muttered to himself as he climbed out of the dry hole as the sun was setting.

Day after day the farmer dug one hole after another, and each time he would get the same results—no water. And as he laid down his shovel and walked home, head hung low, he would wonder if he was crazy to believe there was any water to be found. "Am I doomed to spend my life digging and finding nothing?" he moaned to himself. "I must be cursed in some way."

One day a traveling wise man was passing by the farmer's plot of land. To his surprise, he saw the farmer, shovel in hand, digging a hole surrounded by twenty similar holes.

"What are you doing, my friend?" the wise man asked the farmer, who was knee-deep in dirt.

"I'm digging a well—at least, I'm trying to." the farmer replied in a forlorn voice. "But so far, I have only had horrible luck, for I keep hitting rocks and roots—everything but water."

"Dear sir, you will never find water digging that way!" the wise man said kindly.

"What other way is there?" asked the farmer.

"Your efforts at digging are valiant, but they are not working," explained the wise man. "You start digging in one place, and after ten feet when you don't find water, you stop, go to another place, and start to dig all over again. However, the water table in this village starts at least twenty feet below the surface."

"*Unless you dig longer and deeper, you won't find what you are searching for. Stay in one place, dig down deep and don't stop when you get discouraged.* Be patient and just keep digging, even when you hit the hard rock-filled soil. If you persist, I promise you will find the water you seek."

Again and again throughout my life, I have returned to the important lesson contained in this story. Digging deep for wisdom means not giving up when you hit the rocks of discomfort and frustration within yourself. It means being patient and persistent, not stopping at the first insight, the first revelation, the first breakthrough, but going even deeper. It means having trust—that beneath all of your questions and confusion there are answers, there is clarity, there is awakening.

Most of all, digging deep for wisdom means having faith—faith that beyond the hard roots of your fear, your doubts and your disappointments, you will discover a wellspring of wisdom and illumination more powerful and more exquisite than anything you could ever have imagined.

Together, we will dig.

✑ 2 ✑

Turning Points, Transitions and Wake-up Calls

The beginning of wisdom is to call things by their rightful names.
—Chinese proverb

When what was once predictable is nowhere to be found . . .

When what you thought you knew to be certain now appears blurred and distorted . . .

When what you were holding that seemed solid now dissolves as dust in your hand . . .

Then you have arrived at a place on your journey whose name you need to know.

Each of us is offered powerful moments when life invites us, or perhaps quite dramatically forces us, to stop and pay attention to who we are, where we are, how we arrived there, and where we need to go next. Sometimes these moments of awakening manifest as the coming to a crossroads on our path, when we are presented with a choice to turn this way or that. Sometimes, rather than a distinct moment of recognition, we experience these changes as a gradual transition that we slowly or suddenly become aware of, even though it may have been happening for a while. And sometimes there is nothing at all subtle or gradual about these moments—they reveal themselves to us in the form of dramatic wake-up calls, emotional or spiritual emergencies, events or circumstances that force us, ready or not, to face a reality we would rather not face.

No matter how we encounter these periods of intense questioning or difficulty, one theme is the same: our world, which was comfortable, safe and familiar, now seems foreign and even frightening as events, either from inside or outside us, shake up our old beliefs, our usual ways of existing, relating and behaving. We look at the challenges stacked up before us and suspect that we will not be able to survive this time with our "old self" intact, that we will not be able to find our way through the dizzying maze of emotions with anything less than total, brutally honest self-reflection.

"What is happening to me?" we wonder. **We have arrived, unmistakably, at the "here" in "How did I get here?" but where exactly are we?** This is not simply a rhetorical question, but a sincere and urgent cry of the soul, a longing to identify these unfamiliar experiences that fill us with fear, confusion or uncertainty. We really need to know what is going on. We need to give it a name.

. . .

From the earliest recorded times, human beings have had the desire and need to name things. Scientists say that language is the very thing that makes us human. There are 6,500 living languages in the world today, with many more that have died out. That means there are billions of names and words in existence. Estimates of the number of words in the English language alone start at around three million and go up from there.

What is the purpose of all these words? The traditions of many ancient peoples and religions believed in the power of the word or name to bring things into being. *In the beginning was the Word, and the Word was with God, and the Word was God,"* says the Christian Bible. In the Hindu tradition, *AUM* is the sacred symbol that is the source of all existence, the cosmic sound from which the world arose and within which the world exists. In ancient Egypt, it was essential that the parents name their child as soon as he or she was born—otherwise it was as if the child did not exist. To name something made it real. This belief is still an integral part of modern culture—we already have more than enough words, yet we continue to create new ones as we experience, identify and name new realities—in the English language alone, *we still invent up to 20,000 new words and terms a year.*

In ancient times, since names were so important, it was believed that to discover the name of something was to gain power over it and control it: to know the name was to possess the thing. Thus in many cultures the names of deities were kept secret and never revealed. Early writings about the magical arts declare that once a magician knew the name of a thing, he held the secret to its magic. In other traditions, to use the sacred names, as in the recitation of mantras, was to empower oneself, to take on the qualities of the name of the Divine, and to achieve liberation.

In our own lives, we've all had experiences of the power that naming has to define things and actually shift our experience of them. There is a big difference, for instance, between someone you are dating, and someone who is suddenly named your "boyfriend" or "girlfriend." Now, the relationship is "official." Of course, it becomes more so when the "boyfriend" is renamed "husband." You enjoy working for a company, but when you are named manager or assistant vice-president, you suddenly feel more important, and you proudly carry business cards with your new "name." Even unpleasant circumstances became more tolerable when they are named: Your son who does poorly in school, loses his temper with his siblings, and can't seem to pay attention may be seen as a "problem child" until his symptoms are properly named, and he is diagnosed with Attention Deficit Disorder. Now you know the cause of his behavior—it is no longer an exasperating mystery—and you can get him the help he needs.

**Names help us to locate where we are
on our outer and our inner journey,
and to identify *who we are.*
When we are entering unknown territory,
encountering unrecognizable landscapes,
or arriving at unexpected turning points,
we need those names the most.**

The Power of Naming

Not everything can be cured or fixed,
but it should be named properly.
—Richard Rohr

When I was twelve years old, my maternal grandmother told me a priceless story that I have never forgotten. "Mom-Mom," as we called her, was born in southern Russia in 1901, at the height of the Russian Empire's persecution of the Jews. When she was just four, she and her entire family escaped to America to avoid being killed in one of the pogroms that were sweeping through Russia and settled in the then-sleepy seaside town of Atlantic City, New Jersey. The children in the family soon adapted to their new life in the United States, but Mom-Mom's mother, my great-grandmother Ida, spoke no English and, like many immigrants of that time, clung to her old-fashioned ways. Mom-Mom explained:

"One Saturday morning when I was almost thirteen years old, I went as usual to play on the beach with my friends. We only lived a few blocks from the ocean, and I spent as much time there as possible. After a while I got hungry, and decided to go home for lunch. While my mother was making me a sandwich, I stepped into the bathroom to 'go,' and when I wiped down there, to my horror there was blood on the toilet paper! Blood, and lots of it! I shrieked and began to cry. Something was terribly wrong. I'd heard about people with horrible diseases, and now it was happening to me. I was dying.

"Your great-grandmom Ida must have heard my sobbing, and she came running into the bathroom. '*Maidelah*,' (that's Yiddish for little girl), she said, 'what's wrong? Why are you crying?'

" 'Look, Mama, I'm dying.' With a trembling hand, I held the blood-soaked toilet tissue up so she could see the evidence of my impending demise.

"Your great-grandmom Ida's eyes got very wide for a moment,

and then she smiled. 'Darling, wipe your tears—you're not dying,' she crooned as she dried my damp face with her handkerchief.

" 'I'm not?' I asked her in disbelief. 'Then, Mama, why am I bleeding down there?'

" 'Oh, that, well, I'll tell you what that is,' my mother said with a knowing look on her face. I leaned forward in anticipation, anxious to hear her explanation for my horrible plight. '**A crab bit you at the beach!**' she announced triumphantly.

" 'A crab? Bit me down there? But Mama, I didn't feel anything.'

" 'Well, you were probably so busy playing or swimming, you didn't notice, but that's what it was . . . just a crab. Now you wait here, and I am going to get you a special bandage to put on, because you might bleed for a little while longer.' And within a moment, my mother came back with a long, thick white bandage unlike anything I'd ever seen, and she showed me how to attach it to a special belt so it wouldn't fall out of my underpants."

By now I was laughing so hard listening to my Mom-Mom Lilly's story that I could hardly breathe. "Did you really believe that it was a crab?" I asked her, giggling.

"What did I know about these things?" my grandmother answered. "No one talked about it back then, and certainly not my mother, God rest her soul. I just put on the 'bandage' and waited for the crab bite to heal. And five days later, to my surprise, it did. Of course, I stayed away from the beach for the next month, terrified that I'd get bitten again and that this time it would be worse, and the bleeding wouldn't stop after five days."

"How did you finally figure out that you'd gotten your period?" I inquired.

"Four weeks later, like clockwork, I started bleeding again, and since this time I knew it couldn't be a crab, I confronted my mother, and she finally told me that I had become a woman and explained the whole thing. Oh, I was very angry with her, but to be honest, I was also quite relieved. I'd spent the whole month sure that I did indeed have an incurable disease, but that my mother didn't have the heart to tell me. So to finally hear her give my 'ailment' a name, to know it was normal and discover that I wasn't the only one going through it, lifted a huge cloud from my mind."

· · ·

I always loved my grandmother's telling (and retelling!) of this story. However, as the years passed and I grew older, I realized that the tale, which amused me so much as a young girl, contains something more important than just humor and sweet, irreplaceable memories. It teaches a lesson about the power and importance of giving a name to our experiences.

Naming has several important values:

1. *Naming allows us to step back from our experience, to begin to observe it more objectively.*

By giving something a name, we create a sense of separation from ourselves and whatever it is we are experiencing. I am not going crazy because I am experiencing mood swings—my body is going through PMS. I am not a bad parent because my child is screaming and refusing to cooperate—he is going through the "terrible twos." I do not have a bad attitude because I dread going into work each day—I am unhappy with the cutthroat atmosphere at my place of business, and need to make a change. Identifying the experience contains it. Knowing the name makes it somehow more manageable. We become more tolerant and less anxious because we know what it is we are dealing with.

Recently I was scheduled on a very early flight out of town and ordered a cab to pick me up at four-thirty the next morning to take me to the airport. When the driver, Henry, arrived, I thanked him for getting up before dawn so I could catch my plane. "Oh, I'm not starting my shift," he explained. "This is the end of it. I like to work in the middle of the night." I asked him why, and over the next twenty minutes, he told me the following:

In the late 1960s, Henry had spent two years in heavy combat on the front lines of the war in Vietnam. He had seen every kind of horror imaginable and lost many of his buddies. Finally he was sent home. "I was a mess," he confessed. "My girlfriend had waited for me, but when we were reunited, I couldn't feel any emotion. Everything made me jumpy, and the smallest noise, like someone scraping their chair across the floor when they got up or the clatter of dishes in the sink, threw me into horrible anxiety attacks. Worst of all, I couldn't sleep—I would lie awake for hours at night, sweating and hyperventilating. I thought I had gone off the deep end."

It took several years before Henry found some professional help and could give a name to his demon—post-traumatic stress disorder. "You can't imagine what a relief it was to be able to call what I was going through 'something,' he told me. "It didn't really take away my symptoms, but at least I knew what they were, and they didn't freak me out so much. Anyway, that's why I work nights—I still have trouble sleeping in the dark, so this job works out perfectly."

I felt very emotional listening to Henry, proud of him for persevering in trying to make some sense of what had happened to him in Vietnam, but sad for so many other veterans who didn't get the help they needed to name their inner monsters as the first step in taming them. One thing Henry said really stuck with me: "When I was in 'Nam, I thought I was going through the worst thing anyone could in life. But coming home was even harder. At least over there I knew who the enemy was. I knew what I was supposed to do. But to be back here and feel crazy and frightened and angry all the time, and not know why or what to do about it—*that was like an enemy I couldn't ever see or find, but one that never went away*." When the doctors helped Henry name his inner enemy, he could finally begin to find some peace.

2. Naming can calm our irrational fears and dispel the illusion that we are going through something unusual or uncharted.

If naming what we are going through is helpful and affirming in good times, then it is all the more crucial in challenging or confusing times. Imagine, for example, how terrified we would be if the phases in life were not named and explained to us. One day we would notice hair beginning to grow in strange places on our bodies, and we would think we were going through some bizarre transmutation instead of entering puberty. A woman would notice her belly growing bigger and bigger, and would be terrified that she was terminally ill rather than pregnant. My poor grandmother thought she was bleeding to death until her experience was given a name.

This is the second power that naming has—it identifies our experience as something people have gone through before us, and by doing so, it dispels our sense of isolation, connecting us, tangibly or intangibly, with others. "I am not the only one this has ever happened to," we think with a sigh of relief. "I am not alone." And somehow, in an undefined but unquestionable way, this makes whatever it is we are facing more bearable.

3. Naming allows us to arrive more fully in our reality.

Whether a reality is pleasant or unpleasant, exciting or frightening, once we name it, we claim it as ours. It is as if we are pointing our finger at a spot on a map and declaring, "I am 'here.'" Even if "here" isn't a place we want to be, even if we are unhappy to find ourselves at this particular "here," still, we feel a comfort and security in giving it a name, rather than having no idea where we are. Naming it makes it more of a known quantity rather than an unknown, and therefore locates us in time and space. The anxiety of wondering where we are is replaced by a certainty that clears our minds and in some mysterious way calms our hearts.

I remember reading an interview with an American soldier who had been captured and held as a prisoner of war in the Middle East some years ago. When the reporter asked him about the conditions of his captivity, the soldier explained that the hardest part had not been being beaten or kept in a tiny cell with very little food and water, or even feeling afraid that he would never see his wife and children again. The most terrible moments, he confessed, were when he first woke up in a completely dark room and had no idea where he was, how he'd gotten there or what was going to happen to him. He'd been knocked unconscious during a skirmish with the enemy, who had then transported him to a prison while he was still unaware that he'd been captured. For what seemed like several days, they left him alone in the dark pit. Reality of any identifiable sort had vanished, and he felt as if he had gone crazy. When his captors finally revealed themselves and moved him to a cell, he felt a strange sense of relief, as if his sanity came flooding back. At least now he could name what was happening: "*I am a prisoner. I have been captured by the enemy. I am in some secret camp. I am in a filthy cell. I have two guards who take turns watching me.*" As terrible as these realities were, they were his. According to this brave soldier, those realities became his link to sanity and psychological survival.

Here is the point I have been making:

To go through powerful times of questioning and challenge, and leave our process unnamed or, worse, mislabeled, is to condemn ourselves to feeling frightened, disoriented and as if we are somehow doing something wrong. We must give our times of transformation and rebirth their rightful names.

. . .

Every individual existence is brought into rhythm by a pendulum to which the heart gives type and name. There is a time for expanding and a time for contraction. One provokes the other and the other calls for the return of the first. Never are we nearer the Light than when the darkness is deepest
—Swami Vivekananda

It is easy to see where you are when it is light out. It is easy to discern your location when there are signs posted identifying it. But what happens when we come to places on our path that we don't recognize, or have experiences that we haven't heard described? What do we do when we, like the brave soldier, find ourselves frightened and disoriented and totally in the dark? How do we know where we are? *What name do we give to something or someplace we don't understand?*

For most of us, the name we choose is *crisis*:

"My boyfriend just broke up with me, and I'm in an emotional crisis."

"I just quit my job, and I'm in a career crisis."

"Our daughter has started hanging out with the wrong crowd and taking drugs, and we're going through a family crisis."

"I was just diagnosed with diabetes, and I'm going through a health crisis."

"Crisis" is often the word we use to describe unwelcome experiences or situations that we wish were not happening. After all, when asked if the word *crisis* defines something negative or positive, most people would answer negative. Who wants to go through a crisis, even a minor one? Who looks forward to a crisis? "Can't wait until my next crisis! This one was over way too soon," is probably a statement you will never hear. Many of my friends and acquaintances would describe themselves as "in crisis" right now, going through divorce, illness, career challenges, difficulties with their children, loss of parents, financial hardships, and I am certain that not one of them would speak about these experiences with fondness.

Is crisis the proper name for these times? What does the word actually mean? I was surprised and intrigued to discover that the original and literal meaning of the word *crisis* does not denote a negative condition, in spite of the fact that this is its common usage. The etymology of *crisis* traces the word back to its Greek origins from the root *krinein—to separate, to decide, to judge.* The Greeks first used the word *krisis* in a medical sense to describe the turning point in a disease, and then to indicate a moment in judicial proceedings when a certain direction was taken. A *"krisis"* was a critical juncture, a time of decision.

I like this expanded definition of crisis. It resonates with my own experience, and those of thousands of people with whom I have worked over the years:

What feels like a crisis is, in truth, *a turning point,* a moment of judgment, of decisiveness, of transformation, when we have an opportunity to separate from an old reality and chart a new course.

Perhaps, then, the naming of our challenges needs to begin with these questions:

What if that which you've been calling *a crisis, a mess, a disaster, a bummer, chaos, confusion, mayhem or madness* is actually something else?

What if there is something here for you to do other than just endure and survive, rather than feeling condemned to resist or suffer, rather than concluding that you are stuck or thwarted or lost?

What if this place in which you find yourself is not a roadblock, but a true *krisis*—a turning point?

Turning Points and Transitions

You seldom sit at a crossroads and know it is a crossroads.
—Alex Raffe

One of my first solitary adventures as a young girl was taking the train from the small suburb of Elkins Park, Pennsylvania, where I had lived since I was born, to downtown Philadelphia. I would walk to the station on Saturday morning, buy my round-trip ticket, and wait with excited anticipation for the train to arrive—I

was going into the city all by myself! I didn't do anything very original when I was in town, just things that seemed exotic to a twelve-
year-old in the innocent times of the early 1960s. I'd go to Sam
Goody and look through the latest records. I'd stop at Woolworth's
drugstore and admire all of the cosmetics, potions and makeup
that I knew I would be using one day soon. I'd order a root beer
float and French fries for lunch at a soda fountain. Then I'd walk
back to the station and wait for the train to take me home. I never
ventured more than three or four blocks from the main terminal,
just to be sure I didn't get lost, but as far as I was concerned I
might as well have been thousands of miles away in Paris or Venice
or some other magical city—for at least a few hours, I was free and
completely on my own.

It doesn't take much for me to recall the sights, sounds and sen-
sations of those expeditions downtown, particularly those memo-
rable train rides. I can still feel the rough wool fabric of the hard
seat, scratchy against my legs as I pressed my face against the soot-
covered window and watched the landscape appear to stream by. I
can see the conductor standing in the aisle punching my ticket with
his silver implement, the tiny white circle floating to the ground
to join hundreds of others in a carpet of paper snow. Most of all,
I can hear the conductor's singsong voice as if triumphantly announcing the name of each station as we approached: *"Melrose
Park! . . . Tabor! . . . Fern Rock! . . . Wayne Junction! . . . North
Broad Street! . . . Last stop Reading Terminal downtown Philadelphia!"* As each station was announced, I knew I was getting closer
to town, and my exhilaration would grow. Those names became
like a string of soothing mantras I would recite in my head. I had
never been to those places and had no idea what they were like, but
the repetition of each one reassured me that I was, indeed, on the
right train, going to the right place.

Those were simple times and simple journeys. Now, many years
and many challenging times later, I look at my life odyssey and
shake my head at how different it has been from that comforting
and predictable ride from Elkins Park to downtown Philadelphia.
There have been no announcements identifying what emotional

terrain I was traveling through, no warnings to let me know I was about to enter this or that station, no one telling me when I was supposed to get on or when I was supposed to get off, no schedule to consult to make sure I didn't miss the right train.

It would be so much easier, wouldn't it, if our lives were like my childhood train rides, and if those important transitions we needed to be aware of were announced in advance. I can just imagine how it would sound: *"Relationship Reevaluation coming up in three months!"* . . . *"Next stop, Career Change!"* . . . *"Now approaching Health Crisis!"* . . . *"Arriving at Turning Point—all passengers must change trains. . . ."* But this is *not* how it is.

How, then, do we know we have arrived at a turning point in our life? How do we correctly identify and name what feels like a crisis as actually an important crossroads?

First, it helps to understand that not all turning points look or feel the same.

Turning Points That You Know Are Probably Coming

Some turning points are obvious. You know you're approaching them, even if you don't admit it to yourself or to anyone else. You've been unhappy in your job for too long, and the company itself is being reorganized, with firings about to be announced. You and your romantic partner can't agree on the direction you want your relationship to go, and all you're doing is arguing. Your elderly mother has been less and less able to care for herself, and is beginning to need full-time care. In spite of what your instincts tell you in these situations, you still hope for some last-minute miracle, something to change the course of events so you won't have to get to a difficult crossroads, make a painful decision or a face a frightening change.

Even though you may dread these turning points, you are not completely surprised when they happen. They are what we might call the "expected unexpected." *On some level, you have been aware of the transition taking place all along.* This doesn't make the experience any easier or less agonizing, but you are a bit more prepared than you would have been if you hadn't seen it coming. Therefore, you can navigate through it more easily. In these cases, the lament *"How did I get here?"* is more of a rhetorical question. You *do* know how you got to where you are. *You're not disoriented—just disappointed.*

Recently I bumped into an old friend of mine at a fund-raiser. I hadn't seen or spoken to her for some time and noticed she was there without her husband. I knew their marriage had been extremely rocky, and had always sensed that it was just a matter of time before they split up.

"How are you?" I asked, suspecting I knew what the answer would be.

"I've been better," she replied with a grimace. "It's been a really difficult year. Larry and I separated last summer."

"I'm so sorry. I realize how hard that must be."

"Thanks, but I know you aren't surprised," she admitted. "Neither was I, actually. I kind of knew it was coming for a long time, but hoped somehow it wouldn't. I kept waiting for something— don't ask me what—to intervene and prevent the inevitable. Does that make sense?"

Of course it did. I'd been there—we all have.

Turning Points That Sneak Up on Us

Sometimes turning points can be quiet, almost invisible, and therefore, hard to predict and easy to miss. They sneak up on us day by day without our even realizing they have arrived, so that when we come face to face with them, at first *they don't look like turning points at all.* Perhaps we simply feel bored, restless, somehow unsettled within ourselves. We may feel sad for no reason, even depressed, and seem to have lost our passion for love, for sex, for work, for living. Something is not right, but we aren't sure what it is. If someone asked us, "Are you at a turning point in your life?" we'd probably answer, "No, I'm just overworked," or "No, I'm just worn out from having two toddlers at home with me." We don't even suspect that we might be at some important crossroads—we just don't like how we are feeling.

What is happening here? *By way of some underground pathways in our psyche, we have been going through a transition and reached a turning point without even knowing we were approaching it or that we have reached it at all. Deep within us, something has been shifting so slowly that it has been virtually imperceptible.* As we will see later in this book, we are often so skilled at ignoring what has been happening inside us, especially if we feel that it threatens our known reality, that we don't even recognize we've come to a cosmic intersection in our life even when we're standing right in the middle of it.

My friend Pamela just went through this kind of turning point. Pamela owned a children's clothing store, and for months I'd been hearing her complain about myriad situations in her life: her employees were driving her crazy; remodeling of the store was taking longer than she'd anticipated; her nine-year-old son was doing poorly in school, and she was having trouble helping him as much as she wanted due to her busy schedule; and she was too stressed to think about dating, even though it had been five years since her divorce.

Late one evening Pamela called me and, as usual, began telling me about how horrible her day had been. "I just don't know what to do," she lamented. "Why do things have to be this hard?"

"Maybe the Universe is trying to tell you something," I suggested.

"Like what—that my life sucks?" she responded with a sarcastic laugh.

"No, like that maybe you're at an important crossroads. You haven't enjoyed the store for some time now—it's doing well financially, but it's a burden rather than the creative challenge it was when you first opened. You have no time for your son, and no time for yourself. Perhaps you're supposed to be making a change."

Pamela was silent for a moment. Then, in a very calm voice, she replied, "Like selling my business."

"Have you thought about it?"

"To tell you the truth, I actually haven't. But as I hear you describe it, suddenly the pieces are fitting together. Everything in my life is screaming 'SELL!'—I just haven't been listening. I worked so hard to make the store successful, and couldn't ever imagine I wouldn't want to be doing this."

"It is financially successful," I reassured her. *"But if you don't want to be doing what you are doing every day, then you're not succeeding on the inside."*

"And that's why I have been so miserable," Pamela admitted.

Soon after our phone call, my friend sold her business, took two months off to spend more time with her son and reevaluate her life, and in a burst of inspiration decided to start a new company specializing in remodeling and decorating children's rooms. Pamela runs the business out of her house and is happier than she's ever been. She's even dating a furniture designer she met working on one of her new projects.

Like Pamela, **we become so attached to the road we are on, to the itinerary we have mapped out, that when a new road appears we may not even see it.** Often in these circumstances, it does take someone else—a family member, a friend, a therapist—to point out to us that we are indeed at some kind of crucial turning point.

Turning Points Disguised as Dead Ends

Last week I was driving to an appointment at a healing center in the foothills of the nearby mountains. I'd never been to this place before, but had clear directions that told me to follow one road for a while, and then look for the turnoff to the center, so I wasn't concerned about getting lost. It was a beautiful afternoon, and I was enjoying the serene atmosphere of the countryside.

Suddenly the road stopped and there was nowhere else to go. DEAD END, the sign read. "How could this be possible?" I wondered, utterly perplexed. I hadn't seen the turn I was supposed to take, and I was sure I'd looked carefully for it. There was nothing to do but slowly retrace my path. Sure enough, several miles back I noticed that there was a very small lane winding up the mountain, its identifying sign partially hidden behind an overgrown flowering bush. I remembered passing that road but dismissing it, certain it couldn't be the one I was looking for. Now I understood how I had missed the turnoff—I'd assumed it would be a well-paved street, and clearly marked. I didn't recognize it when I saw it because it wasn't what I was expecting.

Sometimes in life we come to what appear to be dead ends, but are actually missed turning points. Suddenly it seems we can't go any farther in the direction we were traveling, and we feel trapped, lost. We don't remember seeing any alternative routes; we don't recall being confronted with a choice. We simply feel stuck. "What am I supposed to do now?" we lament as we stare at the emotional equivalent of a NO WAY OUT sign. The answer is to do just what I did on that country road—we need to retrace our steps, to go back and see if we can find the turning point we missed because we weren't expecting it.

One of my clients is a very successful and well-known film producer. When we first met, I asked him how he got started in the entertainment business. *"I was desperate,"* he answered with a grin and went on to explain his story. Nelson was a struggling screenwriter who moved to Los Angeles with his wife and newborn son in hopes of breaking into the film industry. For two years he tried to sell his scripts with absolutely no luck. Soon he had gone through all of his savings and didn't even have money enough to pay the next month's rent on his apartment. He had reached a dead end and didn't know where to turn.

"I was about as down as a person could get," Nelson confessed to me. "I'd had these big dreams, dragged my wife away from her family in Texas, and here I was with nothing to show for it. I knew what I needed to do—pack up everything that could fit into the car and drive back to Texas to get a job selling cars or insurance or something. But I felt desperate at the thought of actually going through with this."

Then Nelson had an impulse to call his friend Jimmy, whom he'd met in a screenwriting class. Jimmy was always very upbeat, although he, too, hadn't ever sold a script. The last time Nelson had spoken to Jimmy, he'd been excited about some independent film he had agreed to help produce, and asked Nelson if he wanted to get involved. "It doesn't pay anything now," Jimmy explained, "but it is great experience." Nelson remembered thinking what an optimist Jimmy was and what a sucker—he was working for free, which surely couldn't get him anywhere. "At least I should call and say good-bye before I leave town," Nelson told himself.

That phone call changed Nelson's life. Jimmy talked him into working on the tiny film, which ended up becoming an underground hit. Nelson realized that he loved producing and had a talent for it, and soon he and Jimmy formed their own production company. Within a year, they'd produced a movie that became a surprise success and went on to create a multimillion-dollar business. *"If things hadn't been so bad,"* Nelson reminisced, *"I would have missed that doorway."*

This is often how it is with turning points—they seem to occur at crucial moments, moments in which we could easily get stuck unless we look for the opening they offer us. The word *crucial* is derived from the Latin root *crux,* or cross. Again, through ancient language, wisdom is revealed:

**Hidden within crucial, challenging times
are crossroads, transitions and turning points,
easy to miss, but promising us wonderful journeys
to places of delight and fulfillment
we cannot even imagine.**

Wake-up Calls

Great occasions do not make heroes or cowards;
they simply unveil them to the eyes of men.
Silently and imperceptibly, as we wake or sleep,
we grow strong or weak; and at last
some crisis shows what we have become.
—Brooke Foss Westcott

The night after your twentieth wedding anniversary party, your husband suddenly announces that he is leaving you for another woman. . . . Your doctor discovers a clogged artery in your heart during a routine checkup and schedules you for immediate open-heart surgery. . . . Your wife confesses that she's addicted to prescription painkillers and needs to be admitted to rehab. . . . Your business partner of eight years breaks down and tells you that that he badly mismanaged the company assets, and that you will need to declare bankruptcy.

You have just had a *wake-up call.*

A wake-up call is pushy. It's rude. It is a kick in the butt that sends us flying before it knocks us down. It is neither gentle, nor subtle, nor unhurried. Rather, it is demanding and dramatic, forcing us to pay attention to our lives, our relationships, and our own inner selves in a way nothing else does. It is stubborn, compelling us to face what we wish we could avoid, insisting that we deal with those things we are reluctant even to imagine, let alone endure.

If a turning point is a moment when we find ourselves standing at a crossroads, a wake-up call feels more as if we have been hit by a truck and are lying on the ground in a state of shock.

If a turning point is a big storm that creates some dust and disorder, a wake-up call is the tornado that slams into our life and appears to blow everything to smithereens.

Transitions and turning points can be gradual, unfolding over time, but wake-up calls do not afford us this luxury. They often like to wrap themselves in shocks and surprises when they show up at our door. The term *unexpected* doesn't begin to describe how it feels when we are suddenly jolted out of our old reality, confronted with circumstances, challenges and issues we hoped we would never have to face. One moment you're going about your business, and suddenly you look up and to your utter astonishment, everything has changed. You can't believe how you're feeling or where you are. You have no memory of any kind of conscious transition. "What happened?" you ask yourself in disbelief. "I don't remember being aware that I was even heading in this direction."

Wake-up calls are never on our itinerary. So when we find ourselves in the emotionally wrenching situations to which they inevitably deliver us, we cannot help but cry out: *"How did I get here?"* Even if we believe that eventually we will learn, grow and improve our lives because of the wake-up call, still, when it first assaults us, the experience is painful, frightening and emotionally overwhelming. My dear friend and fellow author Lorin Roche calls this "being shattered awake." It is the kind of awakening that we do not readily welcome.

Years ago, when the man I loved at the time suddenly announced that our relationship of ten years was over and he was leaving me, I totally fell apart. For weeks on end, all I could do was weep—actually, howling was more like it. I was in a state of complete shock, incapable at the time of figuring out what had happened or why I, of all people, hadn't seen this coming. One night, unable to sleep, I turned on the television and began watching a show about men and women who claimed to have been abducted by aliens from outer space. They all shared similar stories: one minute they were driving in their car or asleep in their bed, and the next thing they knew they were on an alien craft undergoing some horrible medical procedure. I remember listening to their descriptions and suddenly realizing that this was exactly how I felt— as if I'd been kidnapped, mysteriously abducted from my old life, only to wake up in some nightmare. And all I wanted to do was to go back home.

This is why wake-up calls can almost have a surreal, dreamlike quality to them. *They feel more like a transportation than a transi-*

tion, as if you've been whisked from one reality to another. At first
we may even be in a state of denial, unable to grasp what has occurred. "This can't be happening," we whisper to ourselves in disbelief, but it *is* happening. And now, where you are is unmistakable
and impossible to ignore.

These kinds of wake-up calls—extreme loss, illness, accidents
or tragedy—wake us up to our deepest questions about the meaning of life, our faith, our values, about who we are at the very core
of our soul. Others act as warnings, forcing us to focus on situations we have been ignoring that need our attention—the marriage
that will end unless we take immediate action, the disease that will
progress unless we start taking care of our body. **But all wake-up
calls have one thing in common: they test who we are and reveal us
to ourselves like nothing else can.**

· · ·

I cannot write about wake-up calls without telling you the story of
my friend Dr. Glenn Wollman. For thirty years, Glenn has been
a highly respected specialist in emergency medicine, and the Re-
gional Chief Medical Director for several emergency departments
in California as well as the Director of Integrative Medicine at a
large medical center. When I first met Glenn, I was impressed by
his knowledge of both Western and Eastern medicine, and by his
holistic approach to health and well-being. In our many conversations, it became clear to me that although Glenn loved his profession and was completely dedicated to it, he felt frustrated that he
wasn't able to really work with patients to focus more on preven-
tive health care.

During the next two years, I watched Glenn's dissatisfaction
grow worse and worse. "I need to make a big shift," he'd confess
with a sigh. The question was how. Glenn was very loyal and committed to those with whom he worked, and the idea of letting them
down was unthinkable to him. By his own admission, Glenn was
also a cautious, precise and analytical person. This was part of
why he was such a good doctor, but it didn't make it easy for him
to radically transform his life. The thought of setting out on his
own after so many years in institutional settings was daunting.

Whenever I got together with Glenn, this was one of the main topics—was Glenn ever going to make the change he needed to make in order to be truly fulfilled?

Late one night, my phone rang. It was my friend Marilyn. "Glenn has been in a terrible car accident," she told me. He'd been driving his sports car on the freeway and was getting ready to exit when a car smashed into him from behind at seventy miles an hour, and then sped off. Miraculously, he wasn't killed, although he had to be cut out of his demolished car. Glenn sustained very serious injuries—his back was broken in two places, and he fractured his ankle. For almost a month, he was unable to move. Slowly, with rest and rehabilitation, his body began to heal, although it would never be completely normal again.

The first time I saw Glenn after his accident, he could barely walk, stand or even sit, and he was in horrible pain. I recalled so many other conversations in which we'd talked about his life, his desire to make a drastic change, and the lack of clarity he felt about what to do. Now the decision had been made for him. Glenn's doctors told him what he already realized—he could never work in emergency medicine again, due to its intense physical demands. His career as he had known it was over. "I did say I wanted some time off to re-create my life," he joked. But beneath the humor, we all knew the truth. *Glenn had been hit by a dramatic wake-up call. In the span of a few seconds his entire life had changed, unexpectedly, radically and irrevocably.*

A year and a half has passed since Glenn's accident. During that time, he's been writing a book, developing holistic health and integrative care models that can be used by hospitals and physicians, and producing a series of CD's that offer relaxation and meditation techniques for waking and sleeping set to his beautiful playing of the Native American flute. I just saw Glenn a few nights ago, and he proudly handed me his first CD. I've never seen him look happier.

There are many ways to look at Glenn's story. Some might say that the accident was just that—an accident—and that it was purely coincidental that Glenn had been contemplating leaving emergency medicine. A more psychospiritual view would argue that perhaps if Glenn had taken the initiative to make the changes he wanted to, he wouldn't have been "forced" to change by the universe. Another theory would explain that this was just the way Glenn's life was meant to unfold, and that he was already feeling the change coming but wasn't sure what it was going to be. I've often teased Glenn that he was hit by his destiny, and he agrees.

What is most important is not that the accident happened, but what he has done with it since it happened: Glenn is using his wake-up call to renew and re-create himself in every sense of the word. He has discovered the gift hidden within the crisis and is enthusiastically and gratefully unwrapping it. The healer is healing himself.

Waking Up from the Inside

That's the way things come clear. All of a sudden.
And then you realize how obvious they've been all along.
—Madeleine L'Engle

It is nighttime. You are fast asleep in your bed. Your everyday reality still exists around you. The wind blows the branches of the trees so that they rustle outside your window. The cat makes her way from the living room to the kitchen for a 2:00 A.M. snack. The clock on the wall in your den ticks as it keeps track of the hours that pass. But you are completely unaware that any of this is going on. You are in another world, dreaming of other realities. You are riding a horse in a beautiful meadow, or looking for something you can't remember on a familiar street, or having a delightful conversation with someone you love, or running from something frightening that is chasing you, or visiting a relative who died many years ago.

Suddenly, from far away in your waking world, you hear a loud ringing sound. It is your alarm clock. You'd set it, as always, to get you up in time for work. Instantly, your consciousness is whisked from wherever you were, and you become aware that you are lying in your bed. It is the morning of a new day. You stretch, yawn and open your eyes. You are back in this reality once more.

Sometimes our wake-up calls are not much different from the experience of being woken from a dream by our own alarm. In these instances, it is not something or someone outside of ourselves that is responsible for the radical shift in our awareness, but rather something that wakes us up from the inside out.

Some wake-up calls are not initiated from something outside of ourselves, but from within.
It is as if a timer has been set to go off inside you at a certain moment,
and suddenly, without any warning, it does, waking you into realizations
that will be radical, disruptive and life-changing.

Why does that inner timer suddenly go off? Because it is time—some process has completed itself, and you are ready. Ready for what? That's the thing you find out once you wake up.

Four years ago, I moved to Santa Barbara, California, from Los Angeles where I'd lived for more than twenty-five years. A move like this was a big deal and a major turning point for me—I was leaving behind the place where I'd spent most of my adult life, the location of my business, all of my familiar references and connections. "How did you come to this decision?" people would ask me, assuming I'd been pondering it for some time. The truth was that I hadn't—at least consciously. I had always loved visiting Santa Barbara, but never could imagine leaving Los Angeles after so many years of living there. As far as I was concerned, I was in L.A. to stay.

Then one day, in one moment, everything changed. My partner

was visiting me from the East Coast, and we decided to go to Santa Barbara for my birthday. I hadn't been there for many years, and since he'd lived in Santa Barbara when he went to graduate school, I asked him to give me a complete tour. It was a spectacular California spring day, and the air was fragrant with jasmine blossoms. He drove me through the lush tree-lined streets, up into the hills, past eucalyptus groves, and finally to a beautiful beach where the ocean met the mountains in a picturesque cove. We got out of the car and walked over to the sand to take in the view.

I remember standing there bathed in sunlight, breathing in the exotic blend of sea, wind and mountain grasses, watching people having lunch at beachside tables. I was utterly intoxicated by it all. Then, as if on cue, I spotted a school of dolphins leaping in midair as they frolicked in the ocean, their silver bodies gleaming against the turquoise sky. Suddenly I felt something inside of me shift, and without even thinking about it, I turned to my sweetheart and said, "I'm moving to Santa Barbara."

"When did you decide that?" he asked.

"Just now," I replied, utterly surprised at my own answer. And it was the truth. I hadn't been planning on moving. I hadn't thought about the consequences it would have on my business. I didn't have a place to live. I didn't even know anyone here. But in that moment on the beach, I had somehow suddenly woken up and found myself at a crossroads that I hadn't even been aware was approaching.

The truth about internal wake-up calls that seem to happen suddenly is that there's actually nothing sudden about them at all. Looking back now, I can see that I had indeed been in a transition building up to my decision to leave Los Angeles—I just wasn't consciously aware of it. For years I'd spent more and more time at home, with less interest in venturing out into the busy, bustling energy of the city, energy I used to love, but that I now found tiring. Very few of my close friends lived in the Los Angeles area anymore. The focus of my work had shifted so that I didn't need to be there on a daily basis as I once had. Every chance I got, I found myself escaping to more serene environments out of town. The fact was that I was unhappy in L.A.—I just hadn't wanted to face it.

In that moment standing on the beach in Santa Barbara, I woke up to the truth about what I needed to do. Maybe the alarm clock just happened to go off during my birthday trip. Maybe it had already been ringing, but I'd been too preoccupied or too resistant to hear it until I actually got some distance from my familiar world in Los Angeles. Or maybe something about that beautiful day triggered an awareness inside me suddenly to turn on like a bright light. Whatever it was, one thing was clear: *I had woken up into a truth from which I could not retreat.*

As we will see in the chapters that follow, all wake-up calls demand that we stretch ourselves beyond what has been comfortable and relinquish what has been safe and familiar for the promise of growth, deeper wisdom and fulfillment that may remain untasted for a while. My description of that moment on the beach may sound inspiring, almost romantic, but let me assure you that the impact this wake-up call had on my life was nothing short of frightening and terribly disruptive. It took almost a year for me to make my move from Los Angeles to Santa Barbara, a year filled with complications, anxiety, painful good-byes to several longtime employees, and financial challenges. Moving here may have made sense for me emotionally, but it didn't make sense professionally or even logistically. I knew it would require a lot of compromise, flexibility and a certain degree of sacrifice, and to this day, it still does.

I did not know what called me to this sun-drenched, sparkling town. Somehow, I just knew that I was supposed to come. Waiting for me here were gifts I could not have imagined: friends I felt I'd known for lifetimes, a serenity I had never experienced anywhere else, healing I did not even know I needed, experiences that would become priceless treasures. And if it wasn't for that wake-up call on the beach. I might have missed out on all of it.

. . .

Just when I think I have learned the way to live, life changes.
—Hugh Prather

*I*f you are truly alive, if you are truly growing, you will undoubtedly come to many difficult transitions and crossroads in
your life journey. These twists and turns are not arbitrary. If you
hadn't traveled so far down the road, you wouldn't have come to
this new set of paths, choices, and challenges. *It is because you
have been so courageous, so determined to learn, to seek the truth,
that you are here at all.*

How, then, are we supposed to behave when we collide with
the unexpected, when we find ourselves at a terrifying crossroads, when we have been shattered awake? What is left for us
to do after we yell and moan and cry out and protest, after we
swear and sigh and scratch our heads, after we have exhausted
our anger and our tears? The great thirteenth-century Sufi mystic
and poet Jalal ud-Din Rumi, whose writings have illuminated
many a dark corridor in my own life, offers us a suggestion in his
classic poem "The Guest House." Read it and see what you
think:

> This being human is a guest house.
> Every morning a new arrival.
>
> A joy, a depression, a meanness,
> some momentary awareness comes
> as an unexpected visitor.
>
> Welcome and entertain them all!
> Even if they are a crowd of sorrows,
> who violently sweep your house
> empty of its furniture,
> still, treat each guest honorably.
> He may be clearing you out
> for some new delight.

The dark thought, the shame, the malice.
meet them at the door laughing and invite them in.

Be grateful for whoever comes.
because each has been sent
as a guide from beyond.

For now, let this be enough—to name this place you find yourself
in and welcome these unexpected visitors, as Rumi invites us to do.

Know that this "crowd of sorrows," these troubles and trials,
are positioning your soul for great wisdom and, in time, will reveal
themselves to be hidden doorways into a new and illuminated
world.

&ℰ 3 &ℛ

Getting Lost on the Way to Happiness

Not until we are lost do we begin to understand ourselves.
—Henry David Thoreau

Imagine for a moment that you decide to travel by car to a particular city—let's say Miami Beach, Florida—and you buy a map to help direct you. You study the map and mark all the roads you have to drive to get to Miami, which is 1,500 miles from where you live. Then you begin your long journey. As the days and hours pass, you eagerly look for the signs on the highway that will indicate where you are and reassure you that you're going in the right direction: MIAMI: 1000 MILES, MIAMI: 500 MILES, MIAMI: 300 MILES, MIAMI: 50 MILES and finally MIAMI: NEXT EXIT. "At last!" you think to yourself, "I have arrived."

Now imagine that as you enter the city, expecting warm, tropical Miami, you are shocked to find that it is bitterly cold and snowing heavily. People are rushing around bundled up in scarves, gloves and overcoats. Ice covers every inch of the frozen ground. No matter where you look, you can see no signs whatsoever of anything resembling an ocean or a beach. When you ask the passersby if this is Miami, they look at you strangely, as if you were crazy.

You sit there in your car, utterly bewildered. You stare at the map, which you followed diligently. You look out the window at the snow. You stare back at the map, shaking your head in disbelief. Obviously, you're not in Miami. But if not, then . . . where the heck are you? Was your map wrong? Were the road signs incorrect?

"How did I get HERE?" you ask yourself. And you feel as if you must be going mad.

. . .

In the process of living, there often comes a time when we suddenly look around at where we've ended up in our lives and it looks nothing like what we expected it to. We remember mapping out where we wanted to go with our relationships, our work, and our accomplishments, but instead, we inexplicably find ourselves in places and circumstances that bear no resemblance to where we hoped to be. We feel like a stranger in a strange land, except that this strange land is the life we are leading. Somehow, we've gotten lost on the way to happiness.

For each of us there was a starting point in our adult life when we designed a blueprint of dreams we hoped would lead us to a happy future. Sometimes we are very conscious of this personal life map, setting specific goals for ourselves and attempting to achieve them: "I will get married, have two children and live happily ever after." "I will start my own business, become financially independent and retire in Arizona." "I will go to college and earn a Ph.D. and become a successful research scientist." Other parts of our life map are less conscious or even unconscious: "I want be more successful than my brother." "I always want to be the one in control in my relationships." "I want enough money so that I never have to depend on a man for anything." We're often not even aware that these subterranean desires exist, yet they, too, guide our actions and determine our choices.

Time passes. We are busy working, loving, living as best as we can. We are following our map to each hoped-for destination. Everything seems to be going as planned. But then come those moments we've been talking about—the turning points, the wake-up calls—when we look around at where we've arrived, and realize with a sinking feeling that it's not where we thought we were going.

Perhaps in spite of our efforts to make our hopes and dreams come true, we have ended up in a very different reality. We wanted

to be married but are still single, or divorced or widowed. We
wanted to accomplish a certain goal but have been prevented by circumstances beyond our control from achieving it. *We wanted to be
living one kind of life, but feel trapped in another.*

Or . . . perhaps we have, indeed, arrived exactly where our map
was supposed to take us, only now that we're here, we aren't sure
it is where we want to be after all. The career we worked hard for
feels devoid of meaning or not in tune with our core values. The relationship we committed to is passionless and missing the intimacy
we crave. Our possessions and accomplishments leave us unfulfilled and wondering what it is we are missing.

Whether, in these unwelcome moments, we look around at our
lives and are disappointed because of where we find ourselves or
where we *don't* find ourselves, the effect on us is the same: *we feel
confused, frightened, thrown off-balance.* Like the perplexed trav-
eler who believed he would end up in Miami, we look at the map
we've been using to navigate through life and can't comprehend
how it led us here. *How did we get so lost when we were so sure
we were going in the right direction?*

The Maps That Lead to Someone Else's Dreams

If you want to know your past, look at the present.
If you want to know your future, look at the present.
—Pahmasambhava, eighth-century Tibetan Buddhist sage

When and how did we acquire these maps we use to navigate
through our adult life? And why do they sometimes take us
to places we don't want to be? Pahmasambhava advises us correctly that what we see in our present, good or bad, is very much a
reflection of our past. Upon hearing this, we may strongly disagree. We might insist that no one influenced us to do what we did
or pursue the paths we traveled or choose the directions we chose.
We may sincerely believe that we have mapped out the course of

our lives up to this point freely and consciously. And we would be shocked to find out how wrong we are.

**Until we become aware
of how deeply and thoroughly we have
been entangled in our past,
we cannot unravel ourselves from it.**

A story about maps that lead you to someone else's dreams:

Robert, my old boyfriend from college, called me one day out of the blue. It had been almost twenty years since I have spoken with him. We lost touch when Robert married his girlfriend after me, Alyssa. When I knew Robert, he was a poet, an adventurer, a philosopher and a young man committed to being a free spirit. We had deep conversations about the meaning of life and how we could make a difference in the world. I had been surprised when Robert got together with Alyssa, who was the antithesis of him in every way, and with whom, he admitted to me back then, he could not connect intellectually. I was even more surprised when he married her, became a high-powered attorney, bought an expensive home, had four children and settled into a very conventional life.

Decades had passed since I'd heard Robert's voice, but still, when he called, I knew immediately that something was troubling him. We were so close that we did not need any preliminaries, and when I asked him what was wrong, he answered: "Everything." Robert had recently left his wife after years of a rocky, strained and unfulfilling marriage. He felt choked by the constraints of his law practice, trapped by the enormous financial burden of his luxurious lifestyle, cut off from himself and who he remembers he used to be. This is why he was calling me, he explained. I was his connection to his authentic self. With me, he was always more "Robert" than he could ever be with anyone. Now he simply felt lost.

Robert and I spoke for a long time. He was in pain about the breakup of his family, about being alone, but most of all, he admitted, about feeling he wandered so far off-course from where he wanted to go. "I always told myself I didn't want my father's life," he mused, "that I wouldn't become tied down to a marriage and a job that wasn't making me truly happy. So how did I end up doing exactly that?"

I listened, and gently explained to Robert what I suspected had happened. It was as if years ago he had two maps, one in each pocket. The first map was marked with pathways of adventure and independence, destinations characterized by vision rather than convention. The second map laid out traditional routes to expected places, roads that would meet with everyone's approval—Robert's parents, Robert's girlfriend, Robert's peers. Robert didn't even consciously know that this conventional map was in his pocket and believed he was following the first map. But he wasn't.

Robert grew up with an impossible-to-satisfy, controlling mother who never seemed to be happy with her children or husband no matter what they did, so Robert spent his adult life trying not to disappoint anyone. He didn't want to disappoint Alyssa, so he married her against his better judgment, moved to the suburbs and bought her everything she wanted. He didn't want to disappoint his father, so he went to law school even though he longed to be a writer, and became a well-known corporate attorney. He didn't want to disappoint his partners and employees even though he wanted more free time, so he expanded his law practice. So no one was disappointed, except for Robert. Everyone was happy, except for Robert.

Robert had woken up and realized that he lost himself somewhere on his road to happiness by following a map that led to someone else's dreams—his father's, his wife's, the little boy desperate for approval. Now he was reaching into his pocket to retrieve that second map and finding his way back to a place of authenticity and autonomy from which he could begin again.

. . . .

We must be careful to build our life around our visions, rather than building our visions out of our history," says my colleague Alan Cohen. This is not an easy task. Most of us map out the course of our lives while we are still young; still too influenced by family and friends, by unresolved issues from childhood, by values imposed upon us by the society in which we live; and still not wise enough even to realize that this is the case.

"I must be like my parents."
"I won't be like my parents."
"If I do what I want to do, I will be different from my friends."
"Everyone else is getting married, so I guess it's time for me, too."
"I never want to be tied down to a man like my mother was."
"Everyone in my family goes to graduate school, so I should, too."
"Both of my sisters and their husbands already have children, so I guess my husband and I are next."
"Money will corrupt me as it did my father, so I'm never going to have any."
"No man who is really successful should need his wife to work, so neither should I."

Hundreds of these kinds of directives swirl around in our unconscious. Whether they compel us to conform or to rebel, they all conspire to rob us of the freedom to map out our own true destiny.

It is a dreadful shock to realize that the life map we've been using is totally outdated—ten, twenty, forty years old—based on ideals and values that reflected who we were a long time ago, ideals that aren't even ours anymore. Perhaps those values never belonged to us—we inherited the map from our family, a blueprint for the way we were expected to live. We followed its formula and arrived into a life with which we are not happy, one that feels foreign to us. Perhaps, like my friend Robert, our map was designed to take us to destinations that would please other people—our friends, our mate, our mentors. Now everyone else is happy with us, but we feel terribly unfulfilled.

**We may believe we are looking at the world
through our own eyes,
and not those of our parents, family or society,
but that will only be possible when we
do the hard and brave work
of learning to see for ourselves.**

Secret Timetables and Missed Deadlines

When I was eleven years old, I attended a summer sleepaway camp in the Pocono Mountains of Pennsylvania. One of the activities our counselors would organize for our amusement was a scavenger hunt. These were the days before video games, personal computers and DVD players had been invented, so preteens like myself actually found something as simple as a scavenger hunt to be highly entertaining. We'd be divided into teams, and given the task of acquiring an eclectic list of objects in a limited amount of time. *"Okay, girls! You have thirty minutes to find the following items: a pair of size 10 sneakers; a spoon; a photo of a dog; an Archie and Veronica comic book; a unopened box of Cracker-Jacks; a size 32AA bra; a live frog; five packs of Bazooka bubble gum; a bite plate; a Beatles record; and finally . . . a boy's jock strap! Ready . . . you have one half hour . . . GO!"*

Off we would run, squealing and shrieking all over camp, rummaging through one another's trunks, begging older campers who possessed sought-after items to give them to us in exchange for some promise ("I'll do your laundry for a week!") that we'd have to fulfill later, and, inevitably, approaching the boys in camp with giggles of embarrassment as we attempted to procure the most coveted and challenging item on the list—the jock strap. Eventually one team would win, and we'd all march off to the canteen to drink our sodas and laugh about how much fun we'd had.

Many of us are aware of our dreams and goals, but we may unconscious of the secret deadlines we've attached to them. We spend our adult lives on what amounts to an extended scavenger hunt, complete with a map of "must-haves" and very specific time limits. I call this our secret timetable. It tells us not only what we should achieve or accomplish, but also by when it should be completed:

"I should finish college in four years and find a job right after I graduate."

"I should be able to afford my own apartment by the time I'm twenty-two."

"I should find the right person and get married by the age of thirty at the latest."

"I should own my own home by the time I'm thirty-five."

"I should have several children before I'm forty."

"I should be running my own business by the time my kids are school age."

"I should be making X amount of money by the time I'm forty-five."

"I should be able to buy X and have traveled to Y by the time I'm fifty."

"I should be able to retire by the time I'm sixty-five."

Your secret timetable will reflect your own values and lifestyle. Some items will be psychological goals, rather than material ones:

"I should have healed my pain from childhood before I have my own kids."

"I should get over my anger at my father before he dies."

Some will reflect spiritual goals:

"I should reach enlightenment after meditating for twenty-five years."

"I should have conquered my lapses in faith by the time I am an ordained minister."

Still others will actually involve not only your timetable, but those of people close to you:

*"My daughter should have children before I turn seventy, so I can
still be healthy enough to enjoy them."*
*"My boyfriend should find a new job that pays more before I'll
agree to marry him."*

I have my own timetable. You have yours. They are tyrants,
these "shoulds," breathing down our neck, peering over our shoul-
der, counting down the time, making us feel pressured, late, behind, never enough. **And yet we usually aren't even aware that these
secret timetables exist—that is, until we miss one of our unconscious deadlines. Then we go into crisis.**

. . .

My friend Emily is having the worst year of her life. Emily
lives in Washington, D.C., and works as a consultant for the
federal government. She is attractive, bright and spunky. Men find
Emily appealing, and she's had a long string of romantic involvements since I've known her, but nothing really serious, which
didn't seem to bother Emily that much. The big dream in her life
was to buy her own home in the country where she could raise and
ride horses.

Several months ago that dream came true. About this same
time, Emily turned forty. And suddenly, with no warning, Emily
fell apart. "This wasn't the way it was supposed to turn out,"
Emily sobbed to me on the phone. "I was supposed to be living in
my beautiful house with my wonderful husband and have fantastic kids, and everything would be fine. Instead I'm here in this big
house in the middle of nowhere all alone, and I'm forty years
old!"

Emily practically screamed these last few words, which gave
me a clue to her emotional collapse. Her map and timetable stated
that by forty, she should be able to buy her dream home and be
married to her dream man. She had been aware of wanting the
house, but had never admitted, even to herself, that she wanted a
husband. In fact, she only dated men who weren't very serious
about commitment. The impact of moving into her home alone and
turning forty produced a sudden and painful wake-up call for

Emily. She had missed an enormous secret deadline, and in spite of all she had accomplished, she felt like a failure.

**When we become aware that we don't have
the life we had mapped out
for ourselves, we may feel horribly disappointed.
We may feel as if we've failed. Why?
Because we did not meet our arbitrary timetable.**

When the Right Life Doesn't Feel Right Anymore

You have consciously mapped out your life with goals you truly wanted for yourself. You have followed your map scrupulously. It has taken you to exactly where you hoped it would. But now that you are here, you discover to your great dismay that you are unhappy, unfulfilled and desperate to escape from your life as you know it, even though it is the life you thought you wanted.

Sometimes it's not difficulties that stop us in our tracks but disillusionment, not challenges but disorientation. In these cases, the unexpected that hits us is the astonishing realization that we just aren't happy where we are. This is especially disconcerting if we are where we always thought we wanted to be.

It is one thing to be unhappy when circumstances don't match our expectations. That is a kind of acceptable, tolerable unhappiness. We assume we would be happy if we had a lot of money or if we were married or if we had the career for which we'd worked so hard. We're still hopeful that these things could happen. This hope allows us to endure our unhappiness, at least for a while. "I hate my job," we think to ourselves, "but it is great experience for when I have my own business." "I feel so insecure in this relationship, but I'm willing to hang in there in hopes that he will ask me to marry him, and then I'll be able to relax."

But what happens when we have the things we hoped to have, and we *still* aren't happy? That unhappiness is tortuous because we feel bewildered by it and trapped in it. "If all this isn't going to make me happy, then what is?" we ask ourselves. "What am I supposed to do now?"

An excerpt from a letter I received from one of my readers illustrates this predicament:

> . . . I feel guilty even writing to you because everyone would say I have the perfect life, the perfect husband, the perfect house and kids, and they are right. **But if it is all so perfect, then why do I feel so crappy?**
>
> There is nothing wrong with my husband, and I really can't complain about how he treats me or anything like that. He is a good man and a very good dad to the boys. Honestly, he has done everything I've asked him to, even going to church with me, which at first he didn't want to do. So it is not him—it's me.
>
> The thing is, I feel like I am playing a part in a show, the wife, the mom, the good housewife. But I want to scream because this is not really who I am. I thought it would be, I really did. I thought if I just found a guy to marry I could get away from my folks and have a nice life, the kind I always wanted as a girl. I know you would say I was too young when I met Tim, only nineteen and never been out of this little Kentucky town, and now I think I would agree with you. I just turned twenty-five **but I feel so old, like happiness is over, life is over, and I am just going through the motions.** And I am tired all the time like I just want to sleep and sleep and I keep hoping when I wake up each day that things will be different, but they never are. . . . **It wasn't supposed to be like this.**

This sweet and sad girl is so obviously unhappy in the life she herself carefully designed and constructed. Even worse, she is bewildered by her unhappiness, and feels guilty for even feeling it.

What she thought would be her golden pot at the end of the rainbow now just looks like a plain old depressing dead end. And this is the only map she has ever known, the only life she has ever imagined.

How many times have we uttered that same line in a moment of shock or despair, when we come face to face with the unexpected destination to which our maps have taken us: "It's not supposed to be like this!" Now we must confront that terrified and disappointed part of ourselves and ask:

Who or what says it's not supposed to be like this? An outdated map you designed years ago? An arbitrary timetable? Someone else's idea of how you were supposed to live your life? It's not supposed to be anything. It is supposed to be what it is.

Unprepared for Loss and Unequipped for Imperfection

We're the middle children of history . . . no purpose or place.
We have no great war, no Great Depression.
Our great war is a spiritual war.
—From the film *Fight Club,* screenplay by Jim Uhls

This is a book for the complex times we are in. And I am a product of these times, a "middle child of history." I, too, believed that if I worked hard, I would get everything I wanted. If I planned well, nothing would go wrong. If I did everything I should, I wouldn't get lost. But like you, like so many of us, I got lost anyway.

There is nothing unique about this, or about us—human beings have known misery, braved difficulties and faced horrible disappointments for as long as we have existed. Indeed, most of the problems and challenges we face in our times pale in comparison to what our ancestors went through. Many of our parents, grandparents and great-grandparents came to America with little or nothing. Once here, they went through the catastrophic events of the Depression and world wars, tolerating tremendous personal hardship and sacrifice. A feisty eighty-four-year-old friend of mine says it like this: "These young people and their complaining about this thing and that thing—I tell them, 'Don't talk to me about suffering. *We* knew suffering.' "

This is true. My grandparents and their parents encountered difficulty, devastation and loss in much more severity than I have in my lifetime. Yet I suspect they were better at coping with it. Why? *They were not brought up to expect perfection. They were brought up to endure. And so they endured.*

Only during the emerging optimism of the postwar 1950s did the idea of creating a picture-perfect life emerge. The baby boomer generation was taught that we could and should have it all. Consumption replaced caution as our philosophy, and prevention, rather than endurance, was the value we revered. We immunized ourselves—against flu, against disease, against boredom, against deprivation, against unhappiness.

We have fine-tuned our obsession with eliminating pain, discomfort and deprivation at all costs and as quickly as possible. We take drugs so we can eat what we want with no consequences, so we can have sex without performance anxiety, so we can develop muscles without exercising. We can speak to anyone we want at any time from anywhere with our cell phones. We can create the perfect photos instantly with our digital cameras—if we aren't pleased with the picture we took, we just erase it and try again until it turns out right.

And we are not patient about getting what we want—we like to get things *on demand.* I'm not sure when that phrase first appeared in our language, but my computer's browser just found 8,570,000 references to it for me—in .09 seconds—on demand, of course: on demand pay-per-view movies, news on demand, books on demand, gossip on demand, football scores on demand, credit on demand, astrology on demand, sex toys on demand, recipes on demand, medical advice on demand, erections on demand, divorce on demand. These are all actual listings of real products and services. When we want something, we want it now.

We may look at our parents and grandparents, and smugly think we are so much more emotionally sophisticated than they are. After all, we have our self-improvement seminars, our therapy, our life coaches, our twelve-step programs, our yoga classes. *The more honest truth is that in many ways, we are much less equipped than they were to deal with the unexpected, much less resilient to suffering. Our ability to be patient, to endure, to do without, is not as formidable as the generations that have gone before.*

The consequence of all we've been discussing reveals a dangerous psychological mix:

Our expectations for ourselves are higher than previous generations, and at the same time, our ability to endure is less.
This renders us unprepared for loss and unequipped for imperfection either in ourselves or in the world around us.

We don't expect things to go wrong, so we are shocked when they do. The result is a lot of very anxious and unhappy people.

. . .

Consider these statistics and signs of unsettled times:

- One out of every four women and one out of every five men in America will have a clinically significant bout of depression in their lifetime, according to a recent study conducted by Columbia University and published in the *Journal of the American Medical Association.*

- In the past ten years, one out of every eight Americans has taken antidepressant medication. That means up to 20 million people regularly use antidepressants, and this in spite of new research indicating that antidepressants may have only a small advantage over placebos in studies.

These numbers are getting worse every year, and not better:

- Between 1987 and 1997, the number of Americans treated for depression soared from 1.7 million to 6.3 million. Additionally, the number of those taking antidepressants doubled. Depression and anxiety disorders—the two most common mental illnesses—each affect 19 million American adults annually, numbers from the National Mental Health Association reveal.

It appears that many of us are unhappy and cannot get by without some kind of substance to make our unhappiness go away:

- 22 million Americans suffer from alcohol or drug abuse, reports the Substance Abuse and Mental Health Services Administration.

Apparently Americans are also so anxious that we cannot sleep:

- According to the National Sleep Foundation, 48 percent of Americans report insomnia occasionally, and 22 percent experience insomnia almost every night. Again, it is drugs to the rescue: sleeping aids are a 14-billion-dollar industry. Every year, one in four Americans takes some kind of medicine to help us sleep.

Perhaps the saddest and most shocking statistics of all are those about children, revealing that even they are not immune to this epidemic of worry and anxiety:

- The National Mental Health Association reported that one in five children has a diagnosable mental, emotional or behavioral disorder. *The Journal of Psychiatric Services* reports that use of antidepressants continues to grow by about 10 percent annually among American teens and children.

• The most alarming information, however, is that U.S. preschoolers age five and under are the fastest-growing segment of the nonadult population using antidepressants today. Between 1998 and 2002, antidepressant use among preschoolers doubled.

This is a complex subject we cannot examine thoroughly here. Yet it is impossible not to conclude that something is very wrong. **We have more comforts, more possessions, more of everything than ever before in the history of humankind. And yet in spite of all of this, we appear to be more miserable.**

Waking Up a Stranger in Your Own Life

The greatest hazard of all . . . losing one's self,
can occur very quietly in the world, as if it were nothing at all.
No other loss can occur so quietly; any other loss—
an arm, a leg, five dollars, a wife, etc.—is sure to be noticed.
—Sören Kierkegaard

What are we so anxious about? What is keeping us up at night? What is it that haunts us so relentlessly that we need to tranquilize ourselves so as not to feel it?

Perhaps it is as the great existentialist philosopher Kierkegaard states: Just like someone returning home to discover that he's been robbed, *we suddenly become aware of the quiet loss of ourselves, a loss that occurred without our even noticing it.*

But now we do notice it.

Maybe this is what is so painful for us, why we shift and squirm at the strangeness we feel in our own life, shaken by the shifting landscape around us. Our disorientation is understandable. It stems from our search for pieces of ourselves that got lost along the way—pieces of our dreams, our passion, our purpose that we are unable to find in the life we are presently living.

Have you ever gone back to take a drive through your child-hood neighborhood after being away from that town for many years? You can't help looking for anything that seems familiar, at-tempting to conjure up comforting memories, to feel at home. "There's my elementary school," you exclaim. "And look, that's the house my friend Bobby lived in. I'd go there every day after school and watch TV." You delight in each rediscovered location, reminiscing about the past.

Soon, however, you start noticing what's missing. "There used to be a building here," you explain with a frown to whoever is with you. "And see that new apartment house? That used to be a drugstore where we would go for sodas. . . . Oh no! I can't believe they got rid of that great park where we'd play on the swings and turned it into this strip mall!" You sigh as you pass yet another landmark from the past that no longer exists and reluctantly admit: "Things sure have changed."

This is just what happens when we lose pieces of ourselves. **We scan our lives for comforting landmarks, and are dismayed to find that we feel distant and detached from the very things, the very people with whom we used to feel safe and familiar.** "Why did it have to change?" we wonder.

· · ·

It's an amazing dilemma when one begins to discover
that . . . you're living your life in a trance—in a dream . . .
When that occurs, there's a kind of amazing thing
that takes place.
One is despair, and the other is a sudden awakening.
—Sam Shepard, playwright

Initially there is a surreal, dreamlike quality to everything when we become aware, even to a small degree, that we are lost in our own life. Suspended between two identities—between past and fu-ture, between what is solid and what is amorphous, between how we thought things were and how they actually are—we flounder, so dizzy and off-balance that we are afraid we might fall. To one side of us is despair. To the other side is awakening. We can go either way.

As we will see in our next chapters, falling into despair soon leads to a kind of deadness and denial. It is like pushing the snooze button on the alarm clock and going back to sleep after we have already been wakened. We can do this if we want, but trust me when I say that eventually the alarm is going to go off again.

The opportunity here is to realize that you are already awake—perhaps startled, perhaps grumpy, perhaps disoriented—but awake just the same. Your senses are sharpened. You are raw, even hurting, but you are alive. Now you can look around and begin to discover where you are on your path and what is at hand.

There is an authentic you beyond what you have known as you, a you beyond what others have expected of you, a you that transcends your past, your patterns, your discarded maps. Perhaps it is a you that you lost along the way to happiness and need to retrieve; or perhaps it is a you that has yet to be discovered, unearthed from its shroud of habitual disguises collected over a lifetime.

This is the true purpose of these turning points and wake-up calls: they are attempts to initiate a powerful process of self-renewal, to point you in the direction of your true destination— not a new road, or a new, improved map, but a whole and awakened you.

Recognizing Your Rite of Passage

Recently I spent an hour on a plane talking with a very sweet man named William who happened to have read several of my books. "I thought it was you!" he exclaimed. "Don't worry—I won't start telling you my problems, because that would take hours."

Something told me this was one of those fated meetings, and I asked William what was going on in his life. His answer was: *"Everything!"* He explained that in the last two years he had quit his very prestigious job, moved away from his hometown where all of his family and friends lived, decided to go back to school and become a social worker, and stopped going to his old church and joined a new one, "I'm thirty-six years old," he revealed, "And everyone thinks I'm going through some raging midlife crisis. 'Why are you messing up your life?' people keep asking me. I don't really know the answer. It's hard to explain what happened—I just know when I looked at how I was living, I realized that I didn't feel like the real me anymore, and that I needed to make some big changes."

"Have these choices made you happier?" I asked William.

"I think they will eventually. It's just that right now my life is so cluttered with drama—it's been nonstop for the past few years."

"Sometimes life looks cluttered when a lot of learning is going on," I suggested. *"Your life may appear to be cluttered with experiences because you have lived the lessons of so many lifetimes in one. It may look like it's cluttered with drama, but I think it's just cluttered with learning."*

For the first time in our conversation, William smiled. "I never thought of it that way," he admitted. "So you don't think I'm having a midlife crisis?"

"No. I think you've gone through a powerful rite of passage without realizing it. You've come into a new time of wisdom. You're different on the inside, and so you're feeling compelled to make your life on the outside more completely reflect your new awareness."

The look on William's face brought tears to my eyes. I had obviously said what he needed to hear. No one had been there to greet him on the other side of his rebirth, to honor his courage in facing so many painful truths and making so many leaps into the unknown. I was the first to welcome him into his new life.

Whether we know them by name or not, rites of passage are an integral part of our life journey. *They are the doorways through which we leave one phase of our life and enter into another.* Traditional societies understood and honored these times of coming into wisdom with formal ceremonies and rituals. Seekers went through mystical, spiritual initiations designed to open and shift their consciousness. In ancient Native American cultures young people were sent out on a Vision Quest. These rituals were integral parts of human societies for thousands of years, helping individuals navigate their transitions with understanding and meaning.

Our modern Western society does have its own versions of rites of passage. Most of these involve some form of party—lavish birthday celebrations for children, extravagant junior high and high school graduation proms, expensive weddings, anniversary luncheons at country clubs, office retirement dinners, for example. All of these are superficial markers in that they acknowledge transformations that occur on the outside—our arrival at a certain age, our participation in accepted social customs, or obtaining a level of economic achievement.

Here is the problem as I see it:

Many of us go through undefined, unmarked and unnamed rites of passage without realizing it. Our society has no rituals for honoring a true inner passage of transformation.

As we discussed in chapter 2, we have no names for what we are experiencing. Without recognizing our own rites of passage, we can become more easily disoriented and disheartened on our life journey. We may be in the midst of powerful moments of transition and transformation, but misinterpret these as moments of failure, weakness of character, or a even a kind of insanity. We may have no way within ourselves of saying good-bye to the past, letting go of the old and fully embracing the new. *And upon emerging from our initiation by fire, we may not even realize that we have*

*emerged at all, or be fully aware of the profound transformation
that has taken place deep within us.*

When a society has no understanding of these inner rites of passage into wisdom, it wrongly identifies them as something else.
That is why William's friends and family decided he was falling
apart. Too often, legitimate self-inquiry is disparagingly labeled a
"midlife crisis."

**The midlife crisis is an experience that is misnamed.
It should be called a midlife awakening.
It is the emotional alchemy that rebirths us
at a crucial point in our life journey.**

To dismiss a moment of great soul-searching as a midlife crisis is
to insinuate that the life circumstances that came before this were
"normal," and that deep self-reflection and reassessment is some
sign of mental instability or temporary confusion, rather than a
moment of great awakening. Who's to say our life before wasn't the
crisis? Perhaps it's more accurate to suggest that it is those who
never question their lives, their choices or themselves who are in a
crisis.

Rites of passage are sacred, mysterious and life-transforming
times. They take you on a journey deep within yourself by way of
roads that may at first appear unfamiliar and confusing. "Where
am I going?" you wonder nervously as the path swerves off in yet
another unexpected direction. Would you believe me if I told you
there are magnificent surprises waiting for you just up ahead?

. .. .

My next-door neighbor and friend, Tom Campbell, is one of
the world's best-known marine wildlife photographers and
filmmakers, and one of the most fascinating people I know. He
spends his time diving in exotic and remote locations in order to
capture the wonders of the world beneath the sea, especially
sharks. As I was sitting here trying to decide how to finish this

chapter, I heard a knock on the door—it was Tom, stopping by to say hello and to tell me an amazing story.

Tom recently took a trip to New Zealand with the intention of buying some property there. Before he left, he described what he was looking for: a house in a serene, isolated spot situated on a large lot with a view of the ocean. Tom didn't know anyone in New Zealand, but had the name of a realtor whom he hoped would show him what was available.

After arriving in Auckland on North Island and renting a car, Tom met with the realtor, who took him to view several properties, but none of them were what Tom had in mind. "They were all too close to the city," he explained. "So I decided to drive a few hours further north to the less populated part of the island. I didn't have any property to see, but I figured I could at least get an idea of the type of countryside that was up there." Equipped with a map, but with no real plan, he set off.

Tom drove for four hours, stopping at sites that looked interesting, intent on making his way to the northeast section of the island, which from the map, looked to be an area that had spectacular views. There was one particular bay that fascinated him, and according to the map, he could reach it if he followed a small road that forked off the main highway. He found the turnoff, which turned into another turnoff and another, and soon it became clear that he was lost.

"I was so frustrated," Tom said. "I had no idea where I was, and the map was obviously not helping much. I stopped my car on the side of the road to see if I could at least figure out how to get back on the highway to Auckland.

"Suddenly a car drove up and the woman inside rolled down her window. She asked if she could help me, obviously wondering who this strange guy was lurking about in her neighborhood. I told her that I was from California, and here in New Zealand looking for property to purchase, but that I'd gotten lost trying to find a bay I'd seen on the map. She looked at me strangely for a minute, and then told me that she was a realtor, and that she just happened to be meeting a couple at their home at the top of the hill who had just decided to put their house on the market.

"I asked her if it was a nice home, and she said it was a beautiful house on a large lot with panoramic views of the ocean and of that same bay I'd been looking for. It sounded so much like the place I'd envisioned, and I asked if I could possibly see it. She said she'd have to ask the owners, who hadn't even listed the house yet, but she'd see what she could do.

"Somehow she convinced this couple to leave their house for half an hour so this crazy guy who she'd just found on the side of the road could come look at it," Tom said with a big grin. "Five minutes after seeing the property, I knew it was exactly what I was looking for. I turned to the realtor and said, 'I'll take it.' She thought I was kidding until I convinced her that I was serious. The owners came back and we negotiated the sale on the spot."

Tom reached into his briefcase and pulled out a photograph. "This is it," he said proudly. And there it was, just as he'd imagined— a sprawling home isolated on a lush green hilltop overlooking the sea. Tom had found his house. And I'd found the ending for this chapter.

"It's pretty spooky, really," Tom remarked as he turned to leave. "How did I go from being totally lost to somehow finding this beautiful house that I didn't even know existed?"

"The answer is obvious," I replied. *"You weren't really lost. You just thought you were. In reality, you'd arrived at your true destination."*

. . .

The story of how Tom found his house—and how it found him—is moving, magical and profound. If he hadn't been willing to go searching for his dream, and to get lost along the way, he would never have found what he was looking for.

Sometimes what we're looking for comes knocking on our door. Sometimes it's right around the corner from where we've stopped, sure that we are lost and will never find it.

Sometimes it's waiting for us to look up from our old map long enough to see that there, not so far away, is something wonderful we couldn't even have imagined existed.

You're never really been lost.

You aren't lost now.

The road you've been on will take you to the next road, and the next, and the next, delivering you to many miraculous and surprising destinations that aren't even on your itinerary, but are waiting for your arrival just the same.

❧ 4 ❧

Playing Hide-and-Seek with the Truth

Men occasionally stumble on the truth, but most of them pick themselves up and hurry off as if nothing had happened.
—Sir Winston Churchill

Here is a fable I wrote to begin this chapter:

Deep in the jungles of India, an enormous angry elephant has gone on a rampage through many towns, and now has been spotted moving toward a tiny village situated near the narrow part of the river. When they hear this news, the men and women of the village become alarmed and unsure of what to do. "We should seek the advice of the wise Guru and his disciples," one person suggests. And so it is decided that a group representing the townspeople will bring offerings of food to the modest hut in which the Guru resides with his students.

Late in the afternoon, just after the Guru finishes performing his evening worship, the group respectfully approaches and asks if they can speak with him. The Guru smiles sweetly and invites the villagers to sit with him and his four disciples and discuss whatever they wish. In trembling voices, they relay the information about the angry elephant. "Oh, Wise One," they plead, "we do not know what to do. Please guide us in the correct course of action to take."

The Guru closes his eyes for a moment and then, opening them, he speaks: "I would like to hear what each of my disciples has to say about this matter of the elephant." Thrilled at the opportunity to show off their knowledge, the four disciples sit up straight, brush the dust off their robes, and clear their throats.

The first disciple begins:

"The fact is, we do not know when this elephant might be arriving. Indeed, it isn't here yet, and who's to say it will come anytime soon? Elephants are quite large, and can't move that quickly. Therefore, there is no need for panic. In the meantime, I suggest that we make preparations for the elephant's arrival, perhaps form one committee to figure out how to trap the elephant, another to cook foods to tempt the elephant, and another to devise ways to scare off the elephant. We have much to do, so I suggest we stop talking and get busy."

The second disciple takes his turn:

"It pains me to hear how quickly we assume this is a bad elephant. Perhaps it is coming here to give us its blessings! The scriptures clearly state that the presence of elephants is a very auspicious sign. Perhaps the poor elephant is only running around because some ignorant villagers scared it off. I'm sure the elephant means us no harm. It will probably pass by our village without incident. So there's nothing for us to be concerned about."

Now the third disciple speaks out in an angry voice:

"I resent your coming to us like this and expecting us to do something about some crazy elephant. Are you blaming us for this turn of events? Are you accusing us of not performing the proper rituals to protect the village from harm? How dare you insult the Guru in this manner! You are the ones who should be performing your daily prayers rather than pointing the finger at us. Go back to your chores and leave us alone."

The fourth disciple goes last:

"This is obviously some kind of trick. You can't possibly be telling the truth. There is no elephant. I don't see any evidence of one. I refuse to believe such an outlandish tale. I am having a perfectly lovely day sitting here in the shade, and I will not allow your lies to upset my serene state."

Confused by the four conflicting answers, and more upset than ever, the villagers turn to the Guru, who has been calmly listening to the conversation, hoping that somehow he will enlighten them with the truth. "Master," one begs, "we implore you—tell us what you think."

Suddenly the Guru leaps up from his mat, grabs his walking stick and announces:

"What I think is this: THERE'S AN ANGRY ELEPHANT COMING! GATHER YOUR BELONGINGS AND RUN!!!"

Human beings are stubborn creatures. In spite of very loud warnings and wake-up calls, we don't always pay attention. In spite of clearly marked turning points, we don't always change direction. In spite of something unmistakable that cries out from within us for a change, we rigidly cling to what is familiar. How is it that we do this? How is it that we can stay so long in relationships that make us miserable or jobs we find totally unfulfilling or situations that are not healthy for us? How is it that we don't notice the wild elephant approaching? How is it that we don't move out of the way? How is it that we get so stuck?

We tune out.

. . .

When I was in my second year of college, I went through an extended period of tremendous self-reflection. During this time I preferred being alone. I lived in a tiny one-room apartment that was part of an old house, and used to spend day after day by myself—reading, writing poetry, meditating and trying to make sense of life. I had made many friends in my freshman year, some of whom also lived in the house, and several times each day they would knock on my door asking, "Barbara—are you there? We're going out. Do you want to come?" As soon as I would hear someone at the door, I would panic and freeze, becoming as quiet as possible so they wouldn't know I was home. My friends would knock again, and eventually, when I didn't answer, they would give up and leave.

I can still remember how I felt sitting there hearing people on the other side of the door—my heart would pound, my breathing would accelerate and I would count the seconds until they left. And when they finally did, I would breathe a sigh of relief.

Why didn't I just answer the door and tell my friends I wanted to be alone? Why did I have such a strong reaction to their knocking? What was I afraid of?

The answer is simple: I didn't want to deal with them. It would have been too complicated to try to explain how I was feeling. It would have taken too much energy, energy I needed just to get through my own introspective process. Looking back, I realize I was being rude and even somewhat agoraphobic hiding in my apartment afraid to answer the door—but at the time I didn't care. It was easier for me to ignore my friends than to try and face them.

This story describes the precise way in which many of us approach unpleasant or challenging realities now, in our adult lives: *We don't want to deal with them, so we tune them out.*

Like an unwelcome visitor, Truth knocks on the door of our awareness, attempting to reach us, to wake us up, to invite us out of places in which we've hidden, to reveal new pathways and new directions. We know Truth is there, but we don't answer. We panic. We freeze up. We hide, hoping either consciously or unconsciously that if we ignore whatever is trying to get our attention for long enough, it will go away.

Sometimes we do open the door just enough to see what's out there, but don't let whatever it is in. We close the door again and go about our business pretending the Truth isn't still standing there on our doorstep. And sometimes we get so habituated to disregarding the Truth that we even tune out the sound of its knocking, and convince ourselves that it has gone away for good.

Here is something else I've learned: if human beings are stubborn, then Truth is more stubborn. It is also infinitely patient. It will knock again, and again . . . and again until we cannot ignore it anymore and are forced to get the message.

Ultimately, we will lose this power struggle with the Truth. In the meantime, we become masterful at skills that are not good for us: we become experts at avoidance, experts at evasion, experts at tuning out. This kind of expertise is one without which we would be better off, for as we will see, it inevitably leads to suffering:

**Avoidance sabotages our ability to have meaningful
and truly intimate relationships. It undermines
our clarity and creativity. It robs us
of our capacity to be fully present in each moment.
We think we are tuning out to avoid pain,
but in the end, avoidance delivers us into
the very pain, confusion, and unhappiness
from which we are fleeing.**

Playing Hide-and-Seek with Reality

*Who is more foolish, the child afraid of the dark
or the man afraid of the light?*
—Maurice Freehill

When we are children we love to play hide-and-seek. We command our friend or parent to count to twenty, and then run to find a hiding place. Once in the closet, or under the bed, or behind the couch, we do our best to stifle our nervous giggles and wait with excitement to see if the person looking for us will discover where we are. At first, we feel triumphant when we remain undetected, but after a while we grow restless and start to worry that the seeker has given up the game, forgotten about us, and gone on to something else. Should we come out of hiding? Should we shout out some clues? Where is he, anyway?

Why are we so impatient? Because it's not the hiding itself that fulfills us, but that moment when we are discovered—the sudden thrill and delight when the door is opened or the pile of clothing is removed or the curtain is pushed back. "You found me!" we shriek gleefully. This is the real secret of hide-and-seek: ultimately, we want to be found.

Now we are adults, and we often learn another kind of game, one I call Hide-and-Seek with Reality—**reality tries to find us, and we do our best to *avoid it*.** Perhaps the reality we are facing doesn't fit our picture of what we expected or hoped things would look like. Perhaps we're frightened of the consequences it will have on our life. Perhaps the truth knocking on the door of our awareness is so painful that we will do anything to avoid answering its call. Unlike the child who enthusiastically longs to be discovered, we do not want to be found. So we create sophisticated strategies for ensuring that we can remain undetected and that any unpleasant realities stalking us will not succeed in penetrating our psychological hiding places. We become experts, through our thoughts and behavior, at tuning out, experts at the art of denial.

What is so threatening about the truth? Why do we so often flee from it? What are we afraid of?

We are afraid that we will discover we have wasted time.
We are afraid that we will have to admit we've made mistakes.
We are afraid of what other people will think when we change direction.
We are afraid of losing what is familiar, even if it is causing us pain.
We are afraid that once we let go of what we are holding onto, we may never find anything worth holding onto again.
We are afraid that we will look foolish/stupid/laughable/inferior/worthless to others and to ourselves.
We are afraid of hurting and disappointing the people we love.
We are afraid of so many things, some we cannot even name.

· · ·

The comical and everyday adventures of Mullah Nasrudin, a beloved Sufi character and folk hero, have been used by Sufi masters for centuries to illustrate profound spiritual teachings. Here is my telling of one of my favorite Nasrudin stories:

In his travels far from home, Mullah Nasrudin arrives in a small town. Thirsty from his journey, he makes his way to the plaza, where all kinds of food is for sale. He spots a man off to one side selling large, shiny, red exotic fruits. "This looks like exactly what I need," thinks Nasrudin, entranced by the unusual fruits.

"These unusual fruits look wonderful," Nasrudin proclaims as he approaches the vendor. "I will take a whole basket, since I am very hungry and thirsty." The vendor says nothing, but takes Nasrudin's coins and hands him a large basket of red fruits. Nasrudin leaves, very satisfied with himself for getting so much for his money, and finds a spot down the road where he sits down and begins to eat his basket of fruits.

As soon as Nasrudin takes a big bite of the first red fruit, his mouth feels like it is burning up, as if he has just swallowed a bowl of fire. Tears stream down his cheeks, and his face turns bright red. He can barely breathe. Still, he keeps right on eating, stuffing the contents of the basket into his burning mouth.

A local man passing by notices Nasrudin in distress, and stops in front of him. "Sir, what are you doing?" he asks.

"I thought these were delicious fruits," Nasrudin gasps, "so I bought a large quantity."

"But they are hot chili peppers," the villager warns, "and they will make you sick or worse."

"Yes," cried Nasrudin, popping another chili into his burning mouth, "but I cannot stop until I have finished every last one."

"You are an obstinate fool!," scolds the villager. "If you know they are chilis, why do you keep on eating them?"

"I am not eating chili peppers," Nasrudin explains mournfully. *"I am eating my money."*

Like all Nasrudin tales, this one uses an apparently silly and unlikely scenario to impart a serious lesson.

**When we invest a lot of time and effort in something—
a relationship, a career path, a decision, a choice—
and then come to realize that things haven't turned out
as we expected them to, we often
stubbornly insist on continuing to do what
we've been doing, rather than
admitting that we have made a mistake.**

Even after we ask ourselves, *"How did I get here, and what do I do now?"* and even after we begin to understand the answer, it still can be very painful to face a new truth, take a new direction and release that in which we are so emotionally invested, whether it be a person, a job, a friendship, a belief, a habit or a basket of hot chili peppers mistaken for sweet fruits. Our ego doesn't want to feel we have made a mistake, or wasted time, energy, money, love. Our pride doesn't want anyone else to see us look as if we've done something wrong. And so we do just what Nasrudin did: we tune out what is really happening and go into denial. *We keep eating the chili peppers, even while our mouth, our heart, our soul is on fire.*

The Four Denials

Much has been written about denial and the role it plays in our lives, our addictions and our unhealthy behaviors. The term *denial* was first commonly used to describe people who deny that they have a problem with drug or alcohol dependency, but more broadly, it describes the psychological defenses all of us use to reject painful realities that appear to threaten our self-worth and sense of emotional survival.

The most blatant manifestations of denial are easy to identify: the addict who can't get out of bed but insists he's just tired from the pressures at work; the battered woman who assures her friends that the bruises on her face weren't put there by her husband, but by accidentally walking into a door, for the third time in a month; the girl who tells herself her boyfriend is probably just busy and that's why she hasn't heard from him for a week, even though she's called his house in the middle of the night and he is never there.

We read these examples and reassure ourselves that we would never be this heavily in denial—we are too aware for that. But denial is tricky. Sometimes its most insidious and dangerous forms are the most disguised, and even those of us who consider ourselves conscious and awake may not even recognize them as denial at all. It is always easier to see how others tune out, and more difficult to notice our own patterns—that is because we tune out the ways that we have been tuning out!

In my work, I've identified and named *four common ways of tuning out*, which I call The Four Denials:

1. **Preoccupied Denial**
2. **Idealistic Denial**
3. **Angry Denial**
4. **Unconditional Denial**

Each of these is a strategy we use to deal with what we'd rather not deal with—unwelcome realities, unexpected wake-up calls, difficult turning points, and confusing crossroads.

Remember the four disciples in my elephant story at the beginning of this chapter? Each represents one of the Four Denials. The first disciple becomes too preoccupied with preparing for the elephant to deal with the actuality of its arrival, *Preoccupied Denial*. The second disciple is blinded by his idealistic vision of the elephant and therefore does not take the threat seriously, *Idealistic*

Denial. The third disciple becomes angry and defensive at hearing about the elephant and, imagining the villagers are attacking him, he attacks back, *Angry Denial.* The fourth disciple, obviously terrified, unconditionally refuses even to consider the truth of what the villagers are saying and shuts them out completely, *Unconditional Denial.*

The wise Guru, who is enlightened and free from all limiting patterns and reactions, is the only one who really hears the truth in what the villagers are saying: there is an angry elephant approaching the village, and they must get out of its way if they want to save their lives.

As you read about these Four Denials, you will undoubtedly recognize behavior patterns of many people you know . . . and some of your own as well.

Preoccupied Denial

The truth knocks on the door and you say,
"Go away, I'm looking for the truth,"
and so it goes away.
—Robert M. Pirsig,
Zen and the Art of Motorcycle Maintenance

I once joked to a friend that I was thinking of manufacturing T-shirts with this saying printed on the front: *Don't Bother Me with the Truth Right Now—I'm Busy!* She laughed and said that if I did, I'd probably be a multimillionaire, since everyone would buy one. I came up with this phrase after many years of observing one of the most common ways we deny the realities with which we are faced: **we make ourselves too busy and preoccupied to deal with them.**

One might even say that being busy and always occupied is the American way of life. We are constantly doing, going, buying and planning how we can do even more. Even our children are over-scheduled, running from ballet lessons to soccer practice, from play dates to math tutoring, all the while instant-messaging their friends from their cell phones. Being busy, then, becomes one of the most respectable and accepted methods we use to tune out. After all, we tell ourselves, it's not that we don't want to deal with what's facing us—we really just don't have the time right now. We are too busy for reality.

At first glance, Preoccupied Denial doesn't look like denial at all. In fact, it usually looks like something much more admirable. We're *responsible, committed and ambitious* because we are so preoccupied by our work; we're *devoted, caring and selfless* because we are so preoccupied by our children; we're *altruistic, humanitarian and visionary* because we are so preoccupied by our church, synagogue, charity, foundation or benefit. Who can argue with this? Who can criticize it? We're not in denial—we're just being a good person.

> **Here's a favorite phrase practitioners
> of Preoccupied Denial use often:
> "I know I need to (<u>fill in the blank</u>),
> but this really isn't a good time
> because (<u>fill in the blank</u>)."**

I use the following chart in my seminars to illustrate that when we are in Preoccupied Denial, we can choose any item from Column A, and any item from Column B, and what we're saying will sound reasonable and understandable to most people. Try mixing these up and you will see what I mean.

I know I need to:	*But this really isn't a good time because:*
Deal with my marital problems	I'm under a lot of pressure at work
Stop smoking	I'm recovering from my father's death

I know I need to:	*But this really isn't a good time because:*
Work on controlling my anger	We're remodeling the house
Get a divorce	My daughter has two years left before she graduates
Quit my job	My mother just moved in with us
Get help with my childhood trauma	I'm getting married next year and need to plan the wedding
Confront my husband about his infidelity	Our ten-year anniversary is next month
Go back to work again	I'm going through menopause and dealing with hot flashes
Deal with my son's drug use	I just got promoted at the office and have more responsibility
Go to the doctor and deal with my health issues	I'm in charge of this year's school food drive
Start dating again after my divorce	My son's grades have slipped and he needs my help
Move to a safer apartment	I am studying for my graduate school entrance exams
Go to therapy for our sex life	My husband has a back problem
Start an exercise program	Christmas is coming up
Break up with my boyfriend	We have reservations to go to Hawaii in three months

All these reasons for our preoccupations are legitimate activities. I am sure that you, like me, can make your own list and fill in your own blanks. But the bottom line is that they are also excuses for tuning out what we should be paying attention to—impressive excuses, but excuses just the same. As we said in chapter 1, there's never a good time to face the unexpected or the unpleasant. It is always inconvenient, always disruptive and always inconsiderate of our to-do list.

Those who are prone to Preoccupied Denial are often achievement junkies and attention addicts who have a difficult time doing less than just about everything and find it practically impossible to stop and be still. They need the constant rush of accomplishment and the praise that goes along with it to fill a deep void that has probably been with them since childhood. They become tireless workers, volunteers, friends, parents, helpers—you name it. They say yes to everything and everyone—except the call of their own hearts.

. . .

My friend Mary Jane is a well-known artist who married her husband, Lawrence, when she was quite young. At the time she was impressed with everything about him—he was fifteen years older than she and very successful. Once her own career began to take off, they quickly grew apart. From the first moment I met Mary Jane, I knew her marriage was in trouble. She barely mentioned Lawrence, flirted with every man within fifteen feet and scheduled her life as if her husband didn't even exist. "I know our marriage isn't working," she confessed to me within four hours of my knowing her, "and after my next show, I am going to deal with it."

Several months later, after Mary Jane had returned from a triumphant exhibition of her paintings, she called me to say hello. "So, have you spoken to Lawrence yet?" I asked.

"You know, I meant to, but I've just been swamped," she answered, "I have to prepare some paintings for a new hotel that is opening in the Caribbean, and my son just made it to the finals of a martial arts competition—isn't that exciting? And did I tell you I'm hosting a reception at our house for some Tibetan monks who are doing wonderful work? But when this is all over and I can catch my breath, I really am going to talk to Lawrence about a divorce."

Mary Jane is an expert at Preoccupied Denial, so good, in fact, that eight years and dozens of similar conversations later, she is still impossibly busy, horribly overcommitted—albeit to wonderful things—still unhappily married to Lawrence, and still insisting that she will address her practically nonexistent marriage . . . when things slow down in her life. Only they never do, and as long as she is in denial, they never will. Mary Jane has had several affairs and so has Lawrence. They sleep in separate bedrooms. She has frequent anxiety attacks and pops tranquilizers as if they are breath mints. He is rarely without a drink in his hand. But to the world, they are still a happily married couple.

What is Mary Jane working so hard to tune out? What is she afraid to face? That she will have to sacrifice much of her luxurious lifestyle if she goes through with a divorce. That she will have to relinquish her image as being half of such a powerful couple. That she will disappoint her children. And perhaps most of all, that she probably should have left Lawrence years ago.

Idealistic Denial

The problem is not that there are problems.
The problem is expecting otherwise and thinking
that having problems is a problem.
—Theodore Rubin

If pessimism is seeing a glass filled halfway with water as half empty, and optimism is seeing the glass as half full, then perhaps **idealism is seeing the glass as completely full in spite of the missing water.** This is what I call Idealistic Denial.

Those of us who are experts at Idealistic Denial, and I readily admit to belonging in this category, would argue that we aren't in denial—we're just very positive people who like to hope for the best in every situation, see the best in every person and strive for the best in everything we do. We do not like to rush to judgment, declare failure prematurely or throw in the towel unless absolutely forced to.

Practitioners of Idealistic Denial are often perfectionists who insist on high standards for ourselves and for the reality we are living in. We don't like it when things go wrong, especially when we see how they could have gone right. Like Preoccupied Denial, Idealistic Denial often disguises itself in the cloak of other redeeming qualities: compassion, patience, support, concern, consideration, kindness. But when our compassion turns into codependence, our patience into stagnation, our concern into enabling and our support into sacrifice, we are no longer being kind—we are being blind.

There's nothing wrong with looking for the silver lining in the dark cloud, hoping for a miracle, believing in the power other people have to change or expecting the best. The problem with Idealistic Denial is that we can use these traits to avoid confrontation—either with other people or with ourselves. After all, we hate confrontation, because Idealizers are also harmonizers. We will do everything in our power to elude conflict and unpleasantness, even if it means sacrificing our own happiness.

When we are in Idealistic Denial, we don't start out trying to run away from reality. We simply get trapped by our own idealistic tendencies, which don't leave much room for the existence of the imperfect.

. . .

Dennis is one of the kindest, most intelligent, judicious people I know. His work as a pediatric oncologist requires an enormous amount of compassion, wisdom and love as he does all he can for very ill and dying children and their families. Every day, he is in a battle with the cancer ravaging the bodies of his young patients and with the despair eating away at their loved ones. He takes on both of these with a fierce determination and a belief that to hope for the best will be of more benefit than to fear the worst.

Dennis is no stranger to heartbreak. When he was in his late twenties and engaged to be married, his fiancée broke up with him one week before the wedding, confessing that she had fallen in love with another doctor who worked in Dennis's building. Completely devastated, Dennis threw himself into his work and soon became one of the top physicians in his field. For two years Dennis avoided any romantic involvements until one of his nurses fixed him up with her friend, also a nurse, named Ginny. Dennis was drawn to Ginny because she seemed so lighthearted and uncomplicated. Having spent the past few years depressed and isolated, he welcomed Ginny's bubbly personality. True, she was a bit high-strung, and they didn't share many mutual interests, but Dennis told himself that his former fiancée had possessed all of the right qualifications for his perfect mate, and look how that turned out. So when Ginny pushed to quickly move in together, and soon after to get married, Dennis didn't resist.

Dennis says it was sometime during the first few months of marriage when he realized that Ginny's bubbly personality came out of a bottle of prescription pain medication, and that she'd had a serious drug addiction since she was a teenager. He had thought she was taking pills for a bad back, but somehow hadn't paid attention to how many pills and how often. Even without this discovery, the marriage was off to a very rocky start. It was painfully obvious to Dennis that he and Ginny had nothing in common and were totally mismatched. Ginny swore she would stop using the pills and begged Dennis not to leave her, claiming if he did, she wouldn't survive. Dennis sought out a therapist and poured out his heart about the impossible situation he found himself in.

Dennis was psychologically trapped—how could he leave Ginny as his fiancée had left him, knowing it would destroy her? How could he abandon her in her hour of need as she tried to kick her addiction when he prided himself on being there for even the most tragic of his patients in the worst of circumstances? How could he disappoint her when she was counting on him to rescue her? And just as devastating, how could he live with his stupidity in not having seen Ginny's obvious addiction? How could he explain his poor judgment in believing she was the kind of woman with whom he could be happily married?

All of these realities were too painful for Dennis, who had worked all of his life to be wise, loyal and dedicated. And so he tuned out and went into a prolonged state of Idealistic Denial: he spent even more time on his work and research than before. He watched Ginny go on and off her pills, and told himself that he was being too hard on her, that she didn't really have a serious addiction. He reminded himself whenever Ginny had one of her frequent meltdowns that she'd had a very unhappy childhood and was doing the best she could. He convinced himself that having a romantic relationship wasn't that important and that being in love and sexually fulfilled were for young guys but not him. He could do without it, and besides, soon Ginny would get it together, and things between them would improve.

Dennis's Idealistic Denial lasted ten years, until he woke up one day and found he just couldn't go on suffering and sacrificing anymore. This is how Dennis describes the end of his marriage to Ginny:

> It took me ten years to leave my wife—one hour in that very painful and honest conversation with my therapist during which I admitted to myself that I'd made a mistake when I married Ginny, and nine more years, eleven months, twenty-nine days and twenty-three hours to finally face the fact that, no matter how long I waited, it wouldn't change what I'd realized in that first hour years ago.

Angry Denial

An angry man opens his mouth and shuts his eyes.
        —Cato

Have you ever been in the midst of a deep sleep when suddenly something unexpected startles you awake—the phone rings, your cat knocks over a delicate vase that crashes to the floor, someone's car alarm goes off right outside your window? Your first reaction is usually shock: "What's wrong? What was that noise?"

you mutter, fumbling for the light switch as your heart rapidly pounds. Your next reaction might very well be to get angry: "No, this is not Red Top Cab. You have the wrong number and you woke me up!" "Fluffy, you know you are NOT supposed to jump up on those shelves!" "Those damn neighbors—that's the second time their car alarm went off this week!"

This is exactly how some people feel when they are startled by the unexpected, cornered by the truth, or jolted by a wake-up call in their lives—they are angry that they've been ripped from their comfortable state of existence and forced to pay attention to something they'd rather not deal with. *They feel attacked, and so they attack back.*

If those practicing Preoccupied Denial avoid the truth, and those who favor Idealistic Denial sugar-coat the truth, then people who make a habit of Angry Denial become furious at the truth—as well as with those who deliver the truth to them. The saying *"kill the messenger"* applies here. They become hostile, defensive, belligerent, outraged and punishing, as if somehow their fury will scare off the news/revelation/difficult choice/painful reality facing them.

Intense anger is often a reaction to intense fear—the more afraid we are, the more hostile we often become. This behavior is seen in animals living in the wild, who, when they feel threatened, instinctively protect their territory with any means they have at their disposal: the bull charges; the lioness snarls and leaps; the snake releases venom; the porcupine shoots its quills; the bee stings. Sadly, throughout history, human beings have imitated these same primal instincts for survival in our attitudes and behaviors toward other human beings. What we fear or do not understand, we attempt to condemn and destroy.

Angry Denial renders us blind—blind to the truth that is trying to reveal itself; blind to the new roads of insight, experience and discovery that are available if only we would see them; blind to the love, support and goodwill of others; and most tragic of all, blind to what lies within our own hearts—our dreams, our fears, our longing to truly see.

. . .

Jocelyn, the owner of a successful advertising agency with offices in several major cities, sat across from me and told me a dramatic story. Two years ago she hired Patricia, a motivated young woman a few years out of graduate school, to run her Chicago office. Patricia had started out as an assistant account executive, but quickly proved herself to be a hard worker and aggressive in acquiring new accounts. "I was impressed with her," Jocelyn explained, "and I needed someone who could really infuse the Chicago operation with a lot of energy. I fly in from New York once every few weeks to check on things, but with so many new campaigns, I just can't micromanage each office. She seemed perfect for the job, and reassured me that I could back off and let her handle things. So I did."

A year passed, and business was booming in all of Jocelyn's branches, so much that she decided it was time to bring in a highly regarded international business management firm to oversee the financial operations of her entire company. They planned to spend two months assessing every aspect of Jocelyn's business and offering her recommendations that would help things run even more smoothly. Jocelyn sent out a letter to all of her employees announcing her affiliation with the management group, and asking them to cooperate in helping them gather all the information they needed.

"One morning," Jocelyn said, "I got a call from the vice president of the management group. He told me, 'We've got a problem in Chicago.' When I asked him what sort of problem, he said one word: Patricia. When he had contacted her and asked her for information on her accounts, her financial records and her expense vouchers, she'd gone ballistic, threatening to have him fired, accusing him of trying to steal her job, and even bad-mouthing me for sending him to 'spy' on her. I was stunned and decided there must have been some misunderstanding. Why would Patricia behave this way?"

Jocelyn asked Patricia to fly to New York for a meeting, and things went from bad to worse. "It was so bizarre," Jocelyn told me, "because I was the one who should have been upset with her, and yet she showed up furious at me. She said things like 'How dare you mistrust me!' and 'I consider this harassment.' I honestly felt like I was watching a movie with bad dialogue, only it was really happening. I tried to reassure her that no one was accusing her of anything and that we were simply trying to streamline our procedures and record-keeping in all of our offices. Patricia's setup had always been very informal, and that's why we had brought in professionals. But she couldn't hear any of that—it was as if she had already made up her mind about what was happening and was reacting to that, and nothing else. At the end, she just stormed out."

Two days later, Patricia filed an enormous lawsuit against Jocelyn, charging her with everything and anything one could imagine. The suit was baseless, but it still took Jocelyn six months of time and expensive attorneys' bills to make it—and Patricia—go away. "I haven't quite recovered," she shared with me. "I feel like I accidentally stumbled onto a hornet's nest and got stung all over."

Jocelyn's analogy was actually quite accurate. Unknowingly, she had trespassed into the minefield of Patricia's secret fears—fear of losing her job, of making mistakes, of being too inexperienced and disorganized, of failing. Patricia's bravado and veneer of confidence had always covered up her vast insecurities, which she herself refused to acknowledge or face. She had been in denial—until she was asked for her records. Terrified that her imperfections would be found out and afraid of being attacked, she struck first. Patricia's Angry Denial compelled her to avoid acknowledging her fears and flaws by becoming unnecessarily defensive and hostile. She ironically punished the very person whose approval she was so afraid of losing.

Those people who indulge in Angry Denial are masters at hiding their own sense of inadequacy from themselves as well as from others. They become furious at anyone or anything that even inadvertently finds a way to make them feel the vulnerabilities they have spent their lives working so hard to eradicate.

Unconditional Denial

There are some people that if they don't know, you can't tell 'em.
—Louis Armstrong

Leave it to the inimitable, outspoken Louis Armstrong, regarded by many as the most influential jazz musician in history, to say it better than I ever could—some people have no interest in knowing anything they don't already know, even if it is staring them in the face. This is Unconditional Denial.

Unconditional Denial is the refusal to recognize the truth or to acknowledge reality in spite of any evidence with which we are confronted. Unconditional Denial is the real thing, pure and un-adulterated by any sense of reason or rationality. It is not partial denial—it is absolute. Unlike the other forms of denial, it leaves no room for doubt, no possibility of getting around to the truth at a future date, no other point of view we might consider. It is uncom-promising and unrelenting.

The human mind is amazing in its ability to distort reality to the point at which we actually believe that our altered version of the truth is the right one, and other people's versions of that same reality are false. In the case of Unconditional Denial, this powerful mechanism of blocking out reality is operating at full force. It is the person with his hands covering his own eyes claiming, "I don't see anything." This philosophy is summed up in the bumper sticker I've seen on cars that reads: "Don't Confuse Me with the Truth— I'm in Denial!"

All forms of denial are, to a large extent, a sort of survival mech-anism that kicks in when we feel frightened or threatened. People who fall into Unconditional Denial believe on an unconscious level that their very psychological survival depends on their unswerving adherence to their version of the truth, with no room for negotia-tion. *Their denial becomes a life raft to them in what feels like a ter-rifying sea of painful realities. As long as they remain in denial, they tell themselves, they will not drown.* Sadly, of course, the opposite is true—they are already drowning, drowning in denial so thick and tough that one wonders what, if anything, can ever penetrate it.

. . .

Here is an e-mail I recently received from one of my readers:

Dear Dr. De Angelis,

I am writing you out of desperation, and hope you can help me. My name is Shawna. I am thirty-four years old, and happily married. I am also a twin, and my sister Sheila is the one I am so worried about. Sheila and I have been very close all of our lives, although we are very different. Maybe because I came out first, I've always had more confidence, and Sheila is more insecure. Also, her judgment hasn't been the greatest. In high school, she got mixed up with a bad crowd, lots of partying and drinking, and even though she cleaned up her act after that, she still never took very good care of herself.

This is about Sheila and her husband Bobby. They got married when we were all in college and have two boys. I was so happy that Sheila found Bobby, because he is a nice guy, very stable and makes a good living. I always worried that her insecurities might cause problems, and I guess I was right. About five years ago, Bobby told Sheila that he wasn't happy in their marriage and wanted to go to counseling to work on it. She got angry with him and acted like he hadn't said anything. She never even told me about it, and she tells me everything, or so I thought. Only later after everything blew up did I find out from Bobby. He says that every few months he would bring it up, and she would cry for a while, and then pretend everything was fine. By now I knew something was wrong whenever we'd see them, but when I'd ask, she insisted nothing was going on.

One day about three years ago, I went over to Sheila's house so our kids could play early one morning, and noticed that Bobby's car was gone. I asked her where he was, and she said he was away on business. Now I knew this was fishy because Bobby is a plumber and never takes business trips. Sheila seemed totally normal, baking cookies and doing chores, so I just dropped it. But each time I went over in the next few weeks, Bobby wasn't there.

Dr. De Angelis, I am sure you already know what I am going to say. *Bobby had told Sheila he wanted to separate and had moved out.* I only discovered this when he called my husband later that month and confided in him. He said he loved Sheila, but couldn't live with her anymore. He was tired of trying to make things work on his own. He was pretty broken up about it, and as much as I love my sister, I understood where he was coming from.

Sheila was still pretending nothing had happened, and even when I confronted her, she made up some excuse that Bobby needed his own apartment so he could work on his accounting late at night. I told her I'd spoken with Bobby several times, and he'd told me they had separated, and she just laughed and said, "He didn't really mean it. He's planning to move back in as soon as his business gets back on track. This way he can concentrate better."

Things only got worse from here. Everyone knew Bobby had left Sheila except Sheila! Even her boys, ages ten and twelve, told me they knew their Dad and Mom were getting divorced, in spite of the fact that I overheard Sheila several times saying right in front of them that Bobby was just going through a little "crisis" and that he'd be back. Christmas came and Sheila sent out cards from Bobby and Sheila complete with one of those printed newsletters about how everyone was doing, and she talked all about Bobby! He'd been gone almost a year, and she still refused to admit it to anyone, especially herself. She even sent him an anniversary card on what would have been their wedding anniversary, and I know this because he showed me, and she wrote "Happy Anniversary Baby! From your true lover and wife Sheila, here's to many more years together." I cried when I saw this card.

A year and a half ago, Bobby started dating a very nice woman named Helen who he met in church, and they got very serious. Everyone likes Helen a lot, and she and Bobby are good for each other, and he looks real happy. When I try to talk to Sheila about this, she refuses to even acknowledge that it is true. *"I cannot accept this,"* she always says. *"As far as I am concerned, Bobby is still my husband. I refuse to take his thing with that woman seriously. It's just about sex, I'm sure."* She still calls Bobby all hours of the day and night, like they were still together. She pretends Helen doesn't exist. Bobby doesn't know what to do any more. He's tried to be nice and civil and keeps waiting for Sheila to face the truth, but she never does. She still acts like he is coming back any day now. She even still wears her wedding ring, though I've begged her to take it off.

We have tried to get Sheila to go to counseling, but she refuses and insists she is fine. *She is living in a complete dream world, and I cannot live in that world with her.* It is breaking my heart to see her like this. Please tell me if there is anything I can do for my twin sister.

.   .   .

Sheila's tale is a sad one. Until she gets professional help or hits bottom, she probably won't find the motivation she needs to heal herself. Reading Shawna's letter about her sister's unstoppable denial, I was reminded once again of how powerful each of us is, beyond anything we could imagine. Sheila certainly was a disturbing but unquestionable example of this power. Day after day, year after year, in spite of all evidence to the contrary, she has persisted in her denial of the truth, using every ounce of her will, her strength, her intention to block out reality. Of course, this is no accomplishment to be proud of—it is destroying Sheila's life—but I can't help but wonder what great achievements Sheila would be capable of if only she chose to focus all of that stubborn determination in a positive rather than destructive direction.

. . .

Truth hurts—not the searching after: the running from!
—John Eyberg

I n whatever manner we do it, for whatever reason we do it, and
for however long we do it, one thing is certain: running from the
truth is an exercise in futility. Eventually, and inevitably, truth will
catch up with us, and by that time we will be exhausted.

**Tuning reality out takes a tremendous
amount of energy.
When we use our time, our will and our efforts
to run away from truth, we become exhausted—
physically, mentally, emotionally and spiritually.**

We don't even realize how much of our life force we've been using not to see, not to feel and not to know . . . until we stop doing
it. Then, suddenly, we are flooded with waves of strength, vitality
and optimism. We feel revived, renewed and in many ways reborn.
And this is as it should be, for when we relinquish our denial, parts
of us will have died—our struggle, our blindness, our resistance to
that truth that has been patiently waiting for our embrace.

Tuning Back In

*We must care to think about the unthinkable things,
because when things become unthinkable, thinking stops
and action becomes mindless.*
—James W. Fulbright

T his is what we are beginning to understand: **Nothing matters
more than being awake to the truth that is around you and the
truth that is inside you.** To tune out these truths is to move through

life like a sleepwalker, eyes closed to what lies behind you and what lies in front of you. You, and I, and all of us who long to live enlightened lives, must, as the great politician and visionary James Fulbright reminds us, find the courage to face the truths that have been stalking us, to recognize the wild elephants stampeding over our expectations and to think about "unthinkable things."

Imagine how our lives would look if we became as adept at running toward the truth as we are at running away from it.

Imagine how much insight, wonder and revelation would flourish in our awareness if we put our intention into fully waking up, rather than in remaining asleep.

Recently I came across the remarkable story of Katharine Butler Hathaway, an American writer born in 1890. As a child Katharine was diagnosed with spinal tuberculosis. In an attempt to cure her deformed spine, her doctors strapped her to a board and kept her immobile for ten years, until then she turned fifteen. In spite of the horrible suffering she endured, the treatment did not work. Katharine realized, although no one would come out and say it, that her disability was a forbidden topic: She was hunchbacked and considered "deformed" by her family and society, and expected to lock herself away from the world and live as a dependent spinster.

Katharine made a courageous choice—she chose to embrace the truth about her condition and to embrace life. She moved away from her family. Defying all expectations, she became an artist, traveled throughout Europe, bought and restored a home in Maine and eventually married. Her memoir of her struggles, *The Little Locksmith*, was published the year after she died at the age of fifty-two.

Katharine wrote:

The change of life is the time when you meet yourself at a crossroads and you decide whether to be honest or not before you die.

Perhaps this is the real and only crossroads we all come to—not the decision to go this way or that way on the outside, but the decision about how we want to exist on the inside; not what we are going to do about our career, our relationship, or our problems, but whether we are going to turn away from the truth or turn toward it.

These are the brave choices waiting to be made:

The choice to tune back in and hear the insistent knock of the truth.

And the choice to answer the door.

✑ 5 ✎

Turning Off and Freezing Up: Where Did the Passion Go?

*People who live and act mindlessly run the risk
of being trapped in unlived lives.*
—Jeff Cox

Sometimes, in trying to avoid suffering, we make ourselves suffer more. Sometimes, in turning away from what we wish to avoid, we end up slamming into something worse. We attempt to escape from the unpleasant realities relentlessly hunting us down, and so we run blindly in another direction, only to find ourselves ultimately trapped by the discontent of our own unanswered questions and the disappointments of our own unlived life.

Here is my next story for you:

Long ago, there was a stonecutter who lived in a small village at the foot of a mountain. He was a simple man, a hard worker and a steady provider for his wife and three children. However, the stonecutter had a flaw—although generally good-natured, he hated being disturbed by a lot of noise when he was working. His family learned to be very quiet when the stonecutter was deep in thought about how to cut a particular rock, but the neighbor's dogs were another story. Whenever the stonecutter worked, the three rowdy dogs would begin to bark and howl loudly, driving him to distraction. No matter how often the stonecutter complained to his neighbor or shouted at the dogs to be quiet, the animals continued to torture the stonecutter with their incessant racket.

Finally the stonecutter had an idea: if he couldn't shut the dogs up, he could at least shut them out. So he fashioned two balls of wax and he pushed then deep into his ears. Silence! He was ecstatic. He could barely hear much of anything, but he didn't care. For the first time in years, he worked on his stones in peace.

When the stonecutter's wife noticed that he was unusually cheerful, she couldn't imagine what could be responsible. For several weeks, she felt relieved that her husband had stopped complaining about the dogs and appeared to be in a peaceful frame of mind. But after a while, she became irritated because it seemed that no matter what she said to him, he totally ignored her. "Good morning, dear," she'd say when he came to breakfast, but he would say nothing back. "The horse is limping—he might have a pebble in his shoe," she'd announce, but her husband would walk by as if she hadn't said a word. "Have you seen my bucket?" she'd ask, but he'd simply smile and walk away. "Why is he treating me like this?" she wondered in despair.

The stonecutter's wife wasn't the only one becoming exasperated with him. His customers, too, were having problems. A wealthy landowner visited his workshop and asked if the stonecutter could build a fountain in his courtyard, promising to pay him well, but the stonecutter never came to the man's estate. The farmer down the road, who'd known the stonecutter since they were children, stopped by one day and offered to hire his friend to build a new stone wall around his fields, but the stonecutter acted as if he didn't hear him, and the farmer left furious. Soon the stonecutter had almost no work, and was running out of money.

The stonecutter did sense that people around him seemed

more agitated than usual, but he was so content enjoying the new peace and quiet of his world that he didn't give much thought to anything else. "I can't remember ever being this happy and calm," he remarked to himself. ·

Finally, the stonecutter's wife was at the end of her rope. Her husband had barely spoken to her in ages. She'd pleaded with him to tell her what was wrong, begged for him to remember how much they had once loved each other, and implored him to open his heart to her again. When that didn't work, she'd tried yelling at him and threatened to leave, but this, too, seemed to have no effect. One day she decided that enough was enough. She packed her belongings into the wagon along with her children and told the neighbors she was going back to live with her parents in the next village. All that was left for her to do was to say good-bye to her husband.

By now you probably have figured out that the stonecutter had not taken the wax balls out of his ears ever since he put them in. In fact, he'd forgotten all about them. But this particular day in summer was unusually warm, and the wax, having grown softer over time, suddenly began to melt. The stonecutter noticed the thick liquid dripping out of his ears, and just then, his wife appeared at his workshop door. "Good-bye," she said in a cold voice. "I'm leaving and taking the children with me."

A jolt ran through the stonecutter's head—it had been so long since he'd actually heard his wife's voice—or anyone's—clearly. Then what she said registered in his brain. "Leaving?" he asked in a puzzled voice. "Where are you going, my dear?"

"Don't play dumb with me! I'm leaving—for good! I can't take this hell with you anymore," she cried.

"But . . . but . . . I don't understand! Is something wrong? Are you unhappy?"

"Am I unhappy?" she shouted. "It's a little late to ask me that now. For three years I've tried to talk to you, tried to explain how miserable I was, but you shut me out. It was as if you didn't hear a word I said! No more!" And with that, she turned and left.

Suddenly, the stonecutter heard another sound he hadn't heard in three years—the neighbor's dogs barking loudly. And in that moment, his heart broke as he realized what a foolish thing he had done: by making himself deaf to the noises of the dogs, he had shut out everything else. He had not only been deaf—he'd been blind to the truth.

. . .

We usually do not realize the high price we pay for tuning out until it is too late. At first, like the stonecutter, we may breathe a sigh of relief that we no longer have to deal with the truths we've been dreading. Our relationship isn't really that bad, and things are calmer now that we aren't talking about our problems. Ever since we've accepted the fact that we will never get a promotion at work, we've stopped caring so much about our job, and therefore have more time for ourselves. Since we've decided that our friend who's upset with us is just not worth the trouble and stopped calling her, we don't have to worry about what to say to her.

Soon, however, we discover the unfortunate truth—**we cannot tune out selectively.** When we shut off the ability to see one thing, we create the habit of shutting off our ability to see anything. When we shut down our willingness to hear, whether our own inner voice of discontent, our partner's complaints, or the messages coming to us from others, we shut down our capacity to hear anything. Without noticing that it is happening, without intending it to happen, the outcome of tuning out repeatedly is the same:

When we tune out for long enough, we inevitably turn off.

What does turning off feel like? *Numbness. Flatness. Disconnection. Coldness. Deadness.* That is, if you even are aware of feeling much of anything.

Most of the time, however, being turned off feels like *nothing*. *That's because you are turned off*. The stonecutter had no idea he had shut out the world, and even though my story isn't meant to be realistic, the pattern is the same: when you begin to turn off to what is happening inside you and what is happening around you, it is as if you begin very slowly and imperceptibly to retreat from the world. Others may notice that you are more distant and less present, but you are often oblivious to how you are retreating. You even become angry with anyone who accuses you of pulling away, which will probably encourage you to pull away even more.

A fourteen-year-old girl describes her process of turning off in this way:

> You just switch off because you don't like how the story is going. Like closing a book before you finish, or turning off a program, or switching off a CD.

A thirty-four-year-old husband says it like this:

> I never made a conscious decision to shut my wife out. After a while, it was just easier for me to turn off to her criticisms and her coldness than it was for me to deal with them. I'd tell myself I was just giving myself the weekend to chill, and I'd retreat into my own little world. Soon one weekend became a month of weekends, and then years of feeling totally disconnected. And now, I just feel a million miles away from her, and I can't figure out how to open back up.

From a forty-eight-year-old divorced woman:

> The only way I knew how to survive my husband's drinking for so many years was to turn myself off and just go on automatic. What else could I do, with three small children? When he was drunk, he was like the fourth kid. I was

taking care of everybody, trying to hold things together even though I knew they were falling apart. Once we got divorced and the kids got into high school, my friends told me it was time to get a life again. And I would think, "How the hell do I that, just start caring again?" 'Cause I felt pretty close to dead inside.

Turning off the television or your DVD player or your cell phone doesn't have serious or lasting consequences—when you are ready to watch or listen or talk again, you turn them back on. This is not how it is when we turn ourselves off.

**We don't realize how turned off we've been
until we try to turn back on again
and discover that we can't find the switch.**

Living a Turned-Off Life

*Our lives begin to end the day we become silent
about things that matter.*
—Martin Luther King

For all the courage I have shown in my life, there have been as many moments when I've kept silent out of fear. For all the love I feel for myself, there have been as many moments when I've allowed others to treat me without kindness. For all the vision and clarity I possess, there have been as many moments when, hoping to avoid conflict and loss, I have closed my eyes to the truth. And for as much as I have fought always to keep my heart open, I, too, confess to having turned off—not for long, but for long enough to look back and mourn every lost hour that I spent in the thick fog of sacrifice and self-deception.

It is clear to me now, standing as I do these days on a safe and stable shore, *that my most agonizing suffering has all had its source in me.* No lover's lies or dishonesty has been more devastating than my own refusal to honor what I knew to be true in my heart. No enemies' attempts to harm or hinder me have been more damaging than my own choices to allow these dark forces to temporarily fill me with fear and cause me to falter. Nothing anyone has unfairly taken from me—recognition, money, ideas, opportunity—has been more of a loss than that which I have willingly relinquished by ignoring what I needed and deserved.

This has been an essential and hard-earned awakening, one that has rewarded me in ways I could not have anticipated—healing me, liberating me, empowering me.

All of us are taking part in this same kind of personal excavation, struggling to recover pieces of ourselves we thought were stolen from us, but that in fact we ourselves have buried or locked away—lost emotions, hidden dreams, forgotten longings, self-respect and faith.

Katherine Anne Porter, a Pulitzer Prize–winning American writer of short stories who gained renown in the early part of the twentieth century, writes about these necessary but painful moments of revelation in her famous work "Theft." In it she tells the compelling story of a woman who, for all of her life, has completely turned off her own needs, giving pieces of herself away to one man after another. In the final moments of the story, when a stolen purse is returned to her, the woman contemplates her life and her losses and realizes that she feels robbed, not by the purse snatcher, but by her own decision to ignore the longings within herself. She confesses:

"I was right not to be afraid of any thief but myself, who will end by leaving me nothing."

Each time I read this line, I am struck by how powerfully it captures a truth that, like the heroine in the story, too many of us discover too late: we spend so much time trying to protect ourselves from hurt and loss, worrying about what other people could do to us, or take from us, when in fact we are the "thief" who is the most likely to steal from ourselves.

When we tune out and turn off,
we rob ourselves of those things
that are most valuable—
our dreams, our feelings, our love, our aliveness.
This self-perpetuated theft is a loss that costs us
more dearly than we can imagine,
for we have stolen from ourselves that which is
more precious and essential than anything we think
others have ever taken from us.

Freezing Up

What other dungeon is so dark as one's own heart?
What jailer so inexorable as one's self?
—Nathaniel Hawthorne

Hidden beneath a turned-off life is a storehouse of despair. Sometimes it is quiet despair, born of the unspoken knowledge of all that we have cut ourselves off from. Sometimes it is a cynical despair, scolding us that it is too late for happiness, too late for change. Sometimes it is despair disguised as anger or blame, and sometimes it isn't disguised at all, and we experience deep sadness and depression that does not seem to go away.

Imprisoned in these dungeons of despair, we often find ourselves in a kind of paralysis, as if we are bound by invisible chains and cannot move. It is difficult for us to make decisions, difficult to get motivated, difficult to reach out, to act, to change. We feel stuck, frozen. And it is hard to tell which is more perplexing to us—the lethargy we're experiencing, or our disturbing inability to snap ourselves out of it.

Recently I read a magazine interview with the late Christopher Reeve, the famous actor and film star who in 1995 suffered a devastating equestrian accident and was paralyzed from the neck down. I had deep admiration for Mr. Reeve's courageous and indomitable spirit. He defied all odds in his quest to breathe on his own without the aid of a respirator and to rehabilitate his body, and at the same time he worked tirelessly raising awareness and promoting research on spinal cord injuries. At one point in the interview, Mr. Reeve said something so powerfully honest that it has stayed with me since:

"Some people are walking around with full use of their bodies and they're more paralyzed than I am."

This blunt, profound wisdom, born of tremendous pain and sacrifice, crystallizes the point as only someone in Christopher Reeve's circumstances could.

We are free to move, but too often we don't. We are free to reach out and touch our loved ones, but too often we pull away. We are free to speak, but too often we remain silent. We are free, but we freeze up.

.   .   .

A good friend of mine had been struggling in her relationship with her husband, who is also my friend, for several years. He was a terrific father and all-around nice guy but had grown detached and distant from her. She knew he was under tremendous pressure at the office, and for a while she blamed this for the distance between them. Eventually, when things got worse and not better, she begged him to work on the relationship and go with her to counseling. She told him that she felt miserable, unloved and neglected, and warned him that she was beginning to fall out of love. "How did we get here?" she'd plead. "Let's do something to save our marriage."

Despite her attempts to get through to him, her husband ignored her requests and did nothing. He didn't disagree with her. He didn't say it was her fault and not his. He didn't become angry. He just did nothing.

I knew this man loved my friend very much, and I was surprised to hear he wasn't fighting with all he had to keep his wife. Each time I'd speak with him, he acted as if everything was fine, proudly sharing stories of his children and not mentioning a word about his marital problems. Even when his wife gave him a last ultimatum, he quietly ignored it and acted as if nothing had happened. When I asked my girlfriend why she thought her husband was behaving this way, she said something very revealing and very sad:

"I think he is so terrified of facing the fact that we are in trouble that, rather than confront the truth, he just froze up. *It is like he's frozen in his own life, unable to do anything.*"

Eventually my friend reached her limit, and made the difficult decision that it was time to end her marriage. Hours after she told her husband, he called me, sounding utterly destroyed. "My wife wants a divorce," he confessed between sobs. "All of a sudden, she said it's over. I can't believe I am losing her. The house, our friends, everything we shared—it's all going to vanish. How can this be happening to me?"

My heart hurt for my friend, not just because of his breakup, but because he had, as she suspected, been shut down, frozen up. The shock of her leaving him had acted like a violent wake-up call, cracking the ice around his heart. He had been turned off for so long, but now he was feeling everything: shock, grief, guilt, anger at himself, fear about his future and horrible regret. Finally he was paying attention, but it was too late.

．　．　．

I magine that every unresolved issue, unchallenged fear and unprocessed emotion is like a tall block of ice in the middle of our path. When there are just a few of these, we can maneuver our way around them. The more we don't deal with in our lives and our relationships, the more ice blocks there are, until at some point we are surrounded by a wall of frozen problems and frozen feelings. We feel stuck, trapped and unable to move.

Anything that contributes to our numbness and our ability to turn off will help keep us in a frozen emotional state: drugs, alcohol, food, shopping, overworking—whatever tranquilizes our discomfort and sedates our unhappiness—friends or family who cooperate with our denial, even a mate who is strongly entrenched in his or her own numbness, making it difficult for us to pierce our own.

This is what happened to my friend's husband. He had a lifetime of frozen issues walling him in, compounded by professional and financial stresses and the fear of failing in his marriage. He dealt with these the only way he knew how—he froze up even more.

When you say to yourself, "I don't want to deal with this," you not only cut yourself off from someone or something else—*you cut yourself off from your own life force, from that source of love, power and wisdom inside you.* You may think that by turning away from what is unpleasant you are protecting yourself, but this notion is false.

Turning off never protects you from hurt.
Freezing up never insulates you from pain.
Instead, it creates a wall of icy numbness between
you and that which you long for—
intimacy, passion and true connection.

There is only one way to escape from the frozen dungeon of our own heart. The ice needs to be melted, block by block, emotion by emotion, truth by truth, dream by dream. That is what my life's work has been about. That is what we are doing in these pages.

Where Did the Passion Go?

Love never dies a natural death. It dies because we don't
know how to replenish its source. It dies of blindness
and errors and betrayals. It dies of illness
and wounds; it dies of weariness, of
withering, of tarnishing.
—Anaïs Nin

Freezing up and turning off is the enemy of aliveness. It is the enemy of passion. It is the enemy of love. You can't remain frozen and have a deeply intimate relationship. You can't remain turned off and expect to feel turned on in your heart, your mind or your body. That's because freezing up stops the flow of love, and turns it into a river of ice.

When you turn off to things calling to you from inside, you turn off in your heart. And when you turn off in our heart, you turn off in your body.

Lately, newspapers and magazines have been filled with articles about "the sexless marriage." Couples confess that it has been months, even years since they have been intimate with one another, and many experts reassure us that this pattern is normal for people who lead busy, complex and stressful lives. In essence this point of view asserts that everything about these marriages is fine—it's just that the couple isn't having sex. Married couples themselves adopt this attitude as an explanation for their lack of physical intimacy. "Some couples seem to accept that sexless marriage is as much a part of modern life as traffic and e-mail," writes Kathleen Deveny in her *Newsweek* cover story "We're Not in the Mood" (June 30, 2003).

I receive countless calls, letters and posts on my Web site about this same phenomenon every day. Here's one that someone just sent me:

> I feel embarrassed admitting this, but my husband and I haven't had sex in almost a year. I'm thirty-two and he's thirty-four, and we have two small children. I used to work full time, but now I'm a stay-at-home mom, which keeps me pretty busy. My husband works hard, and we're also both very active in our church on the weekends. Our marriage seems very harmonious, and I know we do love each other, but the sex has disappeared. We've been married for ten years, and I've read articles that say it's natural

for the passion to disappear after a while. My friends who've been married for a long time tell me they almost never have sex either. I miss how close we used to be, but feel stuck. What I want to know is, do you think this is normal?

My answer to this woman was: Yes, I do think the loss of sexual desire and lack of intimacy is normal, meaning that it is common in contemporary society, *but I do not believe it is natural, nor do I think it should be viewed as a predictable occurrence in relationships that we all must accept.*

Conventional wisdom explains the sexless marriage as simply the inevitable outcome of the hectic and demanding pace of life in the twenty-first century. While circumstances like physical disability or illness can cause sexual intimacy to become difficult if not impossible, I believe that for most of us, the loss of sexual connection is the result of a "turning off" at the deepest levels of our being, and *not* an expected phase in marriage that we must all get used to. Both partners are tuning out and freezing up, cutting themselves off from their own passion, and consequently from each other.

When we are living a turned-off life, we end up having a turned-off marriage.

. . .

Sex is the most compressed set of circumstances that we've got. Everything is in that collision.
—Arthur Miller

I love this quote by the great playwright Arthur Miller. He is right—the sexual dynamic between lovers is indeed a compressed set of circumstances in which all of our issues collide. It is impossible to keep what happens in the office, the living room, the kitchen and our minds and hearts from affecting what happens in the bedroom. It is impossible to be frozen up or turned off in our consciousness without feeling turned off in our body.

Our erotic selves and our spiritual/emotional selves are intrinsically linked. Shutting off to the demands of either one will inevitably have the effect of shutting us off to the other. The price we pay for tuning out and turning off is the sacrifice of the sensual.

Denial is not very conducive to the flow of erotic ecstasy. If we suppress or ignore our erotic and sexual needs within a relationship, we will create an inner tension that will throw us off-balance in our work and in other aspects of our life. In the same way, if we are turned off within ourselves, we will most likely find ourselves turning off sexually with our partner.

Last year, I spoke to a group of high-level executives from an international communications company. The majority of attendees were men, and, as usual in my presentations, I didn't address the standard topics expected of business speakers—sales, productivity, stress management, improving customer relations—but talked instead about what I thought would benefit them the most as people. My lecture was titled *Living and Loving with Passion: How to Keep Yourself Turned On*. You can be sure that there was an excited buzz of curiosity when I walked up to the podium.

I have always loved speaking to groups. It feels as if I am speaking to one person at a time, because that's my style, but multiplied by five hundred or five thousand, depending on the size of the audience. The effect is like an enormous, supersize dose of intimacy. On this occasion I was addressing a very intimate topic and saying things many of these people hadn't heard verbalized before.

At one point during my presentation I said:

"You can take all the Viagra you want, but if you have turned off in parts of your life or your relationship, the only thing that pill will be able to turn back on is your penis, because it can't turn on your passion. That is something only you can do from the inside out."

You could hear a pin drop in the ballroom—that's how quiet it was. As a speaker, I've always been known for being direct and down-to-earth, but I wondered if I'd gone too far this time. I continued with my talk and received a standing ovation. But as I spent time autographing books and meeting people, I was still concerned about how the CEO of the corporation, whom I'd never met, was going to react to the content of my address.

As I packed up my things, the CEO's assistant approached me. "My boss wants to speak to you privately," she said.

"This doesn't sound good," I thought with a grimace as I followed her through the hotel lobby and took an elevator up to the penthouse suite. "Please wait here," she instructed me, and then she left, closing the door behind her.

My mind raced as I anticipated the conversation I was about to have with this high-powered man who was infamous for his steely temperament and impatient approach to everything. Should I apologize? No, that didn't feel right—I'd created the best presentation I could have and believed that everything I had said and how I had said it was valid. Should I try explaining why I'd chosen this topic for his group? No, I wasn't in the habit of defending myself. Besides, the meeting planner had given me free rein to talk about whatever issues I felt the participants would relate to. I was still musing about how I was going to handle this encounter when "Mr. CEO," as I will call him, walked in looking like J.R. from the 1980s TV series *Dallas*, complete with cowboy hat and shiny alligator boots.

"Well, Barbara," he began, "I've been in this business for over fortysome years, and that was a first for me."

"Here it comes," I thought, preparing myself for the worst.

"Yes sirree," he continued, "never have I seen a group of tough, jaded executives so . . . so . . . damn, what's the word I'm looking for . . . so spellbound!" Mr. CEO gave me a broad smile. "You got them to listen, sugar; even better, to think about things they try very hard not to think about. First-class job!"

"I'm very happy to hear that," I replied, breathing an enormous sigh of relief.

"But that's not why I wanted to meet you in private," Mr. CEO added in a quiet voice. "It was to make a confession. My wife and I have been married for thirty-five years. The first ten were as good as it gets, and the last twenty-five have been, well, less than ideal. I know she's been unhappy with me. God knows, I am not an easy man to live with.

"The part that has disturbed me the most has been my loss of desire. You see, I am an old-fashioned kind of guy. My gal is my true love, and I've been faithful to her. However, for a long time, we have been living more like friends, with no sexual relations at all. The problem was with me—I had lost all desire. My doctor prescribed pills, and like you said, they worked on my body, but not on my mind, and that was worse than doing nothing at all. I felt numb and disconnected and I had no idea why—until I heard your speech this afternoon.

"You probably won't believe this—most people wouldn't—but I am one of those people you described who has been living a turned-off life. I am worn out by working twelve hours a day, tired of the responsibility of such an enormous corporate machine, and exhausted by the same old power struggles. Men spend their whole lives trying to achieve what I have, but honestly, I am bored with the whole thing—have been for years. I've built this company into what it is today, and so I believed it would be irresponsible of me to resign."

"So you just run on automatic pilot?" I suggested.

"Exactly," he agreed. "Automatic and mindless. And until today, I had no idea how bad this has been for me. You know, I'm a Texan—I'm a passionate man! I need to feel passionate about what I'm doing and who I'm doing it with! And I've been no better than a tired old bull who's too dawggone bored to do his duty. Well, all that is going to change. First thing I'm doing is taking some time off to figure things out. My wife's been wanting to go to Europe, so I am going to take her on a real fancy trip. Do you think she'll like that?"

Mr. CEO's enthusiasm was infectious. "I think she'll love it," I said, "but I think she'll love hearing everything you just told me even more. You know, a lot of men would be too proud to admit any of this. I really admire you for being so honest."

"Well, when I'm wrong, I'm wrong," Mr. CEO grinned. "As my daddy always told me: 'A smartass just don't fit in a saddle!' "

I had to leave in order to catch my plane, and as we exchanged good-bye's, Mr. CEO left me with a parting thought: "By the way," he said with a chuckle, "there was another first today, besides the standing ovation—in all my years of meetings, that was the first time I ever heard anyone say 'penis'!"

Some months later, I received a postcard from Mr. CEO. It read: *Greetings from Texas!* with a vintage picture of a 1950s cowboy sitting on a horse reared up on its hind legs. On the back of the card, true to the character he was, Mr. CEO wrote me this brief but meaningful message:

> **Just a card to let you know that I'm "Back in the Saddle Again"!**

It was postmarked from Paris, France.

I still chuckle recalling this anecdote, not just because of its entertainment value, but because of Mr. CEO's willingness to ask himself, *"How did I get here?"* and his courage in paying attention to the answer.

The Ghost Lover

He was so invisible to our daily world, so detached
from me, and so distant from our love
that he might as well have been a ghost.
—Barbara's diary entry, 1973

When people live together day after day hardly connecting, barely touching, physically near but separated by seemingly impenetrable barriers, they become what I call *ghost lovers*. According to certain traditions, a ghost is a being caught between worlds, someone who can't move on to the Other Side after death, because he is confused or angry or feels he has some unfinished business he must complete. He is here, but not here. He is present, but unable to touch or feel with the senses. He is longing to make contact, but unable to communicate. He feels robbed of life, but is unable to truly be alive.

So it is in relationships when people have emotionally turned off but are still physically present. They are there, but not there. They are longing to feel, but are detached and numb. They are like ghosts.

There is nothing lonelier than living with a ghost lover. I know—I have done it. You speak, but the other person doesn't seem to hear. You reach out, but the other person doesn't reach back. You share your tender feelings, but they don't make contact with anything solid, passing through your lover as if he or she were transparent. You grasp hold of what you thought was right in front of you, but there is nothing—and no one—there.

Sometimes only one partner is the ghost lover, and the other is the one chasing the ghost and trying to bring him or her back to life. This is a painful and frustrating pursuit. As the chaser, we feel rejected by our mate's disinterest and detachment. Nothing we do seems to penetrate his or her indifference. If the partner who is the ghost lover happens to also be a good dad or a great mom or a stable provider or a terrific daughter-in-law or a kind person, we can become terribly confused, questioning our own judgment and criticizing ourselves for being unhappy. *"So what if we have a sexless, turned-off marriage,"* we reason. *"Maybe I'm being too hard on my mate, too unrealistic."* And if we look away from what our heart is screaming for us to see, and shut down to our longings for intimacy, we soon turn into a ghost lover ourselves.

> **When the intimate and sexual connection**
> **has been gone from a relationship for some time,**
> **both partners simply go into a silent agreement**
> **to live together as ghost lovers.**
> **The foundation of these relationships is**
> **often functional rather than emotional,**
> **logistical rather than loving.**

I see couples like this all the time, not only in my work but everywhere—eating at a restaurant, walking through the mall, sitting on an airplane. They are the ones who appear to be intimate strangers: they are in the same physical space, but there are few connecting energies between them. It's as if most or all of the emotional circuits that once linked them have been severed. Each is in his or her own world. *Whatever "us" remains is a formality, acknowledged out of habit or politeness.*

Then there are the children, often the only thing binding ghost lovers together. Here is where things can get really tricky: often, one or both partners in a sexless marriage unknowingly transfers their sensual and emotional (nonsexual) needs onto the kids, especially if they are preteen and still interested in being close with their parents. Mom and Dad get hugs and kisses and cuddling from the children that they no longer get from each other.

Of course, having a warm, affectionate relationship with our kids is healthy and essential for their own development. *Problems arise, however, when a parent becomes absorbed with connecting with their son or daughter at the expense of a partner.* This pattern has painful, complex and often irreparable consequences:

- Husbands or wives can be secretly jealous of the affection their mate shows to a child.

- Children can become accustomed to being the main focus of Mommy's or Daddy's emotional attention and affection, and unknowingly play the role of substitute spouses.

- A parent can become frozen into a pattern of idealized, unconditional love that results from relating to a child who naturally has the parent on a pedestal. This makes the parent intolerant of conditional love and increasingly incapable of adult intimacy with his or her partner.

· · ·

My friend Margaret agonized for several years before deciding to separate from her husband, Ted, not because of how she felt about him, but because she was worried about the effect divorce would have on her two children. She and Ted had been living like ghost lovers ever since their first child was born. Although she knew they had grown apart in very different directions and would eventually be happier if they weren't together, she still wondered if she was making a decision that was good for her but bad for the kids.

Margaret and Ted had always been very strict about not letting their children watch any unsupervised television. A few months after Ted moved out, Margaret decided that her oldest daughter, Candace, who'd just turned eight, was ready to see family-oriented movies and took her to her first full-length film. The movie was about a family's adventures in Africa, and Candace was mesmerized as she watched the wild animals on the huge screen. At one point in the film, the parents were standing on a hilltop looking out over the beautiful landscape, and the man took his wife in his arms and kissed her passionately.

Candace turned to her mother and whispered, "Mommy, what is he doing with his mouth?"

"He's kissing her," Margaret answered.

"But why is he kissing her there, like that, and not on the cheek?" Candace persisted in a puzzled voice.

"Well," Margaret replied thoughtfully, "Because that's what mommies and daddies do when they love each other."

Candace was quiet for a moment, and then she spoke:

"Well, then, how come I never saw you and Daddy do that?"

Margaret was stunned into silence by her eight-year-old daughter's candor and clarity. With one innocent question, Candace had summed up what had been missing in Margaret's marriage—physical and emotional intimacy. Tears filled her eyes as she contemplated how sad it was that her own children had never seen their parents acting like people in love and had never witnessed their father being romantically affectionate with their mother. To eight-year-old Candace, seeing that couple kiss in the movie was as new and exotic as seeing the giraffes, lions and leopards—all were things she hadn't known existed.

Margaret's heart ached with regret, but along with the regret was enormous relief. After hearing her daughter's comment, Margaret was certain that she had made the right decision in ending her marriage. *"I want my kids to grow up and live passionate lives,"* she declared when she told me this story. *"I want them to think that kind of kiss is normal. I want them to love passionately and be loved back with passion. What kind of role model would I be if I stayed in a relationship and just went through the motions, but felt numb and shut off? Now I just have to find my own passion again."*

·   ·   ·

When you truly grow up
what you will be
is free
—Emmanuel

Ultimately, it is the heart, and not the body, that is the source of all true passion. Once we realize we've been turned off, we face the hard work of figuring out how to turn ourselves back on.

As we will see in the chapters to come, the journey back to

truth, authenticity and passion is one of reawakening, rediscovery and rebirth. Sometimes that journey includes resurrecting a troubled relationship, as partners reconnect to their own passion and reincarnate from ghost lovers to being real lovers again, physically, emotionally and mentally. Other times, the journey demands that we take a different road from the one we've been on, and we *will* have to pass through those turning points, leaving what is familiar behind and making new, courageous choices for ourselves.

What will give you the strength and perseverance for this journey? Your own passion that is alive within you even now.

**Each time you choose to change, to grow,
to improve, or to learn,
you are acting from that inner core of passion.
It is that passion for truth, for happiness,
for freedom that compels you to
dig deep within yourself for wisdom,
to ask the difficult questions, and to hear
the often painful but necessary answers.**

Your passion has not disappeared. It's just been buried, locked away in a hidden place within you to which only you have the key. The nineteenth-century poet and seeker Robert Browning conceived of this when, in his mystical work "Paracelsus," he wrote:

> There is an inmost center in us all,
> Where truth abides in fullness . . .
> And to Know
> Rather consists in opening out a way
> Whence the imprisoned splendour may escape
> Than in effecting entry for a light
> Supposed to be without.

If you listen carefully, perhaps you can hear voices,
    calling to you from your inmost center.
They are the voices of your own imprisoned splendour:
    Your forgotten wisdom,
    your buried joy,
    and your lost passion
Longing to be set free.

❦ 6 ❧

Will the Real Me
Please Stand Up?

"Who are YOU?" said the Caterpillar.
This was not an encouraging opening for a conversation.
Alice replied, rather shyly, "I—I hardly
know, sir, just at present—
at least I know who I WAS when I got up this
morning, but I think I must have been changed
several times since then."
—Lewis Carroll, *Alice in Wonderland*

What is there for us to do during our time on earth that is more crucial to our sense of inner peace and more central to our experience of wholeness than knowing and understanding ourselves? On our path to awakening, the question *"Who am I?"* is our constant and inquisitive companion every step of the way. This inquiry is not a one-time assignment. In spite of our hope that once we figure out who and what we are, we can relax and cruise through the rest of our journey, it does not happen this way. Instead, we change. Circumstances change. Other people change, and all of these changes change us even more. Sometimes so much seems to be changing that we can barely catch our breath long enough even to ask, "Who am I?" let alone try to answer. Just like Alice explained to the Caterpillar, we know who we Were, but as for who we ARE, well, that's another matter.

The quest to know ourselves becomes all the more complex and baffling when we are in the midst of challenges, turning points and wake-up calls.

*How do we rediscover ourselves once we realize parts of us have
    been buried or forgotten?*

*How do we find our way back to hope, happiness and confidence
    once we realize we have been lost and wandering in the wrong
    direction, or that we simply need to take a new road?*

*How do we know who we even are in times when so much of us
    has already disintegrated, and even what remains is unsteady
    and blurred?*

． ． ．

One of the most popular television quiz shows in the 1950s
and 1960s was *To Tell the Truth.* The host would introduce
three contestants, all of whom claimed to be the same person, usually someone with an interesting profession or unusual hobby. The
four celebrity panelists would ask the contestants questions, trying
to determine which one was being truthful and which two were lying. The two impostors would try hard to fool the panelists into
believing that they were the person the host had described. At the
end of the round, the panelists would write down who they thought
was telling the truth.

I used to love guessing along with the panelists, saying to my
mother, "I think number 3 is the real opera singer," or race car driver
or lion tamer—whatever the mystery person was supposed to be.
And I would wait anxiously along with the studio audience to see if I
was right. Finally, the host would say the famous closing line: *"Will
the real——please stand up?"* and someone would. Sometimes the
contestants totally fooled us all; sometimes we guessed correctly.
No matter what the outcome, we, along with millions of Americans, were transfixed by *To Tell the Truth,* and the phrase *"Will
the real——please stand up?"* became part of our popular culture.

On our own journey of self-discovery, we are inevitably led to
this same question: **"Will the real me please stand up?"** Asking this
takes emotional courage, and arriving at an answer is not the
amusing game it was on the quiz show. It is serious business, re-
quiring that we face the question with relentless honesty and sincere perseverance to see through all the ways we, like the imposters
on *To Tell the Truth,* try to fool ourselves. We must embrace parts

of ourselves we've been ignoring, face truths about our life that we've been evading, confront longings, dreams and visions from which we've turned away.

So where, then, do we begin? The answer is simpler than we could imagine:

The truth is not far away.
It is not something you have to chase down.
It is right here, where you are right now.
It always has been, and it always will be.
Nothing else is possible.

This is such a startling and yet enlightening concept, and one that each of us must work to understand. The truth is not some complicated puzzle you must solve by searching for hidden pieces. The truth already exists within you. It *is* you. When you look for it, you can't miss it!

The journey, then, becomes one not of searching for truth, but rather of *uncovering it,* not of wondering if you will ever find truth, but rather *cultivating a willingness to see it.* It is asking yourself the right questions and knowing for sure, like those of us who watched the quiz show, that any minute now the truth, already present but unidentified, will stand up and reveal itself.

When I Grow Up I Want to Be...

What can we gain by sailing to the moon if we are not able to
cross the abyss that separates us from ourselves?
This is the most important of all voyages of discovery,
and without it, all the rest are not only useless, but disastrous.
—Thomas Merton

"What do you want to be when you grow up?" Do you remember being asked this as a child? As children, we project ourselves into an imagined future and choose what we think we want to be: a fireman, a rock star, a doctor, a basketball star, a zookeeper, an artist. At several points along our journey into adulthood, we choose again, adapting our dream to reality, modifying our original vision as we discover new talents and new interests, broadening what is acceptable to us as we deal with the down-to-earth demands of adult life. The nine-year-old boy who wants to be a policeman decides at sixteen to be an anthropologist, and again at twenty-one to get a degree in international business. The seven-year-old girl who is certain that she wants to be a pop star decides at fifteen she really should go into modeling, and at twenty that she wants to get married and have children as soon as possible.

No one questions this rechoosing process while we are adolescents and young adults. In fact, considering the possibilities is encouraged. But at some point, everything changes. *We reach an arbitrary age by which we are supposed to know what we are doing in life.* Perhaps that age might be twenty-one. Perhaps if we go to college, it is when we graduate. Perhaps we have a sense of being allowed to "experiment" with what we want to do until we are twenty-five, at which point we are supposed to "settle down."

Whatever the magic number, we are supposed to get serious once we arrive there. We're expected to choose one way to live, one person to love, one profession in which to work and to stick with these choices for the rest of our lives. We are admired if we appear stable, steady, predictable, established. **We are expected to stop changing. We are expected to stop choosing.**

It is not surprising, then, that many of us have worked so hard to find the "right" role and adopt it. It is part of the American psyche to be politically and socially correct, to know what is in, what is out, what is acceptable, what is taboo. **We are brought up to fit in rather than find out who we are.** Those who are different and do not fit in are often made to suffer and feel somehow inferior or worse, as if they have failed to meet a standard that makes them acceptable.

We've all had the experience of looking back on our teens, and twenties and saying to ourselves:

"I can't believe I: thought that/did that/cared about that/loved that person/was upset about that/wore that outfit/bought into that/believed that was cool/didn't realize that/ate that/said that/ etc."

We laugh at some of these memories and cringe at others; but mostly we feel relieved that we have moved on from who we were in our past. "I was young," we reassure ourselves as an explanation for what we retroactively see as unwise choices or foolish behavior. And we smile contentedly, confident that now that we know what we are doing. We're done with all of the uncertainty and experimentation of youth. We've grown up.

There is one glaring problem with this model—it doesn't work. The reason is simple: as human beings, we are not stable and fixed. We do change, and we keep growing, even if we sometimes resist the process, and kick and scream all the way into a new awakening.

**It is unrealistic for us to expect that
we will remain the same person with the same values,
concerns, dreams and needs for decades.
It is unrealistic for us to expect that we will not change.**

Perhaps centuries ago, when everything in the world moved much more slowly, most people did not radically change within their lifetime. It wasn't unreasonable to expect that the decisions a person made in his twenties would still make sense thirty or forty years later, if he even lived that long.

In these early years of the twenty-first century, when every moment of life seems to be accelerated, moving at a frantic, breathtaking pace, our personal journey, too, is accelerated. It is as if we are packing several lifetimes of living, loving and learning into one. And more living and learning means more change.

The Search for the Authentic Self

*It takes courage to grow up and turn out to be
who you really are.*
—e.e. cummings

Sometimes in our quest for self-knowledge we look with discomfort and disbelief at our reflection in the mirror of old values and past choices, and do not recognize the person we see or the life we are living. Perhaps we realize that what we thought we needed isn't what we need anymore. Perhaps we discover that we're still living a choice we made when we were twenty-one, or thirty-one, and today it no longer fits. In these powerful moments, we feel compelled to make the outer expression of who we are more honestly and accurately represent our inner self. *We are longing to live a more authentic life.*

**Living with authenticity means that who you appear
to be to others is who you really are.
Your beliefs, your values, your commitments,
your inner realities are all reflected
in how you live your life on the outside.
The more you live authentically, as who you truly are,
the more peace you will experience.**

What does living with authenticity look like? Some suggestions to consider:

LIVING AUTHENTICALLY MEANS:

- *Behaving in ways that are in harmony with your personal values*

- *Making choices based on what you believe, and not what others believe*

- *Feeling you can be yourself and be loved, rather than having to act in ways you feel will be acceptable to others*

- *Accepting and honoring all parts of yourself rather than hiding or lying about them*

- *Communicating the truth when you need to, even though it might create conflict or tension*

- *Not settling for less than what you know you deserve in your relationships*

- *Asking for what you want and need from others*

We want this for ourselves, but living this way is easier said than done. Often, when our authentic self calls to us, we stubbornly resist, clinging instead to our old, familiar roles. As uncomfortable and limiting as these roles may be, we are frightened that if we change too much, we will somehow lose our identity and become . . . well, that's the point—we aren't sure. **Relinquishing our old roles makes us feel identityless, placeless, as if invisible.** We ask ourselves:

"Who will I be if I'm not a wife/mother/doctor/good son/reliable person/obedient daughter-in-law/superachiever/loyal employee/self-sacrificing friend anymore?"

We do not know the answer.

There is an irony to this. Frequently, whether we know it or not, by resisting change, by being attached to our investment of time and energy in choices that once served us but no longer do, we have already relinquished much of ourselves—in relationships that are stagnant or passionless, in jobs that are dissatisfying, in life choices that do not serve our highest good.

When Old Roles and New Choices Collide

This is an e-mail I received from a reader:

> I am a forty-four-year old mother of two boys, and I have been married for almost twenty-one years. For the past five years, I have been battling severe depression. I got married right out of college, and gave my identity over to my husband and his field of work. You see, he is a minister and people from his church had this idea of what they wanted me to be as a minister's wife, how I should talk and act, and feel, and even what I should look like, and if I didn't fit the image they shunned me, didn't speak to me, made me feel like I was doing it all wrong. My husband was just as bad as everyone else, and didn't stick up for me or protect me. I found myself battling the very people that should have been my support.
>
> I cried a lot, became really depressed, tried to be all things to everyone, and it just left me angry and miserable. I ended up feeling emotionally, mentally, and physically bankrupt. I tried to start so many businesses so I could escape with my children, but because I was so mentally fatigued and run down, my businesses did not make it off the ground like I wanted them to. I didn't understand until I read your book *Secrets About Life Every Woman Should Know* why I have been so exhausted, too exhausted to make my businesses successful. I was waiting for love from my husband or for him to say the right thing before I would be happy. I was waiting for my boys to respond to me in a certain way before I would be happy. I was waiting for myself to become the perfect wife and minister's spouse.
>
> Now I know I cannot be happy until I am myself again. The problem is, I'm so used to being Mrs. Minister that I don't know who myself is.

I feel like running away and starting over. I want to shake all the anger and bitterness, lose weight, and just chalk this all up to a real big learning experience. My dream is to one day get my own apartment, and to open up a business that will help troubled children to know that there is hope out there. Even though I battle with severe fatigue, I am praying that I can rebound to become a productive woman before my time is up here on earth. I hope it won't take me another twenty years to figure out what I should be doing and who I really am. Thank you—your work is not in vain!

Signed,

Searching for my passion

I could feel this woman's pain like a weight pressing down on my own heart. She is asking herself, *"How did I get here?"* and in hearing the answer, she is discovering ways she has been cut off from her own authentic self. Her need and choice to change has been colliding with her role as a minister's wife, and the battle has been exhausting her.

I see these tragic battles all the time, collisions between old roles and new choices:

· · ·

A stay-at-home mom of twins who has been strongly outspoken against working mothers finds herself fantasizing about going back to her job in the travel business. In spite of her philosophy that women should stay home with their children, with which her husband staunchly agrees, she secretly admits to herself that she is bored and desperately longs to have a career again. Frozen between these two opposing points of view, and afraid to voice her dilemma to anyone, she becomes severely depressed.

· · ·

A young man finally admits to himself that he is an alcoholic, and begins a twelve-step program that supports him in becoming sober and taking responsibility for his actions. All of his friends as well as his parents are still heavy drinkers critical of those who don't share their lifestyle, so he doesn't tell them he's quit. They only know the old fun-loving guy he used to be, and his initial attempts to spend sober time with them are disastrous. Hurt and confused, he isolates himself completely from all social contact and stuffs down his anxiety with food. In two months he gains twenty pounds.

. . .

A middle-aged woman whom everyone always characterizes as the "sweetest person in the world" realizes that she has been locked into playing the role of the helper from the time she was young. Her mother had health problems, and as the oldest daughter, she took on the role of caretaker from an early age, continuing this pattern in her adulthood with her husband, her friends, her relatives and her own children. Now, motivated by her doctor's warning that her self-imposed pressure is probably contributing to her hypertension, she nervously attempts to begin speaking her mind, saying no instead of yes to every request for help, and making choices based on what she wants rather than what will please others. The result is upsetting: her husband reacts by asking, "What's got into you?" and several friends criticize her for becoming "selfish." Unsure of how to integrate her new, emerging self into her old life, she sinks into a depression.

. . .

All of these people are faced with the same dilemma. They have been trying to live one-dimensional lives when in reality they are, like all of us, multidimensional people. Each of them has grown and evolved, and no longer fits into the rigid roles they had built for themselves—they're spilling over the edges of their own self-created boundaries. But their fear of losing the approval and acceptance of their friends, family or community has driven them into hiding their emerging selves. They not only feel unhappy and afraid, but very much alone.

This is the sad irony of trying to live by someone else's values in order to be loved. When you know you're not being yourself, you don't trust the love and approval you receive from others. How can you? You realize if you show the real you, that approval will most likely be withdrawn.

**You cannot feel truly connected to people when your authentic self isn't available to connect with anyone. The love and acceptance gained from playing a role is counterfeit and empty.
It will never fulfill you, for deep inside your heart, you will know it is not even directed toward your true self.**

. . .

*We did not change as we grew older;
we just became more clearly ourselves.*
—Lynn Hall, *Where Have All the Tigers Gone?*

I've always had a fascination with Russian nesting dolls, or *"matroyshka."* You've probably seen these—a brightly painted wooden doll whose outer case opens to reveal another, smaller doll, inside which are many smaller and yet smaller nested dolls. *Matroyshka* have been a tradition in Russia for centuries. They originated as a symbol of fertility and motherhood, and were given as gifts for good luck. In Russian, *"mat"* means *mother*—thus, the name *matroyshka*.

These Russian nesting dolls are a metaphor for our process of self-discovery: the journey toward our authentic self isn't so much a traveling from one role to another, or a choice between an old part of ourselves and a new part, but more accurately a peeling-away of layers. As we grow, we open to reveal more and more of ourselves, parts that have been hidden within other parts. Just as the *matroyshka* doll "gives birth" to one doll after another, we give birth to new versions of ourselves, again and again.

This model is one of wholeness, rather than polarity:

We are not just one static self, but many emerging selves.
This view is inclusive, rather than exclusive—
each part of us is necessary to give birth to the next.
The self is complex, rather than singular.
We are not either this or that,
but an intricately designed, multileveled being
within which many expressions of ourselves coexist.

Perhaps this is what writer Lynn Hall meant when she said that we do not change, but become more clearly ourselves. We unfold, we blossom, we reveal that which, like the smallest hidden doll, was waiting to be discovered.

Getting to Know Your Shadow

Everyone is a moon, and has a dark side
which he never shows to anybody.
—Mark Twain, *Pudd'nhead Wilson*

One of the skills possessed by the artisans who create *matroyshka* dolls is the ability to make each new doll hidden within the other more beautiful than the last. As we open the outer doll and discover the new painted doll inside, we are enchanted with what we find. "Look at this one!" we exclaim. "It is even prettier than the one before!"

Our own process of self-discovery isn't always so delightful. Sometimes what we uncover hidden within us are parts of ourselves we do not want to face. This hidden inner realm is what Swiss psychiatrist Carl Jung named "the Shadow part of our self," a collection of emotions and impulses that lie concealed below the surface of our more acceptable, proper, idealized self. All of us have a shadow self, whether we realize it or not. **The shadow self is everything in us that is unconscious, undeveloped, rejected, repressed and denied.**

Some people mislabel the Shadow self as our "dark side." This is a simplistic misunderstanding. **It is not that our shadow qualities are "bad"**—*it is that we hide them because they do not fit into our picture of who we are or want to be, and do not match what others expect us to be.*

We consider ourselves to be compassionate, but we have a more selfish, sometimes arrogant, impatient side.

We pride ourselves on our self-discipline, but have secret addictive tendencies that we keep under inflexibly tight control.

We preach about morality and purity to others, but constantly battle with our longing to indulge our senses in every possible way.

We fiercely defend our independence from others and claim we want nothing from them, but a part of us desperately longs to find someone who will take charge and let us lean on him.

We fear that if people saw these pieces of our Shadow, they would not love or accept us. So we deny their existence, even to ourselves.

How do we identify our Shadow self? One easy way is to look at the qualities we detest in others—*we will always feel agitated and uncomfortable when we are around people who embody a part of our Shadow.* As horrifying as this seems, the people we are the most critical of are usually the ones who are acting out our own suppressed Shadow qualities. Psychologists call this unconscious mechanism *projection*—we project onto other people qualities that we have totally disowned in ourselves, and then become outraged when we witness them. For example:

- The self-righteous mother who sacrifices all her needs for her children becomes furious when she hears that her sister and brother-in-law are going away for a week and leaving their kids with friends, something she considers selfish, neglectful and irresponsible, but desperately longs to do.

- The strict, punishing father who behaves like a cruel dictator with his own children, not allowing them to be joyful, to have fun, to have any kind of freedom, because he secretly fears his own unbridled self, something he has suppressed ever since he almost killed a friend in a car accident when he was a wild teenager.

• The twenty-something party girl obsessed with wearing the latest fashions, going to the hottest clubs, hanging around with the "in crowd" and known for ridiculing others for being boring, unattractive and worthless, who is secretly terrified that she herself is nothing inside and that without working so hard to stay on top, she will be easily forgotten.

• The "play-by-the-rules," compulsively perfect employee frightened of making mistakes and of being a failure, who constantly puts down the more successful managers as being arrogant, pushy, sloppy and too aggressive, but secretly envies their courage and achievements.

Our Shadow self is also our *unfinished business, unfulfilled needs, unresolved emotional issues, unrealized longings and dreams.* It is all the things that tug at us, trying to get our attention while we do everything we can to ignore them. In addressing our battle to suppress our Shadow self, Carl Jung warns, "Every part of the personality you do not love will become hostile to you."

And this is exactly what happens. One day our Shadow self manages to emerge from where we have kept it carefully controlled and hidden, and suddenly we experience a crisis. *"What is happening? How did I get here?"* we ask ourselves, stunned that we are feeling or doing things we don't recognize as being part of our conscious self-image. "It isn't like me to be this way":

"It isn't like me to be so unhappy."
"It isn't like me to feel so wild and unconventional."
"It isn't like me to not care what other people think."
"It isn't like me to change my mind."
"It isn't like me to want to rock the boat."
"It isn't like me to be so selfish."
"It isn't like me to get so angry."

The truth is, it *is* like you—just not the "you" you're used to showing to the world, or even to yourself. It is the "you" that has been locked away and has finally escaped. It is your Shadow.

. . .

Sometimes what we believe to be our Shadow is actually the very Light that's been missing from our life . . .

Winston, age forty-five, has always worked hard to be the good, stable son in his family. His older brother, Peter, is a musician who has lived a wild, flamboyant and totally unconventional life. While Winston was studying day and night to get into college and become a chemical engineer, Peter was hitchhiking around Europe picking up every girl he could find. Winston got married to his longtime girlfriend and had a traditional wedding and three children spaced a few years apart; Peter has been married and divorced three times. Winston drives an unassuming, practical car; Peter drives a Porsche. Winston plans everything in his life down to the last detail; Peter is spontaneous, jumping on a plane at a moment's notice, starting and stopping projects when he feels like it. "Winston never gave us any trouble, even as a baby," his mother still proudly tells anyone who will listen. As for Peter, "well, he's always been . . . different," she explains, raising her eyebrows for emphasis.

One day, something completely astonishing and unexpected happens to Winston. While attending a conference in Miami, he meets Pauline, a woman staying at the same hotel, and instantly falls head over heels in love. Pauline is a hairdresser originally from Cuba. She is sexy, fun-loving, philosophical and deeply passionate. When Winston is with her, he feels totally alive and awake in a way he never has before. He can open up to her about things he's never even felt safe sharing with his wife. Pauline, too, feels a connection of souls. They both know they are meant to be together.

Walking on the beach with Pauline the night before he is scheduled to go home, Winston is in agony. He knows what he wants to do—leave his wife, quit his job and move to Miami. He realizes how unhappy he has been for a long time, maybe since he was a child, and now it is as if he just woke up from a dream that was his

other life and the other Winston. But how can he dismantle everything he worked so hard to build? He feels torn in two. During a
tearful good-bye, he tells Pauline he needs time to come to the right
decision.

In a phone session with me, Winston explained his dilemma:

> I don't recognize myself. I've never done anything like
> this before. It's the kind of thing my brother Peter does. I
> have always hated his selfishness, his irresponsibility, and
> yes, I admit that I've felt superior to him because my life
> was so orderly. Now look at me—this is worse than any-
> thing Peter's ever done! I feel like I've turned into the worst
> parts of him.
>
> Everyone is going to think I've gone crazy. And this is
> just going to destroy my mother. I've always been her per-
> fect boy. And Peter . . . he'll just love it, because finally his
> little brother is the one who is screwing up.
>
> I know what I have to do. I can't go back to who I used
> to be, and my whole life and my marriage is based on that
> person. I can't let Pauline go now that I've experienced love
> like this. But how could this have happened out of the blue?
> Why didn't I see it coming?

Winston had come face to face with his Shadow self, which in
his case embodies the part of him that is passionate and alive.
Buried for most of his life, it had finally broken free, despite his as-
siduous attempts to keep it locked away. Its arrival in Winston's
conscious world felt shocking and sudden, but the truth is, it had
been there inside him all the time. *He was confused and disoriented, not because he didn't know what to do, but because he
couldn't believe that he, Winston, was doing it.*

Winston did find the courage to leave his unhappy marriage
and started a new life with Pauline. To his surprise, his wife confessed that she, too, had been unfulfilled for some time, and soon
after they split up she found a new partner. The biggest shock for
Winston, however, was the support he received from his family.

His mother reassured him that all she ever wanted was for him to be happy—not to be perfect—and his brother, rather than gloating over Winston's difficulties, reached out in a way he never had before. It was Winston, and not his family members, who had locked himself into a role that had imprisoned his true passion and aliveness. And it was Winston who finally set himself free.

The emergence of our Shadow self may temporarily cause havoc in what we believed was our orderly world, but in the end, it will put things back together in a way that brings us much more authentic happiness, renewed confidence and deep contentment.

. . .

A man will be imprisoned in a room with a door that's unlocked and opens inwards as long as it does not occur to him to pull rather than push.
—Ludwig Wittgenstein

In 1998, playwright Eve Ensler, best known for *The Vagina Monologues,* went to the Bedford Hills Correctional Facility, a women's maximum security prison in New York State, to lead a writing workshop in which most of the workshop participants were convicted murderers. *What I Want My Words to Do to You* is a powerful eighty-minute documentary film that chronicles the inward journey these women take through writing exercises and conversations, exploring their sorrow, their guilt and their attempts to heal themselves. I was transfixed as I watched this film and listened to the words of these women as they described what it was like to be incarcerated, not just by their cells and the penitentiary walls, but by their own pain and their judgments of themselves.

Eve Ensler asked the workshop participants to write about what effect they would like the film and their words to have on the audiences who will see it. Judith Clark, who is serving a sentence of seventy-five years to life for three counts of second-degree murder, wrote this:

"**What I want my words to do to you . . . I want to make you wonder about your own prisons. I want to make you ask why.**"

The hard-earned wisdom of these powerful words touched me deeply.

We are all prisoners to the extent that we have locked pieces of ourselves away, and condemned them to live in the dark recesses of our minds and hearts. And only we can free ourselves by wondering about those prisons and by embracing those shadowy parts of us we have been afraid to recognize.

Facing My Shadow

So now I will tell you a Shadow story, one of mine:

Nine years ago, when I began to reevaluate my life, my spiritual teacher gave me the message that it would be good for me "to be a nothing and a nobody for a while." Looking back, I believe she knew, in the mysterious wisdom great teachers possess, that if I took her advice, I would soon come face-to-face with a part of myself I didn't even know existed, one of my most terrifying and deeply buried Shadows.

When I first heard the message, I thought I understood what it meant, and why she had given me this particular suggestion. I knew I had been working too hard and needed to slow down. I realized this would be challenging on many levels but concluded that it wasn't anything I couldn't handle. "She wants me to deal with my fear of failure," I thought confidently to myself. "If I pull back from working for a while, I will have less recognition and less income, but I've gone through this before, so it shouldn't be a big deal."

And it was true—I had faced failure and challenges all of my life, starting out with nothing, being forced to build things back up several times in my career, overcoming dozens of rejections in trying to sell my first book until I finally found a publisher, having to fight for my ideas in all of my projects. I had worked hard on myself over the years, in therapy, with my spiritual practices, and with the support of guides and mentors. Even though I was sure I still had many issues left, I wasn't too concerned about what might come up if I slowed down my pace and took more time off. "What could be so difficult about working less?" I reassured myself.

When we cannot see, we can't see what we cannot see. This was the case for me. I thought I was conscious of what was in my unconscious, but by definition, how could I have been? That is the nature of our Shadow self—it is hidden, and until we are willing to confront it, it remains cloaked and invisible, even to us. With all of my psychological understanding, and decades of self-inquiry, I was in for a big surprise.

Several months passed. As I cleared my calendar from any new obligations and finished up old ones, I began to experience something totally unexpected, something completely out of character for me: *I liked doing nothing.* I liked spending my days reading, arranging flowers, shopping for groceries, cooking, straightening up, walking my dogs. I liked having nothing planned. I liked not being in a hurry. I liked not having to get dressed in more than shorts and a T-shirt. I liked not having to go somewhere and stand on a stage and inspire people. I liked not having to say anything smart to anyone. I liked not feeling I had to make a contribution to humankind. I liked not feeling obligated to help people. I liked not feeling that I had to make a difference.

This revelation totally shocked me. I had always prided myself on being able to work harder and longer than anyone at anything. I had worked my way up from nothing to where I was in my life with very little help from anyone. I had gotten everything the hard way. (Notice how even now, I've used the words *hard* and *work* twice in two sentences!) Added to this were my deep spiritual beliefs that everything I did had to be significant, meaningful, and purposeful, This was my credo—*to work hard, not expect anyone*

*to do anything for me, and make as significant a contribution as I
could to the planet.*

Now, I found myself doing just the opposite—nothing—and
being just the opposite—nobody. And I loved it. And I hated that I
loved it. Why? Because it wasn't "like me." Even worse, because it
was too much like people I had disapproved of my whole life. My
apologies in advance for this list:

- *People who do nothing to help others or the planet but
  just indulge in their own pleasure*

- *People who didn't have to work for anything they had—
  success, money, fame—but got it handed to them by family, fate, luck, good timing, and were arrogant about it*

- *Women without children who let themselves be supported
  by husbands who work tirelessly, while the wives, who
  somehow never feel the need to help out, sat around choosing new fabric for the sofa, enjoying three-hour lunches
  with friends, and getting yet another spa treatment*

- *Women who only seek out men with money and are bla-
  tantly honest about wanting to be taken care of by a man
  even if he isn't their perfect emotional fit*

- *Experts who capitalize on commercially appealing ideas
  that are big moneymakers but are without originality or
  depth so they can sit back and bask in their wealth rather
  than risk anything*

These were the kinds of people that had always pushed my but-
tons and whose lives made me the most angry. "How spoiled, how
self-indulgent, how ignorant!" a part of me would think in judgment. "Thank God I am not like this." Now, even though I was not
living a life anything like these, and was simply taking a lot of time
off from work, one of my most hidden Shadows had emerged—*the
part of me that envied the people I condemned.*

I dug deeper, and I began to understand that I had always felt heavily weighed down by an overwhelming sense of responsibility to use my time, my talents, and all of my energy to make a difference in this world. *But could I love myself when I did nothing? Could I respect myself if I went for a day, a month or even a year without making a major contribution to society? Was I jealous of people who felt no such cosmic obligation? Did I have permission just to be simple, normal?*

I'd always believed that my drive to do something significant, to work so hard and to achieve so much had its source in a need to prove myself, to earn love and admiration. Now it became clear that I had driven myself incessantly because I was terrified that if I slowed down, I would lose my momentum and stop forever.

My Shadow self was the opposite of an overachieving, self-sacrificing servant of humanity—she just wanted to live a simple life and enjoy herself. She didn't want to work so hard. She didn't want to always be held accountable by others as a teacher. She didn't want to be scrutinized, criticized, projected upon. She didn't want to be responsible for making a difference. She wanted to be invisible.

Years ago, one of my metaphysical teachers told me that my greatest fear was of being ordinary and living an ordinary existence. For the first time, I understood what he'd meant. This had always been my secret inner battle. My driven side didn't trust my Shadow side: "If we let her stop, she'll get lazy and do nothing," it would whisper, "and then what will we accomplish?" And so I would work even harder.

Now, like a general who stands high on a hilltop overlooking the opposing armies on the battlefield, I could clearly see the two forces that had been warring within me for most of my life:

One—The spiritual teacher and visionary fiercely committed to serving other seekers on the planet; the energy of drive, vision and achievement

The other—The human woman longing for love, companionship and the simple bliss of life's everyday sweetness; the energy of harmony, nourishment and wholeness.

These two essential parts of myself had never been at peace with one another, and I had not known it until that moment.

How does this story of the discovery of my Shadow self end? Naturally, it doesn't—it continues, and as it does, I continue to be amazed at what I am shown as more and more of me emerges from the shadows and into the light.

Several nights ago, I had dinner with a very intuitive friend whom I hadn't seen for a long time. "Something is different about you," she said suspiciously after we'd been sitting together for a while. I asked her what she thought it was. She paused for a moment and answered: *"There's more of you here."* Then she smiled and added, *"But it's a peaceful more."*

And she was right. Day by day, the parts of me that used to be at war with one another are finding a harmonious balance as I learn to honor and embrace each of them for the particular gifts they bring to my existence. I am more of myself than I ever have been. And it is indeed a peaceful more.

. . .

When we invite "the real me to please stand up," we should be prepared for not one, but all of our selves to emerge. This is what it means to live an authentic life—having the willingness to recognize and accept *all* parts of ourselves, the ones we know well, and the ones that have been lurking in the shadows. To do this, we will need to transcend our conventional and limiting concepts of good and bad.

Eve Ensler reminds us: *"I think the danger comes when we lock people into being either bad or good and we don't allow for the complexity and ambiguity that lives in each of us."*

Our real enemy is not the darkness within us,
but our rejection and denial of it.
It is not by turning away from the Shadow side
of our self that we find peace,
but in turning toward it, knowing it,
embracing it as a long lost part of our self.

Who Is the Real Me?

The moment you are being, you're nobody but yourself.
To be nobody but yourself—in a world which is doing
its best to make you everybody else . . . [is] the most
wonderful life on earth.
—e. e. cummings

Here is my truth about the real me.

The Real Me:

Sometimes I love being with people.
Sometimes I flee from company and can bear only silence.

Sometimes I am sure people see my gifts, my wisdom and
my light.
Sometimes I think people have no clue who I really am.

Sometimes I will forgive and forgive and forgive and forgive
no matter what someone does to me.
Sometimes a line is crossed, and I close the door.

Sometimes I am the ancient goddess with the power of the
universe flowing through me.
Sometimes I am an insecure, wounded little girl afraid to
make a phone call.

Sometimes I have infinite patience and compassion for
everyone's choices.
Sometimes how people live and behave makes me ill.

Sometimes I see the perfection of the life and purposefulness
in everyone and everything.
Sometimes I think the world is just a screwed-up place.

Sometimes I want to serve the planet with every waking
    breath I take.
Sometimes I want to cash in my retirement account and go
    live on a tiny tropical island where I have no responsibil-
    ities, no commitments and no purpose other than to en-
    joy each glorious day.

All of these are the real me. Some parts I am quite fond of. Some
parts are nothing but trouble. Some parts make people admire me.
Some parts make people wonder about me. Some parts I am certain
I should have included in my list. Some parts . . . well, I am nothing
if not authentic!

As I learn to accept and honor each of these pieces of myself, I
experience an exquisite sense of wholeness for which I realize I
have been searching all of my life.

I used to pray to be certain things, to have certain things and to
achieve certain things:

"Please make me successful."
"Please give me energy to work hard."
"Please find me the right partner."
"Please help me write a great book."

Now I pray for one thing:
    *"Please fill my heart with enough love to embrace all that I am,
and all that others are."*
This is the courage for which I dig deep in myself—the courage
to be willing to live joyfully as a bundle of passionate contradic-
tions.

The real, whole, authentic you won't fit easily into the container
    of other people's expectations.
You will have too many edges.
You will not be a conventional shape.
You will be a unique, one-of-a-kind treasure.

And as you continue to grow, your shape will continue to change
    until you are smooth and sharp,
    dark and light,
    all at the same time,
Like a rare, radiant diamond.

PART TWO

Navigating Your Way Through the Unexpected

From Confusion to Clarity, From Awakening to Action

When you come to the edge of all that you know
You must believe one of two things;
There will be earth to stand on,
Or you will be given wings to fly.
—Unknown

The process of gaining wisdom begins with the asking of questions," I wrote in chapter 1. Once these initial questions awaken us to where we are, the questions themselves undergo an important metamorphosis, transforming themselves into new ones: *Do I turn this way or that way? Do I open this door or that one? Do I leave behind this part of myself, this way of life, this person, or take it along? Do I renovate my reality, or move out and start over?*

"How did I get here?" turns into
"What do I do now?"

These new questions are our focus in the second section of this book:

How do we move from where we are to wherever it is we're supposed to go next?

How do we follow roads that we cannot find, and paths that seem to lead nowhere?

How do we traverse the great chasms of fear, regret, sadness or confusion that we must often cross in order to find our way out of the darkness?

How do we turn dead ends into doorways?

How do we navigate through unexpected times?

. . .

There is a classic Buddhist story I've heard recounted many times that is an appropriate place for us to begin. Here is my version:

> One day a young student at the Buddhist monastery is invited to meditate with two senior monks as part of his spiritual education. The three men take the long walk to the opposite side of the lake from the monastery and sit down by the shore, ready to begin their meditation practice. Suddenly, the first senior monk leaps to his feet. "Oh no, I forgot my meditation mat," he explains. "I need it to meditate properly." Then he goes up to the edge of the lake and walks easily across the surface of the water to the monastery on the other side, returning the same way he came, carrying his mat. The young student is astonished at this miraculous accomplishment but, practicing discipline and respect, says nothing.

> The three settle down to meditate again when the second senior monk suddenly stands up. "I just realized that I forgot my sun hat," he announces apologetically, "I'll just run back and get it—it won't take long." And with that, he, too, steps into the lake and runs across the top of the water to the other side, returning minutes later with his hat.

> The student can barely believe his eyes, and concludes that these senior monks must be showing off to impress him. "Just because I am younger doesn't mean I have not achieved spiritual mastery," he says indignantly to himself.

"I am just as enlightened as these two old monks—and I will prove it." And with that the student runs to the water's edge, preparing to walk across it, and immediately sinks into the deep lake.

Coughing and sputtering, he pulls himself out of the water and tries again and again, sinking down into the water each time. Unwilling to give up, he tries repeatedly to walk on the water's surface as he's seen the senior monks do, and each time, he fails and sinks into the lake.

The two older monks watch the frustrated student's efforts for some time. After a while, the first monk calmly turns to the second monk and says: *"Do you think we should tell him where the stones are?"*

There is a part of each of us that wants someone to give us the answers to life's problems, to point us in the right direction, to tell us "where the stones are." This is especially true when we are in the midst of moving through the murky waters of crisis, challenge and self-inquiry. "What do I do now?" we ask ourselves—now that we've dug deep for wisdom, arrived at turning points, come out of denial, retrieved lost pieces of ourselves, embraced our Shadow, let Truth in the door and tuned back in. How do we move forward? How do we cross the lake without drowning?

Navigating successfully through changes does not happen by chance, nor by luck. As we learned from the monks who crossed the lake, there is more than one way to get to our destination. Rather than making exhausting efforts that only end with our falling flat on our faces, we can learn some basic, universal principles about transformation that will show us how to glide more gracefully through our changes and challenges.

I have fallen into my own "lake" many times, but I never gave up trying to find the path that leads across. Gradually I have learned where many of the stepping-stones are. In the chapters that follow, I will do my best to describe them to you. They are not rocks made of granite, or lava, or any other minerals; these are stones of wisdom and understanding that can help you move from wherever you are to where you long, and deserve, to be.

The Power That Surges You Forward

My inside, listen to me, the greatest spirit,
the Teacher, is near, wake up, wake up!
Run to his feet—he is standing close to your head right now.
You have slept for millions and millions of years.
Why not wake up this morning?
—Kabir

It's morning. You are lying in bed, suddenly wide awake, even though you don't have to get up yet. You would like to sleep some more, but you are too restless and agitated—the awareness of all you have to do today has stirred you out of your slumber and is impossible to ignore. You feel overwhelmed just thinking about the multitude of tasks waiting for your attention. "What should I do first? Which phone calls are essential for me to make? Dealing with that person is going to be so unpleasant—I wonder if I can put it off for a while longer? How am I going to get through the day without becoming too distressed?" These are the kinds of thoughts running through your mind as you toss and turn, hoping that somehow you will miraculously drift back into dreamland. But no, you are too anxious to relax. Whether you like it or not, it is time to get up.

This is how it happens with our inner awakenings as well. When they come, they bring with them a sort of benevolent restlessness that is impossible to ignore:

When we are cut off from our own truth,
disconnected from our own wisdom and shut down
in our heart, we block the flow of power
and universal energy into our lives.

When we reconnect with our truth and authenticity, these obstructions are removed and that power surges back through us.

This universal energy is the life force, the Holy Spirit, the Christ Consciousness, what in Chinese is the "chi," and in the Hindu tradition is the "shakti." Each spiritual and religious tradition calls this energy by a different name, but the definition is the same: it is the power that brings everything to life, like the voltage running through wires that allows a lightbulb to be illuminated. When we are plugged in to that energy, we have access to an infinite supply of energy, wisdom, creativity, wisdom and love. When we turn off our connection to our inner self, we are disconnecting from that source.

There is a tremendous energy that begins to flow through us again when we wake up from an emotional sleep, or from a period of denial, or from a long time of having been lost to ourselves. It is as if we have just had the power turned back on. This surge of the life force can be very disquieting and even disturbing, especially when we have been not used to feeling it this strongly for a long time, maybe even for all of our lives. Like the person lying in bed too agitated to go back to sleep, we become unsettled from the force of our own awakenings, wondering why we are suddenly so anxious. "Something must be wrong with me," we conclude.

Ironically, the opposite is true: something is right. We have woken up into a new level of wisdom, of clarity, of authenticity. When we don't understand that this is the case, *our coming together can easily be misinterpreted as a falling apart.*

• • •

I learned about these surges of cosmic energy the hard way in my own life. I had never heard this concept clearly explained by any mental health professional, rabbi, minister or spiritual teacher. Almost every time I had a major awakening and unblocking of energy in my life, I would initially feel restless, uneasy and worried about myself. In time, my restlessness would subside, and I would experience new levels of achievement, creativity and contentment. **It took me years to figure out that what felt like an anxiety attack was, at least for me, simply a higher frequency of life energy that I just wasn't used to, a cosmic power surge.**

When I became a teacher, I made a point of explaining the phenomenon of the cosmic power surge to my students. I would watch the look of utter relief on people's faces as I described my own experiences and explained how easy it is to misinterpret this increased voltage, mislabeling it as a symptom of some kind of mental disturbance or worse. "I went through that after I got divorced, but I thought I had Adult Attention Deficit Disorder," someone would confess. "As soon as I made the decision to change careers, I became so restless and anxious that my doctor wanted to put me on tranquilizers to calm me down," another would share. These were the voices of men and women who had gone through powerful personal rebirths and emerged, trembling, on the other side with no way to put their experiences into perspective.

Once again we are reminded of the power of naming something. As Kabir eloquently says in his poem, we have been sleeping for millions and millions of years. Now the miraculous has happened— we have opened our eyes. *"I am not going crazy—I am waking up!"* we must say to ourselves as we adjust to a new, heightened energetic frequency born of our expanded consciousness.

Moving from Awakening to Action

There is a time for departure even when there's
no certain place to go.
—Tennessee Williams

A reader wrote me about her dead relationship with her angry, controlling husband who, in spite of her pleading, refuses to get help with his problems. She has wanted to divorce him for some time and has told her family, her friends and even a lawyer about her plan—but not her husband. She's been frozen, afraid to make a move, and now she is realizing the toll it is taking on her:

> I finally admitted to myself that I have been treading water for such a long time in my life. I've been treading not knowing quite where to swim to, where the shore is for me. I'm afraid that if I just choose a direction and begin swimming, I may never find shore at all. Perhaps I'm waiting for a rescue boat to come out and save me.
>
> What I have to face is that all this treading has caused me to become achingly tired. I feel the burn in my muscles. I am exhausted from trying to keep myself afloat. I know I'm not going anywhere like this, and I am faced with two options. One: I SWIM—swim, swim and swim and find shore. Maybe I'm not THAT far away. Or Two: I drown.

This woman painfully articulates a point that is crucial for us to understand on our quest for self-knowledge:

A moment comes when we've seen the truth, we've had the breakthrough, we've understood the revelation, and it's time to do something about it. Continuing to do nothing becomes more and more uncomfortable, like using up our energy treading water rather than swimming to shore.

Transitions are supposed to be temporary. They are a place for passage, not a destination in themselves. We can't just keep analyzing the past. We can't just have the revelation, or attend the seminar, or go through the therapy, or share the confidential conversation with a friend, or write another ten pages in our journal or watch someone else transform on a TV talk show. We need to integrate what we've learned. We need to begin to make a change, a shift, a move forward. We have to *do* something.

The shifts we make on the inside need
to be expressed with action on the outside.

We're awake, but now it's time to get out of bed.

Once we have emerged from the demanding work of an awakening, there is a great temptation to stop where we are and go no further. As difficult as it is to face unpleasant truths, it is that much more difficult to do something about them.

This is where we must be brutally honest with ourselves—have we actually transformed, or are we just talking as if we have? Have we changed our patterns, or have we just become an expert on them? Have we moved, or are we just rearranging the furniture?

Here are two examples that illustrate the difference between looking like we are changing and truly changing:

. . .

Nathan, a life coach, is a powerful and convincing speaker. He specializes in working with South American corporations, training their top executives. Nathan is good at what he does. He can impressively describe the issues we each face in our lives. He can prescribe step-by-step techniques for making changes. He can tell moving tales about people who have applied his principles and transformed their lives.

However, Nathan practices very little of what he preaches. He is known in his industry for being harsh and unconscious in the way he treats his employees, for chronically cheating on his wife and for being nothing like what he appears to be. Nathan knows the truth and is a highly skilled expert at talking about it. He just doesn't live it.

. . .

Celeste collects transformational experiences like other people collect dolls or stamps or baseball cards. She has attended every personal growth seminar in existence. She has had readings with almost all of the country's top psychics. She goes to therapy twice a week, attends a chanting and meditation evening once a week, attends support group meetings on several other nights and on the weekends she visits every spiritual teacher, Hindu guru,

Buddhist lama, Tibetan monk, Native-American shaman or other holy person she can find.

Celeste can talk about all of these teachers in glowing terms, and she can also explain her psychological patterns and emotional issues in this and other lives. But that is all she can do—talk. She mistreats her boyfriend, doesn't take care of her body and is terribly high-strung. She hasn't integrated a fraction of the wisdom she's received and appears only to be interested in finding the next event to attend, as if one day she will win a prize for having the longest list of cosmic experiences.

. . .

You may know people like Nathan and Celeste. You may recognize a part of them in yourself. **To look as if we are changing and to actually change are two very different things.** The irreverent comedian Steven Wright puts it more bluntly, but gets the point across: *"There's a fine line between fishing and standing on the shore like an idiot."* We can dress like we're fishing, have the most advanced fishing gear, go to the best spot to catch fish and stand there and talk about the art of fishing, but until we cast the rod, we are not fishing.

. . .

Life can only be understood backwards
but it must be lived forwards.
—Søren Kierkegaard

A teaching story I wrote about awakening:

Once long ago, a farmer stayed out late drinking far too much ale and, becoming intoxicated, he accidentally fell asleep on a thicket of sharp thorns. As long as he remained asleep, he didn't feel the pain of the thorns cutting into his body, but the moment the effect of the ale wore off and he awakened, he become aware of a horrible stinging sensation swallowing him up from head to toe.

The farmer knew he should get up and get out of the
thicket, but the slightest movement made the pain even
worse. So he just lay there on the thorns, as still as possible,
afraid to move at all.

I will not deceive you. Coming out of denial is painful. Facing
unexpected losses and challenges hurts. And sometimes waking up
from the ways we have been asleep feels like finding ourselves on a
thicket of thorns from which there is no easy escape. Discovering
where we are is bad enough, but the prospect of figuring out how
to move forward seems impossible and overwhelming.

Revelation is hard. Revolution is harder.
Awakening is hard. Action is harder.

This is one of the reasons that it is often so difficult for us go
forward. We feel like we've barely recovered from our revelations
and awakenings, and that if we actually try and integrate them into
our lives, it will be too difficult, too painful. Like the farmer, we remain where we are, uncomfortable, but afraid to move.

Here is the stepping-stone I would like to offer you:

**When you begin to move forward from awakening into action,
be careful not to misinterpret pain as an indication that you are doing something wrong, and turn to go back the other way. You may
find yourself thinking, "If it hurts this much, it can't be right," but
this is not always an accurate assessment of pain. Pain is not always
a sign that you are doing something wrong. Sometimes it tells you
that you are doing something right.**

Several years ago, I had to have oral surgery for a tooth problem. My friend and wonderful endodontist, Dr. Rami Etessami,
performed the surgery in his Los Angeles office, and all went
smoothly. Although I was groggy and uncomfortable when it was
over, I was relieved finally to be out of pain. Two days passed, and
I felt as good as new.

One Friday night a few weeks later, my mouth suddenly began to hurt in the exact spot where I'd had the surgery. "Oh no," I lamented, "something went wrong, and I'm going to have to go through the procedure all over again." I spent the weekend anxious and agitated, with my imagination in overdrive.

On Monday, I called Dr. Rami and explained my concerns. He listened carefully to my symptoms, asked me some questions, and then told me the good news. "There is absolutely nothing wrong with you," he reassured me. "The pain and tingling you are experiencing is very normal after this kind of intense surgery. What you are feeling is the nerve fibers regenerating new pathways. Not only is the sensation not a bad sign, it's a wonderful sign that you are healing beautifully."

I was very relieved to hear Dr. Rami's explanation of my discomfort, and as with everything in life, once I understood the source of what I was experiencing, my concerns vanished, and the intermittent pain didn't bother me as much. Every twinge told me that my teeth were healing.

When we begin to integrate our awakenings into action, we will have moments of discomfort, twinges of uncertainty. This is where the "cosmic power surge" comes in. That fire of restlessness, that divine agitation, is there to urge us on, to make sure we move forward toward the healing and wholeness that awaits us.

Face to Face with the Gap

You've got to jump off cliffs all the time
and build your wings on the way down.
—Ray Bradbury

Even when we want to move forward in our lives, even when we have spent long enough questioning, contemplating, digging and examining, it is not easy. This is especially true when we come face to face with the Gap:

You are standing on the edge of a cliff, high above the ground. Across from you, you know there is another cliff, one you want very much to be on. Perhaps you can see it clearly and can imagine how you will feel when you are finally there. Perhaps the other side is covered by clouds or mist, and even though you believe it is there, you can't see it at all. You know you don't want to stay where you are for much longer; you know it's time to jump.

Then you look down at the huge gap of space between the two cliffs, and in that moment, you become overwhelmed with FEAR—fear of falling; fear of not having what it takes to get to the other side; fear of getting there and changing your mind and not having a way to get back; fear that if you leap, you may have to leave behind something or someone you care deeply about.

You can hear your dreams calling to you, reminding you of how badly you want whatever it is that's waiting for you on that other cliff, that you'll never be happy if you stay where you are now, that you've been putting this off for too long already. But you can also hear the voices of people you know standing near you—some trying to talk you out of jumping to the other side, some angry with you for leaving them behind, still others warning you that you are making a big mistake. And so you remain where you are, looking behind you, looking ahead of you, frozen and unable to leap.

We all come to a moment in our transformative journey when we find ourselves standing on the edge of a symbolic cliff, knowing that we need to find the courage to jump and somehow get to the other side. We stare at a gap between where we are and where we want to be, with no idea of how we are going to get across.

Perhaps we know we do not want to live the life we've had in its old form, but we aren't sure what our new life should look like. Perhaps we've finally come to terms with the fact that our marriage is not as fulfilling as we want it to be, but we aren't sure what to do to make it work again or if we should even try. Perhaps we've lost a loved one or a job or our health or our financial security and know we need to find the courage to move forward in spite of it, but can't seem to figure out exactly how to begin again.

It is our nature as human beings to want to feel safe and in control, to orient ourselves by looking around and recognizing people, places and patterns that are familiar. When we confront what appears to be a void stretching before us, we become frightened and often cling more tightly to whatever it is we need to let go of.

This dread of facing that gap is one of the forces that keeps us from getting out of bed, that keeps us treading water rather than swimming to the shore, that keeps us frozen in inaction.

**All growth requires the courage to let go
as we jump from one cliff to the next,
from who we have been to who we hope to be,
leaving behind our comfort zone
and leaping, at least temporarily, into the unknown.**

Even when we are unhappy in an unfulfilling career or a passionless relationship, still, it is familiar territory, and what is familiar feels safe to us. "At least I know where I'm standing now," we tell ourselves. "At least I'm familiar with my pain, my unhappiness, my lack of contentment. But if I leave this behind and leap, who knows where I will end up?"

Getting Stuck in Confusion

*If we don't change our direction
we're likely to end up where we're headed.*
—Chinese proverb

I'm so confused." I've heard this lament thousands of times in my life—from clients, from friends, from my own inner voice. It announces a state in which we're standing at some kind of crossroads, looking this way and that way with no idea which road we should take. Or perhaps we are standing on a cliff, trying to figure out whether or not to leap. Whether our challenge is about what to do, what to feel or what to believe, the result is the same—we know we need to make a choice, and we tell ourselves we're too confused to do so.

Confusion is one of the most common obstacles we face as we try to make our leap from awakening to action, and one of our favorite ways to get stuck. Many years ago when I first began teaching seminars, I confronted this issue of confusion in my students so often that I came up with the phrase: **Confusion is a cover-up.**

Being confused is always covering up something else. The experience masks emotions we would rather not feel, challenges we would rather not address, realities we would rather not face— so instead we tell ourselves that we're confused.

"I'm so confused about my marriage," a woman says to me.

"If you weren't confused," I ask her, "what might you be feeling right now?"

"I'd be furious at my husband for being so shut down. I'd be scared that he'll never change and we'll get divorced. I'd be angry at having put up with the way he's treated me for so long. But . . . it's all so confusing."

This woman isn't confused at all—she's pissed off! However, it's safer for her to feel confused than to feel angry. Especially for those people who have a difficult time acknowlwedging unpleasant emotions, confusion can be a nice way to express our not-so-nice feelings. Saying we are confused sounds better than saying we are outraged.

The state of confusion is also a convenient place where many of us hide out when we are afraid to make a decision. As long as I'm confused, I can't decide anything that might hurt someone I love, or make a mistake that might hurt me. Rather than feeling my fear

of disappointing others or failing myself, I can just remain confused indefinitely.

. . .

Jody's widowed and elderly mother has been having frequent accidents in her home and obviously can no longer take care of
herself. Just last week, she forgot to turn off the stove and started a
fire in the kitchen. Fortunately, a neighbor smelled smoke and
helped her put it out—otherwise, the outcome could have been disastrous.

For months, Jody has been complaining to her husband and her
friends about how confused she is. "I just don't know what to do,"
she repeats over and over. They listen sympathetically, but to them,
the truth is apparent. *Jody is not confused—she is heartbroken.*
Some part of her knows she is going to have to put her mother in a
retirement home, a decision she dreads making. Although her
mother already has many friends living there, Jody realizes it will
still be an enormous adjustment for her, giving up the house she's
lived in for more than forty years and admitting that she is no
longer self-sufficient.

Jody's sense of confusion is covering up many more authentic
and painful emotions: *sadness* at seeing her mother's health fail;
grief at the loss of the traditional mother-daughter role, which now
will be reversed; *fear* as she contemplates the future, and knows
one day soon her mother will pass away; *guilt* at the thought of
putting her mother in a facility rather than having her share her
home, which would be impossible since Jody is a flight attendant
and travels all the time.

Instead of facing these feelings, Jody lingers in confused limbo,
postponing what, deep down, she knows is the inevitable. Soon she
is going to have to take the leap off the cliff, but as long as she tells
herself she is confused, she can avoid doing the thing she dreads.

For some people, confusion is not just something they face in
times of challenge, crisis or transition—it is a career, a lifelong,
chronic state in which they remain as a way of not having to grow
up and be responsible for themselves or their actions. We all know
individuals like this. For example: the fifty-year-old man who is

still trying to figure out what he wants to do professionally and never has to take any real risks; the thirty-something woman who can't seem to decide on a career and always finds wealthy older gentlemen to help her, usually financially, as she tries to get through this confusing time. Once again, the confusion is just a cover-up. In these cases, it covers up fear, lack of confidence and a need to feel taken care of by others.

The Four Big Payoffs We Get from Remaining Confused

We kid ourselves when we claim that our confusion is making us helpless and impotent. Confusion is very powerful, but it is a negative kind of power. It gets us results, but not ones that are necessarily beneficial to our growth. Here are some of the payoffs we get out of being confused.

1. Attention

Confusion is a great attention-grabber. When we are confused enough, people will feel sorry for us and give us lots of attention. "Poor thing—she is going through such a hard time." Some people don't know any other way of getting love and attention other than playing the helpless victim—and victims are always confused.

If we remain confused for long enough, we get to be a martyr. "*Look* how much I am going through," our painful sighs tell those around us. "But somehow, in spite of all this adversity, I am surviving."

2. Advice

When we are confused, we need lots of advice from everyone. Our daily routine becomes asking the people around us for their opinion about what we should do. This is a covert way of being irresponsible—not only do we not have to make any decisions ourselves, but if the advice others give us doesn't work, we can always blame them for the outcome.

Constantly asking for advice to help us with our confusion is a way to remain a child and avoid growing up. We secretly, or not so secretly, want to be rescued, perhaps by the "mommy" or "daddy" we never had.

3. Addictions

Staying confused is a great way to stay addicted. After all, as long as we are going through such a challenging and confusing time, we have an excuse to indulge in our drugs/alcohol/food/cigarettes, and so forth. "I know I should quit," we say, "and I am going to—but this isn't a good time. I'm just so confused right now."

Of course this sets up a vicious circle—**as long as we are clouding our consciousness with substances that rob us of clarity, we can't get clear enough to get unconfused.** So we feel worse, and tell ourselves we need the crutch of our addiction to help us through. And the cycle continues.

4. Avoidance

This is the biggest negative payoff of confusion. When we are confused, we spend all of our time dealing with our confusion, creating the illusion that we are actually busy doing something. Preoccupied with being confused, we get to avoid whatever it is that we don't want to face:

We avoid the truth.

We avoid change.

We avoid facing our fears.

We avoid disappointing people we love.

We avoid taking risks.

We avoid confrontations with others.

We avoid reality.

We avoid leaping off the cliff.

The Confusion-Clearing Exercise

What follows is a writing exercise—another stepping-stone—one I've used in my seminars that will help you get through feelings of confusion.

On a piece of paper, make two columns. At the top of the first write: *What I feel confused about:* . . . At the top of the second write: *If I were clear I might have to:* . . .

Sit quietly with no one around and ask yourself these questions, and answer as honestly as you can. Do one set at a time, and write down both parts, as in the example below. *Be willing to tell the truth no matter how uncomfortable it feels.*

What I feel confused about:	*If I were clear I might have to:*
My health and which diet is best for me	Choose one diet and stick to it Stop eating junk Exercise
Whether or not I should propose to my longtime girlfriend	Admit to myself that even though I love her, I don't feel she is the right person for me Face her and how upset she will be with me
How to handle my frustration at work	Admit that my supervisor is sabotaging my projects Confront him or his supervisor Quit
Whether or not to put my house up for sale	Admit that I am not happy in my neighborhood Face the fact that my house hasn't gone up in value as I thought it would Downsize my lifestyle

<u>*What I feel confused about:*</u>	<u>*If I were clear I might have to:*</u>
My relationship with my roommate and why we aren't getting along	Admit that we have grown apart Tell her that I don't like her doing drugs in the apartment with her boyfriend Move out or ask her to move

This is a very powerful and effective process. It is predicated on my belief that underneath our confusion, we actually are clear most of the time. The wording "If I were clear I might have to . . ." has an intriguing way of slipping past our conscious mind, and giving our inner self the opportunity to speak.

If you have a friend or partner with whom you feel safe, you can try doing this exercise together out loud. If you would rather write down your answers, you can share what you've written afterward. I've also used this Confusion-Clearing Exercise with teenagers and even young children. They always love doing it and come up with very honest responses.

The Confusion-Clearing Ceremony

Sometimes certain issues in our lives are more stuck than others. If you find yourself unable to get clear about something, try this Confusion-Clearing Ceremony:

Write down your issue on a piece of paper. Beneath what you've written, write a specific date by which you would like to be clear. For instance:

My issue: Whether I should go back to college and get an advanced degree, or keep the job I have now.

I would like to have clarity on this by one month from today, August 5, 2005.

Now take this piece of paper and put it in a powerful or sacred spot in your home: on an altar if you have one; near a candle or crystals; close to a picture of anyone who inspires you or who you feel helps you—a spiritual teacher, your deceased relatives, Jesus or Mary, for example; near a statue of Buddha, Ganesh or Quan Yin, or anywhere else that is a special place for you.

Once you've placed the paper in this spot, close your eyes and offer your request to all the helping and guiding forces you know of, asking them to please bring you clarity by the date you chose or sooner. Offer thanks for their assistance and perform any other rituals that feel right to you.

I have had miraculous results with this Confusion-Clearing Ceremony, as have many of the people I've shared it with. A word of caution: don't overload the Higher Power with a long laundry list of requests! Try getting clear on your own first, and only offer your clearing request for issues about which you can't seem to get unconfused. It is also respectful to just make one request at a time.

The Maori, the indigenous people of New Zealand, have a saying:

Turn your face to the sun, and the shadows fall behind you.

Just past the shadows of our confusion, the Truth, like the Sun, is always waiting to reveal itself to us. We need to be brave enough to go beyond our bewilderment and look within ourselves, to push aside the veils of confusion and discover whatever it is we need to know, learn or feel in order to move forward in our lives. That light of Truth will illuminate our path, and guide us safely to the other side of the shore of our awakening.

The Loving Conspiracy

Your friends will stretch your vision or choke your dream.
—John Maxwell

Sometimes when we attempt to wake up in our own lives and leap forward to new levels of truth, honesty and authenticity, the resistance we encounter isn't only from within ourselves, but from the people around us—family, friends, coworkers, even our intimate partner. I call this the Loving Conspiracy—*what happens when, consciously or unconsciously, those closest to us undermine our efforts to grow or change.*

We would like to believe that all the people in our life want the best for us. We would like to believe that our friends, relatives, partners, parents and children all want us to shine, to grow, to be the best we can be. When we are confronted with reluctance, resistance, disapproval or even anger from our loved ones at the advent of what we consider a change or transformation for the better, it often stuns us. "How could she/he love me so much and yet be so unhappy with my growth?" we wonder in disbelief. Why would people who care for us want to hold us back or keep us stuck in a place where we're obviously not happy?

Remember the Russian *matroyshka* dolls with one doll hidden within the other? A *matroyshka* is wonderful if a person likes nesting dolls, each with a surprise inside, but not everyone does. Imagine the disappointment of a person who expects a solid doll only to discover that it opens up to reveal many other dolls inside. "This is not what I wanted," he or she might complain. "It's too complicated. I just want a simple doll."

Sometimes, if people know the outermost version of you, they will be shocked to find there is more inside, especially if what emerges does not fit their picture of what and who they thought you were or want you to be. "What's this?" they question with unhappy surprise as you reveal another you that has been hidden within the one they know. "I didn't know you: were like this/felt

this way/cared about these things/believed this/wanted this/were interested in this."

Everyone in your life will not celebrate
the unfolding of your authentic self.
Some people don't want "the real you"
to please stand up because,
believe it or not, they were comfortable
with your limitations,
your old roles, your old denials,
all of which got along very nicely with theirs.

. . .

I am in the middle of a divorce right now, so I'm having a hard
time," the man sitting next to me on an airplane confesses. And
he tells me his story. Gus is a firefighter, a down-to-earth kind of
guy who married his wife, Tina, when he was in his early thirties
and she was twenty-four. They had three children in seven years,
and Tina seemed to thrive in her role as a mother and homemaker.
Gus was happy and thought Tina was happy, too. Gus explains
what happened:

> When our youngest child started school, Tina started to
> act differently. She began hanging around with two of her
> old friends from high school, one gal who wasn't married
> and owned some kind of store, and another who was mar-
> ried but lived a very fancy kind of life, traveling all over and
> going to conferences, things like that. All of a sudden, she
> comes home with books about psychology. She never used
> to read that kind of stuff, and even made fun of it. Then she
> announces that she is going off to a self-improvement week-
> end with her friends at some hotel. Let me tell you, I was
> pretty peeved. I told her I didn't want her going to a hotel
> with a bunch of strangers, and we had the biggest fight of
> our marriage. I'd never seen her like this before. So I gave in,
> and she went.

As far as I can tell, the weekend didn't improve her—it made her worse. She came home agitated and angry at me, talking about how she needed to change this and that about herself. I tried to tell her that I liked her the way she was, and that seemed to make her even more angry. She said I didn't "get" her, that I didn't listen to her, and I have to admit, I agreed, because I couldn't understand why she was stirring things up, and told her so.

Things went downhill from there. She went out and got a job, even though I let her know that I wasn't happy about her working when the kids were still so young. "Why are you changing everything?" I'd ask her. "We were doing fine." She'd always give me the same answer—that this is who she was, and I needed to accept it. But I couldn't, because it wasn't the Tina I married. I didn't know where that Tina was anymore. Anyway, you know the end of the story. We're divorced, and I still don't really understand this whole mess.

My heart went out to Gus as he told me his sad tale. Of course, I understood exactly what had gone wrong, even if he still didn't. Tina had searched and eventually found herself, only it wasn't a self that Gus liked. He wanted the Tina he'd met when she was twenty-four years old, not the one that had been hidden inside like the Russian nesting doll.

The original Tina was very conventional, with little personal ambition. She wasn't very introspective. She was content to take care of others and not pay much attention to herself. This suited Gus just fine. He wasn't interested in a self-actualized woman. To Gus, Tina had changed and had somehow betrayed him in the process. But Tina hadn't really changed at all—she had just deepened, unfolded, blossomed into a richer, multidimensional version of her younger self.

As you become more authentic, more awake, more aware, some people will balk at the new you. This is both painful and perplexing when it happens. It is as if you pushed and struggled and finally made it through the birth canal and much to your surprise and disappointment, your arrival was greeted with this: *"I liked you better before, when you were in the womb."*

What they are really feeling is:

"The new you threatens me and the way I am."

"I'm afraid the new you won't like the old me."

"Seeing you so changed reminds me of all the ways I need to change but haven't."

Too often, this is how it is for us as we begin to emerge from our awakenings. We rejoice at our own hard-earned growth, but our triumphs are bittersweet as we try to comprehend why our loved ones not only don't share in our celebration, but appear to be punishing us for having awakened at all.

I hear stories like these all the time:

Sylvia, a fifty-nine-year-old widow, has been suffering deeply since her husband died two years ago. Finally she decides she needs to embrace life again, and joins a singles group from her synagogue, where to her great surprise she meets a gentleman with whom she falls deeply in love. Several months pass, and Irving asks Sylvia to marry him. Elated, Sylvia announces the news to her friends in the Bereaved Spouses Support Group she's been attending. The reaction of several women shocks her: one tells her she is making a big mistake; another warns that the man must be after her money; a third woman even scolds Sylvia, saying she is shaming the memory of her late husband.

· · ·

Julio is proud of himself for finally getting his body into shape. At twenty-seven, he was overweight, with high cholesterol and various health problems. Knowing obesity runs in his family, he joins a gym, changes his eating habits and in six months loses forty pounds. He flies home to see his family for Christmas, excited about showing them his accomplishment, and is shocked when they seem to try to sabotage his health regime. His mother refuses to cook anything but fattening foods and complains when he won't eat what the rest of the family is eating. His younger brother becomes angry whenever Julio goes out for a run. His father makes disparaging comments about Julio's new less-than-manly physique, claiming real men aren't slender like Julio.

. . .

Donna, thirty-six, has been working in the personnel department at the same corporation for eight years, and is tired of always being so timid and self-effacing around her boss and coworkers. This is a childhood pattern that Donna is finally ready to break. After a year of counseling and lot of personal reflection, she feels a new level of confidence and empowerment. Slowly, she begins to take the initiative in her department, offering suggestions at meetings, and becomes a much stronger presence in the company. The vice president notices Donna's transformation and praises her for it. However, Donna's best friend at work, Suzanne, becomes increasingly cold to her. When Donna asks her what's wrong, Suzanne accuses Donna of showing off, trying to make the other employees look bad, and betraying their friendship.

Each of these people is the unhappy victim of a Loving Conspiracy in which their friends and family are using a variety of tactics to discount or sabotage their growth and progress. Here are some of the common methods others might utilize when they feel threatened by your breakthroughs:

- **Convincing you that something's psychologically wrong with you**

- **Creating their own drama or emergency to pull your attention from your soul-searching and on to them**

- **Enrolling other friends or family members to talk you out of your concerns or feelings**

- **Making you feel guilty for your growth by accusing you of abandoning them, feeling superior to them, breaking promises made to them or misleading them**

- Intimidating you by saying that other people are very unhappy with how you have changed but are not telling you this to your face

- Scaring you by predicting a negative outcome for all of your new choices

- Emotionally blackmailing you by withdrawing their love until you change back to the way you were

It is difficult enough to stand facing the gap between where we are and where we want to be, and trying to find the courage to leap. But when people we care about are unhappy with our intention to leave the cliff we've been standing on, their disapproval often holds us back like invisible but powerful ropes. We want to move forward, but we feel the Loving Conspiracy pulling on us to stay where we are.

This unexpected tug of war can fill us with despair. It has taken all the strength and courage we have to battle our own resistance to change. Now it seems we may also have to battle our friends, our family, even those who supposedly love us the most, as we become fully ourselves.

Fear of Contagion: Stop These Changes Before They Spread!

Traditions are group efforts to keep the unexpected from happening.
—Barbara Tober

Sometimes in order to avoid their own wake-up calls, people might discourage us from experiencing any of our own. . . .

I have a former employee and friend who, after suffering for years in an ill-matched marriage, finally got up the courage to admit to himself that it was never going to work. He told his wife he believed the best thing for both of them was to get a divorce. Anyone who knew this man or had ever seen him with his wife could not have missed the fact that he was terribly unhappy. So he was shocked when one of his casual acquaintances called him up and tried to talk him out of leaving his marriage.

"I had never discussed my relationship with this man," Gary explained to me, "and he knew nothing at all about my situation. Nonetheless, he must have called me a dozen times, insinuating that I would be committing some kind of sin if I made the choice to leave my marriage and suggesting that perhaps I was mentally unstable to even be considering it. He even contacted some of my other friends behind my back and suggested they do an intervention. I was already suffering over what was a very painful decision, but this made it even worse. I just couldn't figure out why he was so outraged about what I was doing in my private life."

When I asked Gary what he knew about the man's own marriage, he told me that the couple seemed very disconnected, and that he was surprised this fellow and his wife were still together. "Well, that explains it," I announced: "He's afraid he's going to catch it from you, so he's trying to nip it in the bud. Just wait," I predicted. "I've seen this pattern before, and I have a feeling he will be next."

Sure enough, less than a year later, the man who had berated Gary for considering divorce suddenly left his own wife. Obviously, the demise of this man's marriage was already in the works, and he wasn't directly influenced by Gary's choice to end his relationship. His vehement condemnation of my friend's decision and his perversely paternalistic attempts to stop him spoke loudly of his battle with his own Shadow self and his own repressed fears and desires.

**Some people fear that change is contagious,
like an epidemic with no known cure,
and they are afraid of catching it from you.**

Societies function harmoniously when people follow both spoken and unspoken rules. Most of us honor these guidelines and expect others to do the same. I will obey the traffic signals if you obey the traffic signals. I will pay my taxes if you pay your taxes. I will wear the appropriate clothes to work if you wear the appropriate clothes to work. I will keep my lawn well groomed if you keep your lawn well groomed. We don't like it when people break the rules, especially if we have made an effort to follow them.

We become especially threatened when other people break undefined but very important emotional rules. As long as I have to endure my unfulfilling job or sexless marriage, you had better endure yours. As long as I have to be overweight, you have to be overweight. As long as I have to be in the closet, you have to be in the closet. As long as I have to struggle, you have to struggle. As long as I have to suffer, you have to suffer.

What happens, then, when someone else begins to question those emotional rules, or—gasp—dares to defy them? It's as if the whole house of cards threatens to collapse. If my colleague can break free from a stifling job and pursue something unconventional but satisfying, then why am I still sitting here bored to tears? If my friend can end his incompatible relationship, then why am I still enduring mine? As long as everyone else stayed where they were, I got to stay where I was. But now change is on the loose, and who knows what can happen?

Now we begin to reach a deeper comprehension of the Loving Conspiracy:

Although others may appear to be lovingly "protecting" you from making a mistake or doing something you will regret, they are most likely attempting to protect themselves. "We'd better stop it before it spreads!"—that's the hidden message in their behavior disguised as "goodwill."

"I can't understand why people are frightened of new ideas. I'm frightened of the old ones," said artist, composer and writer John Cage. I share his view, yet this is the way it has been throughout time. What is new and different is perceived as threatening, dangerous and in need of being controlled, supervised or eliminated. As those of us on a conscious journey grow and transform

as individuals, we will not be exempt from this sort of oppressive suspicion, even from those closest to us.

Still, we cannot allow this to stop us from leaping to new heights of awareness and new levels of awakening. As painful and unnecessary as it is that our courageous rebirths and inner victories will not always be cheered and celebrated by some, we must continue to grow new wings and to fly, knowing that we will not be alone on our new journey—*others who have found their wings will be flying alongside us.*

Leaving the Voices Behind

*Life is a process of becoming, a combination
of states we have to go through.
Where people fail is that they wish to elect a
state and remain in it.
This is a kind of death.*
—Anaïs Nin

W hat would you change about your life if you thought you only had one year left to live? This sounds like a question we hear in a sermon at church or are asked to contemplate in a personal growth seminar during a self-discovery exercise. Here is the story of Nicole, for whom this question became very real, told in her own words:

I used to joke that my life was uneventful, and until the day when I was diagnosed with liver cancer, I suppose it was. I went to the doctor for a checkup because I had been feeling so tired, but I never imagined that I would hear him announce that I had cancer, and that I probably only had one more year at the most to live. I remember sitting there in his office thinking, "But I'm only forty-five years old—I'm supposed to live until I'm at least seventy. I'm too young to die." The doctor told me that I would still be able to be active for some time, until my liver began to fail, and then I would go pretty fast. Listening to all this, I felt like I was having a horrible dream, except that I wasn't . . . it was very real."

As my husband and I got up to leave, my doctor came over to give me a hug and tell me how sorry he was. He had tears in his eyes.

"Is there anything at all I can do?" I asked him.

"Just make sure you live every moment the way you want to," he answered.

That night I couldn't sleep, and as I lay in the dark I began thinking about my life, or what I had left of it. The doctor's words echoed in my head, and I began to ask myself, "How do I want to live every moment?" An answer came from deep down in my soul, one that I didn't expect, but that I knew was as honest an answer as I'd ever given to anything: *"I want to leave my husband and try to find true love."*

I know this sounds shocking, but you have to understand that I'd been thinking about doing this for years. I'd been with my husband, Ralph, since we were kids in high school, and for the past decade we'd been more like friends than lovers. Ralph and I were very different people, and in order to keep the peace between us, I'd given up a lot of my own interests. I had always loved Ralph, but I'd never really been in love with him. You could say I'd been living part of a life, but not a whole one.

I've never been the kind of person who makes waves or does anything I know will hurt anyone. I've always worried about what people thought of me. Suddenly, none of this mattered anymore. *I didn't want to die without tasting true love, if I could find it. I didn't want to die without doing all the things I'd been putting off doing.* Tears ran down my cheeks as I realized how much time I had wasted, and how little time I had left.

One week later, I moved out and got a little studio apartment near the beach, something I'd always wanted to do. I don't know what shocked people more—finding out I was dying of cancer or finding out I'd left Ralph! My parents were horrified and warned me that I would need Ralph in the end, and that to turn my back on him now was foolish. My friends were bewildered and thought I was probably having an emotional reaction to the cancer, and would eventually come to my senses and move back in. Ralph's family didn't know how to treat me. They didn't think it was very sensitive to be angry with someone who was dying, but I knew they were furious at me for "abandoning Ralph", as his sister put it.

It's hard to describe what happened next. I started doing all the things I wanted to do, being the way I wanted to be. *For the first time in my life, I felt like the "real Nicole"— pretty sad, I know, considering I was dying—but in many ways, I felt more alive than I'd ever been.* And then something amazing happened. I met a man while we were both walking our dogs on the beach, and fell madly in love.

Aaron was everything I'd always wanted in a partner. He was warm and adventurous and very fully in the moment. I couldn't believe he would want to be with me, a dying woman, but whenever I'd bring it up he'd reply, "Hey, I could die before you, you know!" I'd always been such a cautious person, but now I felt free to indulge my every whim, so when Aaron suggested we take a trip around the world, I thought, "What the hell—let's do it!"

By now, almost no one from my former life was speaking to me with the exception of a few good friends and my parents, who were sure that the cancer had already spread to my brain. What other explanation was there for my crazy behavior? I was the main subject of all the hot gossip at my old job and even at church, according to my girlfriend Sherrie. I was behaving shamelessly, people said. How could I do this to my husband and my family? This was no way for a dying woman to carry on.

Whenever Aaron would hear these things, he would laugh and ask me, **"So, what is a respectable way for a forty-five-year-old woman to die?"** And I'd answer: **"With a smile on her face!"** This became our little joke.

We spent five months traveling to all the places I'd always dreamed of visiting—Australia, New Zealand, Bali, Hong Kong, Thailand, France, Italy, even Africa. Aaron was in the travel business, so it was first class all the way. Every day was perfect, and as strange as it may sound, I forgot about my cancer and just lived and loved as hard as I could.

Finally, we returned home, and I went to the hospital for a day of tests. I felt fine, but it had been ten months since my initial diagnosis, and I was sure that my time must be running out. Two days later, my doctor called me at home. My heart was pounding as Aaron handed me the phone.

"Nicole, do you believe in the healing power of love?" my doctor asked me.

"Is this your way of telling me that I'm near the end?" I replied in a trembling voice.

"No, Nicole," my doctor answered gently, "It's my way of telling you that as of your tests two days ago, *there is no sign of cancer anywhere in your body*. You are in complete remission."

"You mean, I'm not dying?"

"No, dear, you are not dying. From what I can see, you are one of the most alive people I know."

This was three years ago, and I am still here, still with Aaron, and still healthy. I have learned so many lessons from this that I can't begin to list them. The biggest one is this: **There are more ways than one to die.** I look back on my years before I had cancer and can honestly say that living the half-life I did, that's when I was really dying. And when I was diagnosed, and began dying, that's when I started living.

. . .

There are more ways than one to die.

We die a little each time we hold ourselves back from being our authentic self.

We die a little each time we go into denial.

We die a little each time we allow ourselves to be talked out of our dreams.

We die a little each time we refuse to heed the call of our heart that is yearning for love, for intimacy, for joyful passion.

We die a little each time we are too afraid to fully live.

Nicole was told she only had one year left to live and decided that she was tired of dying while she was alive. She leapt off her cliff, in spite of the shocked disapproval of friends and family, and grew new wings that helped her fly free for the first time in her life. She insists that even if her cancer had not disappeared and she'd only had that ten months with Aaron, she would do it all over again. And I believe her.

. . .

You only have fifty years left to live—or forty, or thirty, or twenty, or ten, or maybe one. Only God knows. However long it is, it still isn't much time. But these days and hours and minutes are yours alone to use, as you wish, and no one else's.

Gather them up, this bundle of priceless moments, and hold them close to your heart. Do not lose them or drop them or waste them. Let no one steal them from you. *This is your time. This is your life.*

Little by little, you leave the voices behind.
Little by little, you are left with just your one true voice,
    and as soon as you hear it, you know what you have
    to do.

And then one day, finally, you do it. You leap.
    Your new wings unfurl.
    And you fly.

✥ 8 ✥

Mourning the Life
You Thought You'd Have

Our suffering is caused by holding to
how things might have been, should have been,
could have been. Grief is part of our daily existence.
But we seldom recognize that pain in our heart that
one fellow called "a deep weeping, a mourning
for everything we have left behind."
—Stephen Levine

W hen we are faced with the unexpected in our life, there is a point at which to move forward, we must grieve. Even when we realize that loss is a part of life from which no one is exempt, even when we know that our new life promises to be better, even when we believe we are leaving behind that which no longer serves us, still we must grieve.

What do we mourn for? Of course, for people we lose through death or destiny—this kind of mourning does not surprise us. But there are other, unanticipated kinds of mourning for which we are not always prepared:

We mourn for the innocence we once experienced before life chal-
lenged us.
We mourn for the dreams of love we've had to relinquish.
We mourn our loss of safety, of certainty that we will not be
harmed by life.
We mourn for the parts of ourselves we've had to leave behind.

We mourn the loss of the comfortable and the familiar, even if we
    once cursed them.
We even mourn for things from which we ourselves have deliber-
    ately fled.

My first spiritual teacher from India loved to tell a story about
life, loss and mourning that we used to call *"From the Hut to the
Palace"*:

> Once there was a maharaja, the ruler of a very wealthy
> kingdom, who lived in a huge palace filled with every imag-
> inable luxury. The palace was built on the top of a large hill
> and it overlooked a beautiful valley through which a glisten-
> ing river made its way. The king was a happy man, espe-
> cially since his wife had recently given birth to his first child
> and heir. The baby prince was born with a birthmark on his
> leg, and all of the priests declared this to be indicative of a
> unique destiny.
>
> On the other side of the river far away from the palace
> lay a dense jungle. In this jungle lived many tigers. The king
> was an avid sportsman. Each year he looked forward to the
> traditional tiger hunt. In those times tigers were hunted
> from the backs of elephants. The year of his son's birth, the
> king was especially excited to bring the youngster with him
> on the hunt. "Even though he is just a babe," the king
> boasted to his advisors, "it will be good for him to experi-
> ence this ritual, since one day he will be the king." He
> mounted an enormous elephant, strapped his son behind
> him and was off to hunt tigers.
>
> This was a tragic decision. That year, the tigers, having
> grown tired of being slaughtered, had decided to band to-
> gether. When the hunting party approached, the tigers
> charged the elephants, who became alarmed and began to
> stampede.
>
> "Call off the hunt," cried the king, and the trainers

managed to turn the huge elephants around and make a hasty retreat from the jungle back to the palace with no casualties.

When the king dismounted, he realized to his horror that his young son had fallen off the elephant and was lost. He ordered his army to go back and search for the boy, but they were unsuccessful. The king and his queen descended into terrible grief and despair.

The baby prince had indeed fallen and been knocked unconscious. Miraculously, he wasn't really hurt, and somehow the tigers missed him. Just before nightfall, a simple, poor but kindly tribal man was on his way home through the jungle when, to his great surprise, he discovered the baby and considered this a gift from God. "You will be the son my wife and I never had," the man proclaimed. Gathering the baby up in his arms, he joyfully took him home and adopted him into his family.

The young prince began a new life of great poverty and harsh conditions very different from the wealth and comfort to which he had been born. His memories from his infancy faded completely. Soon the only reality he knew was the one in which he lived in a primitive hut with his tribal mother and father, who never told him how he'd come to be theirs.

Years passed, and when the boy reached adolescence, his adoptive parents told him it was time to build his own hut on the edge of the village, which he did with great difficulty, using mud, leaves and sticks to create a protective shelter from the elements. There he lived, scratching out a meager existence, totally oblivious to his true birth and status.

The old king, who had never recovered from losing his only child, was now close to death. Each year since his son's disappearance, he had sent his armies to search for him, and each year they had returned without finding the prince. Knowing he didn't have long to live, he sent his armies out one last time.

One day, as fate would have it, the king's soldiers came upon the tribal village, and asked the frightened villagers if a male child had been found in the jungle many years before. The tribal elders nodded solemnly and pointed to the miserable hut of the now grown prince.

When the soldiers saw the young man standing by his hut, they immediately noticed the unusual birthmark on the prince's leg. It was him! They bowed to the bewildered boy, and cried out, rejoicing:

"We have found you! Praises be to God. You are the prince, and your father, the king, is dying. You have been lost for all these years. You do not belong here in this miserable place. Come with us back to your glittering palace, where you will inherit your father's kingdom and rule all these lands."

The astonished young man could hardly believe his ears. Could this be true? Was he really a prince, and not a poor tribal villager? Even so, this was the only life he knew. How could he leave it behind?

"Come, great one," the commander of the army said to the prince, "we must return home before your father dies. Say good-bye to this wretched hut in which you lived, trapped in ignorance of who you really were. A grand palace awaits you!" And with that, the commander took a torch and set fire to the dismal hut that the prince had built with such effort.

At the sight of his hut, which had been his safety and protection, going up in flames, the prince fell sobbing to the ground, and let out a wail of grief:

"O my hut! O my hut! What will I do without my hut?"

The commander listened to this lament and concluded that the prince must be in shock—why else would he have such a strange reaction to wonderful news? He pulled the distraught prince, who was still weeping, up onto an elephant, and began the trip back to the palace.

Confused by the young man's sorrow, he tried to cheer him up by describing the lavish life that awaited him. "You are going to live in a magnificent palace," the commander explained with enthusiasm. "It is made of marble and gold, and the gardens are fragrant with every exotic flower, and swans float blissfully on the beautiful lake."

But the prince wasn't listening. He just kept turning his head to gaze back at the burning hut, unable to imagine how he was going to live without it. "O my hut! O my hut!," he cried, certain that this was the darkest day of his life.

. . .

This tale has many wonderful layers of wisdom woven into it. On one level, it speaks about the state of human ignorance, in which we forget our true spiritual nature as Divine, and instead identify with lack and limitation, becoming lost in unnecessary suffering. All along, the prince was wealthy and powerful beyond his wildest dreams—only he didn't know it. We, too, the story suggests, need to remember who we really are, and then we will be restored to our natural state of inner joy and abundance.

The lesson in this story that I have always found to be the most illuminating is about the nature of attachment and grief. *Even as he is ushered out of suffering, even as he awakens to a marvelous truth about himself, the prince cannot let go of his old identity.* He turns his gaze not forward, but backward. A splendid palace and a life of ease and luxury await him, *but all he can see is what he is losing*—his wretched hut to which he has become deeply attached.

How often this happens to us. We look at our old, familiar structures of safety and limitation going up in flames and begin to wail: "O my hut, O my hut!" Perhaps we are being released from our suffering, reclaiming our true identity in our authentic self. But even as we move forward, one part of us still looks longingly behind at whatever it is we are being asked to let go of. Perhaps unexpected events have made us feel as if our very foundation has been burned out from beneath us, and we are lost in the jungle of confusion with no idea where to go or what to do and with no knowledge of something wonderful waiting down the road.

Here is what we need to understand:

**True turning points and transformations
will always contain an element of grief and letting go.
No matter how promising our new life might be,
we will mourn the loss of what we've left behind,
to which we know we can never return.**

True turning points contain a definite before and after: we travel from one place to another, one way of being to another, one state of consciousness to another. Everything is different—not just a little different, but a lot different. And once we arrive at the new destination to which our changes have delivered us, we are unable to return. We cannot go back. We cannot inhabit the old structures, the old ways of thinking and behaving. Our old hut is in flames.

And so we grieve.

Grieving the Invisible Losses

We must embrace pain and burn it as fuel for our journey.
—Kenji Miyazawa

There are moments in our lives when we expect to feel grief, circumstances in which mourning seems appropriate to ourselves and to others: our spouse leaves us; our parent dies; our child is in a terrible accident; we experience an obvious and tragic loss. Sometimes, however, our need to grieve does not fit into what is socially or culturally acceptable. It sneaks up on us, and even we don't realize we are in mourning:

Jack, sixty-six, has just retired after working for forty years as a state employee. He'd started working for the government with the intention to use the money to put himself through veterinary school, but never quite managed to make the transition. At least his state job was stable and provided a nice income. Jack and his wife, Vivian, have been looking forward to his retirement, and Vivian excitedly reads up on all of the places they plan to visit. When she tries to involve Jack in organizing their first trip, she is surprised by his disinterest and soon becomes worried that he has fallen into a depression. All he does is watch TV, walk the dog and eat.

"I thought he'd be happy to finally retire," Vivian confides in a friend, "but he's just gone downhill since the day he cleaned out his desk at the office. I just don't understand."

Jack is in mourning, and no one realizes it, including him. He is mourning the loss of a career in which he never felt he achieved the levels of recognition he deserved. He is mourning the loss of his chance to become something he never became. At a time when he is expected to be celebrating, it is all he can do to get through each day.

. . .

Today was supposed to be a happy day for Larissa, thirty-seven. She is the mother of four children, and this was the first day of school for her youngest. For months she's been telling herself, "Finally, all the kids will be out of the house, and I can get my grown-up life back!" Larissa's girlfriends have planned a lunch to celebrate, and are surprised when she leaves them a message that she can't make it. Instead, Larissa crawls into bed, where she remains all afternoon, crying her eyes out.

Three weeks later, she's still feeling lethargic and overwhelmed with sadness. Her husband is beginning to worry that something is really wrong with Larissa, but every time he suggests that she see a doctor, she becomes furious at him and they end up in a terrible argument. *"What's wrong with me?"* Larissa wonders secretly. *"Why am I so miserable?"*

Larissa is in mourning for a precious time in her life that she unconsciously realizes is over forever. She is no longer the main source of learning and influence with her children, who now have teachers to guide them. Some part of her knows that every day her

children will need her less and less. What looks like her new free-
dom to everyone else feels like a death to Larissa, only she doesn't
understand why she is mourning, or for what.

. . .

Marlene, twenty-two, and Henry, twenty-three, have finally
moved into their own apartment. They began dating in college and eventually lived together in a house with six other friends.
At first the arrangement was fun and their house always felt like
one big party. By their senior year, they were tired of having no
privacy and couldn't wait to graduate and get their own place.
Fortunately they both found good jobs right after school ended,
and are earning enough money to rent a cute apartment in a nice
neighborhood.

The first month living there is spent in a frenzy of unpacking
and decorating. As things settle down, Marlene is surprised to notice that Henry seems very detached and emotionally shut off. He
refuses to tell her what's wrong, and she begins to worry that he is
having doubts about their relationship.

Henry, too, is worried. He's been looking forward to getting
out of school and starting his life for so long, but now that he's actually doing it, it feels strange and mechanical. He's feeling distant
from Marlene, from his work, from everything. "What is wrong
with me?" he wonders.

Henry feels strange because he is in mourning and doesn't know
it. He has finally left behind his childhood, a time of not having to
be responsible for himself, and has entered adulthood. He always
thought this would feel like the beginning of his life, but didn't ex-
pect it to feel like the end of something for which he now grieves.

. . .

There are losses we need to mourn that are difficult to recognize. They smolder silently within us, lacking the heat and
flash of the immense blazes that accompany obvious grief. They
may be invisible to others and even to us. But they burn just the
same. These losses are the fuel for our journey forward. Resisting
them, we find ourselves stuck in frozen pain, unable to move. Embracing them, we begin the process of becoming free.

**We need to give ourselves permission to grieve
the irretrievable losses of our past,
no matter what they look like,
for this will help us move into the waiting future.**

Mourning What Could Have Been

*In the beginning you weep.
The starting point for many things is grief,
at the place where endings seem so absolute.
One would think it would be otherwise,
but the pain of closing is antecedent to every
new opening in our lives.*
—Belden C. Lane, *The Solace of Fierce Landscapes*

Some time ago, I was watching one of my favorite television broadcasters, Larry King, interview the renowned and award-winning actress Lynn Redgrave. I've had the privilege of being on Larry's program myself, and have always been impressed by his unique blend of curiosity, compassion and nonjudgmental intimacy, which allows his guests to feel safe enough to speak from a place of deep honesty and self-reflection. This was the tone of Larry's interview with Lynn Redgrave as she spoke candidly about the challenges she'd faced in her life, including her battle with cancer and her very painful divorce. Asked how she had survived times of tremendous difficulty and loss, she responded:

I had what I called my days of grief . . . I suppose you mourn the loss or the death of what you thought your life was, even if you find your life is better after. You mourn the future that you thought you'd planned.

Mourning the life you thought you'd have is not a grief that simply dwells on the past. It stretches into the future. We not only have to let go of what we have lost, but we must also re-create the road in front of us, since the old path no longer exists.

. . .

When we lose people and things we did not want to let go of, our sadness is understandable, both to our loved ones and to us. But why is it that when we initiate our own losses—when we quit the job, or end the relationship, or move from one city to another, or break off the friendship—we feel so devastated?

**Sometimes we are not mourning what we've lost,
but hopes and dreams that never came true.
We aren't mourning what was,
but what could have been, should have been.**

When I was in my twenties, I had a boyfriend whom I loved very much, although it was clear that our lives were going in two very different directions, and I knew I needed to make the difficult decision to end our relationship. It took me months of agonizing deliberation to break up with this man, and by the time I did it, I expected to feel a huge sense of relief at not being stuck in limbo anymore. So I was surprised and confused when I became overcome with grief.

I remember lying in my bed one night about a week after I left him, sobbing my heart out. "Why am I crying?" I reasoned with myself. "I have been unhappy for so long with this man. I'm the one leaving. I know what I am doing is the right thing for us both. I want to move forward. I feel relieved that finally it is over. So why does my heart hurt so much?"

The answer was simple—I was in mourning, not for the loss of what I had with my former partner, but for the loss of what might have been and never was:

I was mourning the loss of what I had hoped would happen.
I was mourning the loss of how I had imagined things would be.
I was mourning the loss of the lifelong mate I had thought he would perhaps become.

I was mourning the loss of the intimacy I had longed to share.
I was mourning the loss of dreams that would never come true.

It wasn't the circumstances of my new life alone that were painful, nor the loss of my partner. It was the realization of all I'd never really had. *I was crying more about my unfulfilled dreams than I was about him.* Grieving was a healthy way to acknowledge my feelings of disappointment, and for a few weeks, I did. Then I picked up my dreams and moved on.

Temporary feelings of regret are a normal part of the mourning process. This helps us retrieve our lost dreams. If we hold on to regret, we risk trapping ourselves in a prison of unrealized dreams from which it is difficult to escape.

When Loss Comes with Disillusionment

The hardest thing in life is letting go of what you thought was real.
—Author unknown

Loss is difficult and painful. Loss with disillusionment is worse. Disillusionment is a particularly painful variety of grief. It is tinged with lots of other emotions besides regret—anger, self-recrimination, blame, all of which we will get to in a bit. It is more than grieving for what was or could have been—*it's grieving for what may have never existed in the first place.* I came up with a saying that sums it up:

"Dreams die hard. Illusions die harder."

Disillusionment is confusing and sticky. We mourn the death of a situation that was part projection, part deception, part fantasy, so when we grieve, we're not even sure what we're crying about. All we know is that it hurts, and we want it to stop. Perhaps our intimate partner who we thought truly loved us confesses that he was never in love at all and is leaving the relationship. Perhaps the friend we believed was a dear friend betrays us in a way that makes it clear she wasn't the loyal companion we always assumed she was. Perhaps we discover that a teacher, mentor or role model for whom we've had enormous respect is not the person he pretended to be.

In her poignant novel *The Bad Boy's Wife,* author Karen Shepard describes this kind of loss as she writes about a woman whose husband has left her. In this passage, the woman examines her past through the lens of the present revelation: *"When he'd told her he was leaving, of course he'd taken away her future, but her past wasn't hers anymore either."*

This is how it feels when our wake-up calls include the tearing down of illusions. We don't just feel we lost something—*we feel we have been robbed*—of time, of trust, of the sanctity of memories.

**Loss with disillusionment acts like a thief.
It invades your past, steals your memories of it
and returns them to you empty and devoid of reality.
When you look back and see things as they really were,
you not only lose the hope of having that again in the
present, but you lose its meaning in the past.**

Here are two stories about loss with disillusionment:

. . .

Lawrence is a young black attorney who was hired right out of law school by a prestigious New York law firm. They promised that he'd be made a partner in a few years. Five years pass, and Lawrence proves to be successful in every way, although he is concerned that several members of the firm have been made partner, and he still has not. When he finally confronts one of the managing partners, he is told that the firm is actually going to be downsizing, and there is no chance of him making partner, although his job still is his.

Furious and disillusioned, Lawrence faces the truth he's always avoided: He was hired to fulfill a "minority" position. The very traditional firm never had any intention of making him partner. He had been manipulated into working for them with a false promise.

· · ·

Sarah, twenty-nine, is a high school teacher who meets Roberto, a clothing designer, on a summer trip to Italy and falls madly in love. As the summer is about to end, Roberto surprises Sarah by proposing to her and travels with her back to her home in Connecticut, where she introduces her charming fiancé to her surprised but supportive friends and family. Several months later, Sarah and Roberto marry. Now that Roberto can legally reside in the United States, he moves his small business to New York City and commutes each day to his showroom in the fashion district.

Several years pass, and in spite of Sarah's desire to start a family, Roberto insists that it isn't a good time, since he's getting his business off the ground. One day, Sarah discovers that she has become pregnant. Elated, she drives down to Roberto's showroom to break the news in person. To her horror, she walks in on him embracing a young model.

Suddenly, everything becomes clear to her: Roberto never really loved her—he wanted a green card so he could live in America. His reluctance to have children had nothing to do with his work and everything to do with the fact that he didn't plan on staying with her. What she'd thought was a dream come true was all a painful illusion.

· · ·

Lawrence and Sarah both woke up from being deluded, not just by others, but also by themselves. **There is always a part of us, buried deep in our denial, that does know something is wrong, but we tune that voice out, not wanting it to spoil our happiness.** An important step in healing after disillusionment is letting go of our anger at ourselves for not doing a better job of protecting our heart from being broken.

Mourning disillusionment and betrayal is tricky. When we "wake up" from our delusion, the past will suddenly seem very unreal, leaving us with a sense of disorientation and incompletion. There are many emotions we will never resolve, many facts we will never get straight. The temptation is to obsess over what happened and invalidate the entire experience, which can keep us stuck and unable to move forward in our life.

I've been betrayed many times—in love, in business, in friendship. One of the most difficult but essential lessons for me has been to find a way to still regard the relationships positively, to remember the good times that did take place, the achievements that did happen, the caring that did exist, and not let all of the experience be spoiled.

> **Sometimes we get stuck in mourning the past because we've unconditionally condemned it.**
> **We haven't gone back to retrieve parts of the experience that were good, and salvage the sweetness.**

When I look back on my past relationships, now I can remember the sweet times, the moments of connection, of support and of true friendship. These experiences of loss offered me crucial spiritual lessons that, although quite painful, were indispensable in making me who I am today. Those people who disappointed me played their parts in inadvertently helping me learn those lessons, and for that I am grateful.

As for all the love I gave that was not equally returned, I know this: My love was real. My joy was real. My devotion was real. Nothing and no one can take these experiences away from me, not even the knowledge that they may not have been shared. In the end, my heart was made more beautiful for having loved that much. Today, I have more happiness and love in my life than I ever knew was possible, and I know I wouldn't be able to feel this deeply if I had not mourned and then let go.

Discarding Pieces of Yourself

All changes, even the most longed for, have their melancholy;
for what we leave behind us is a part of ourselves;
we must die to one life before we can enter another.
—Anatole France

A few years ago, I sat in front of my television set watching the launch of the first Mars Exploration Rover, named *Spirit*, from Cape Canaveral Air Force Station in Florida as it began its historic seven-month journey to Mars, more than 49 million miles away. The spacecraft sat on top of a Delta II launch vehicle, which provided the tremendous velocity needed to escape Earth's gravity and set the Rover on its trajectory for Mars. With a thunderous roar, the booster rocket rose high in the sky carrying the Mars Rover through layers of the earth's atmosphere until, finally freed of the heaviness of gravity, the Rover could now begin its journey to the Red Planet. Then the Delta II launch vehicle separated from the Rover and fell into the ocean. Thirty-six minutes had passed since liftoff. Its job was done.

It was mind-boggling to realize that each of these Delta II rockets costs hundreds of millions of dollars and can be used only once. So many years of work and so much money had gone into making these few minutes a reality. Yet it was the release of the rocket that would now allow the Mars Rover to move forward on its long journey, unencumbered by the much heavier launch vehicle. As valuable as it had been, the launch rocket had to be discarded.

Sometimes our own journey is like this. *Along the way, we are boosted through layers of learning and experience by certain people or situations and by roles we play ourselves. These are pieces of what we identify with as "us." Without these people, roles and situations, we would not be thrust from one reality to another. Once we reach a new, higher level, however, their purpose has been served, and like the Mars Rover releases its booster rocket, we must release that to which we've been intimately connected.*

There are people, circumstances, and even pieces
of ourselves that serve us for part of our journey.
They are not meant to keep us company
for the whole way— in order to travel
to our next destination, we will need to let them go.

In the process of discovering our authentic selves, we have had
to search for and embrace pieces of ourselves we've discarded or
disowned—to dig deep to find them, to unearth our Shadow Self
and integrate it into our consciousness, to give a voice to what had
been silenced. Now, to move forward, we need to reverse the
process—to discard pieces of ourselves that no longer serve us and
to relinquish roles that keep us stuck in the past, to get rid of anything that is keeping us from flying.

. . .

I love the ocean, and I love watching films with an ocean theme,
especially movies about long and difficult sea voyages. In these
tales, there is usually a classic and predictable scene depicting a terrible storm that threatens to capsize the ship. *The courageous cap-
tain realizes the ship is too heavy, and unless he lightens the load,
it will surely sink. "Throw everything overboard that we do not
need!"* he invariably shouts, and the crew frantically begins to toss
anything that is not nailed down off the ship into the churning and
angry ocean. The camera pulls back to a wide shot as we see an
odd assortment of items—crates of oranges, plant specimens,
metal tools, clothing, books, sacks of grain, even the precious bot-
tles of rum—being carried away by the waves. Finally, the storm
passes, the sun emerges from behind the clouds and the ship is
threadbare but safe. It has survived the storm.

There are times in our lives, often stormy ones, when it becomes
apparent to us that we, too, need to get rid of what is threatening to
sink us. The old roles need to go. It may feel like we are tossing
things overboard that we can't live without, but the truth is the
opposite—if we do not get rid of what is weighing us down, we will
drown in our own frustration, unhappiness and lack of fulfillment.

Even when we know that what we are doing is necessary, discarding parts of ourselves still brings its own kind of grief. When we relinquish the old roles that no longer serve us, it feels like, and is, a death of sorts. Integral parts of us have died. We feel a painful nostalgia for our old identities and patterns, even if we have worked hard to let them go. We may even try to hang onto the roles of the past for a while longer, only to discover that they are no longer available. We cannot be that person anymore, even if we want to.

When the New You Doesn't Fit into Your Old Life

There is nothing like returning to a place that remains unchanged to find the ways in which you yourself have altered.
—Nelson Mandela

When we change, everything around us appears to change. People seem different; places don't look the same; things don't feel the way they used to. Of course, nothing else has actually has changed. As Thoreau says, "Things do not change; we change." *We are seeing through different eyes, experiencing things through a different frequency.*

When we first emerge from a time of personal transformation, we are often so busy recovering from the process itself that we may not realize how much we have been altered. We're just happy to have survived the time of change and challenge. What we don't yet see is that we have gone through a rebirth.

When a soldier is on the battlefield, he does not have time to notice how war is changing him. He is just trying to do his job and survive. Only when he comes home from being deployed does he begin to realize how radically different he is, and how the terrible and unfathomable circumstances of war have transformed him at the most fundamental levels of his being.

This is how it often is for us when we emerge out of our own personal battles. We are so relieved that things seem to have calmed down and the worst appears to be over, and therefore we don't yet grasp that we are not the same person as we were before. **We have changed frequencies; our minds and hearts have been reprogrammed, and our old way of operating feels awkward, or simply no longer works.**

This experience is very disconcerting. "I always loved this person/job/food/music/place, so how come I don't anymore?" we wonder. We didn't realize we had changed this much, or that we would have to give up so much of ourselves. Sometimes we even try to squeeze ourselves back into what used to work—a relationship, a job, a friendship—only to find that we keep bursting out of the edges. **We no longer fit into the constricting containers of our past.**

. . .

For five years, Christie, thirty-two, worked in a famous Beverly Hills beauty salon as a manicurist, attracting a very loyal clientele. Christie grew up in a small town in Oklahoma, so she loved the excitement of her job—the bustling energy of the store, the flamboyant personalities of the hairdressers, the Hollywood gossip. Last year, Christie and her husband decided to start a family, and a few months before the end of Christie's pregnancy, she took a leave from work to have the baby. Christie had a gorgeous little girl and spent six weeks at home falling in love with her new daughter.

Finally, it was time to go back to work. Christie knew she would miss the baby but was excited about returning to the job she loved. She was shocked when, after just a few hours in the salon, she realized she no longer fit there, and decided to quit. "My energy had become so soft, loving and open from being a mother," she later explained to a friend, "and the very things I used to love about my job, now I couldn't stand—the gossip, the crazy frenetic energy, the superficiality. The whole place and the people in it felt jarring to me. I didn't realize how much I had changed until I went back."

We are not always as courageous as Christie, or as quick to admit that things are irrevocably different. Sometimes we try to bargain with the unexpected and haggle with our changes, hoping to get away with not having to transform quite so much. "Couldn't I just change inside myself, without having to disrupt everything else on the outside of my life?" we wonder longingly. "There must be some way for me to have had all these revelations, but to still keep everything else the same."

Of course, there isn't. I always remind my students that **a chicken can't squeeze itself back into the egg,** Neither can we squeeze ourselves back into old roles that we have outgrown.

This doesn't mean we don't try. All of us have done this at one time or another—with a lover, a friend, a business situation or lifestyle choices:

- *Maybe I can still sleep with him, even though we have broken up.*

- *Maybe I can still hang out with her even though I'm sober and she's always loaded.*

- *Maybe I can tolerate being mistreated at that job because it pays so well.*

We attempt to convince ourselves that we're simply making compromises, being flexible, and that we're not really going backward, even though it may seem that way. It never works, this backsliding. We cannot pretend to be who we no longer are. We cannot pretend not to know what we now know. We cannot make compromises with our soul.

Dangers on the Road: Anger,
Guilt and Self-Reproach

Holding on to anger is like grasping a hot coal
with the intent of throwing it at someone else:
You are the one who gets burned.
—Buddha

I'd just finished autographing books at the conclusion of one of my seminars when I noticed a nervous-looking woman off to the side, obviously waiting to speak with me.

"You've been very patient," I say with a smile. "Do you have a question?"

"Yes, Dr. De Angelis, I want to know if it's natural to be in mourning for a while after a man falls in love with someone else and leaves you."

"Of course it's natural," I reassure her. "It takes time to mourn the heart's losses, and endings in relationships are never easy. But when you're done grieving, you will be able to move on to create love in your life again."

"That's just it," the woman explains, "I'm not done grieving yet."

"Well, you can't rush these things. How long has it been since the breakup?" I ask.

The woman replies, "Six years."

"Six years!" I exclaim. "And tell me, please, how do you know you aren't done mourning yet?"

"Because I still want to kill the bastard!" she says proudly.

I take a deep breath, and as gently as possible, I say to the woman: *"My dear, that's not mourning—it's seething!"*

On the road that leads from your past to your future, and from limitation to freedom, one of the most treacherous stops is anger. The late psychiatrist Dr. Elisabeth Kubler-Ross, one of the foremost authorities in the field of death, dying and transition, identified and named five stages of grief:

1. **Denial**
2. **Anger**
3. **Bargaining**
4. **Depression**
5. **Acceptance**

Anger is an important stage in the grieving process, whether we are grieving the loss of a person, the loss of a part of ourselves or the loss of our dreams. It is easy, however, to get stuck in and even addicted to anger, because it feels good to the ego. When we are angry, we are aggrieved, righteous, indignant and bitter, and these emotions give us a false and temporary sense of empowerment. After feeling so disempowered by loss, change or unexpected situations, feeling powerful again is a welcome change, even if that power is an illusion.

By remaining angry, we are avoiding our grief, and we become stuck in midstream in the healing process. We are the opposite of powerful and free—we are imprisoned by our anger and bitterness. This anger is the kiss of death to our passion, to the new relationships we are trying to create, and to our ability to experience true peace. *"To carry a grudge is like being stung to death by one bee,"* said William H. Walton.

Anger is meant to be moved *through,* not moved *into.*

When we stay angry about a situation, we never get to fully mourn it. Buried beneath our anger is always hurt, fear and sadness—anger is sadness turned inside out. The result of clinging to our anger is that these other emotions don't have an opportunity to be released, and consequently become trapped inside us. When enough pain and sadness accumulate on the inside, we suddenly notice that we feel *"depressed."*

The poor woman who spoke to me after my seminar had been stuck in her anger for years. It had consumed her, immobilized her and kept her from the one thing she truly wanted—to mend her wounded heart. *"Go home and cry,"* I advised her. *"Cry and cry and cry until you have no tears left. And on the other side of those tears, your future will be waiting for you."*

. . .

> *There's no problem so awful that you can't add*
> *some guilt to it and make it even worse!*
> —Calvin, from the comic strip *Calvin & Hobbes*
> by Bill Watterson

"If only I'd paid more attention to my wife, she wouldn't have left me."

"If only I'd helped my husband more, he would have stopped drinking."

"If only I'd been more creative, my business wouldn't have gone bankrupt."

"How could I not have seen this coming?"

"I wasted so much time, but now it is too late."

"How can it be right for me to move forward when it is hurting someone else so much?"

"If I had tried harder, maybe I wouldn't have failed."

"I must be a bad mother for my son to have turned out this way."

"How could I have done something so stupid?"

These are the voices of guilt and self-reproach. When we mourn the loss of the life we thought we would have or even the one we did, we often hear these voices like a relentless, wailing chorus in the background of our awareness. These are not loving voices, nor are they helpful ones. Their purpose is simple—as the cartoon character said, it's to make us feel worse than we already do.

Guilt has the power to keep us trapped in the past
by convincing us to feel bad about ourselves,
and tricking us into believing that
until we get rid of that bad feeling,
we cannot move on.

In this way, guilt is like quicksand, pulling us down into a place of self-recrimination from which it is difficult to escape. We decide that we are not allowed to move forward in our lives until we don't feel guilty anymore. But the more we indulge in our guilt, the more it grows, and soon we cannot move at all, and we don't understand why.

Guilt is a very convenient place to hide out from the things we need to confront. After all, as long as we feel guilty, we have an excuse to avoid facing the consequences of our revelations, breakthroughs and wake-up calls, and can put off the risks involved in making decisions about how to move forward. This is especially true when we convince ourselves we are so worried about how our actions might affect others that we'd better not do anything at all for the moment.

This is where we can easily become confused. We think that to feel guilty is to somehow demonstrate, to ourselves and to anyone else watching, that we care and that we never meant to hurt someone we may have hurt in the process of making changes in our lives. *Feeling guilty becomes a penance we assign ourselves for our transgression.*

I remember talking about this with a friend who had left her husband, but could not break free from her guilt. The marriage had been dead, and her husband had a chronic drug problem he refused to face. Still, she felt guilty leaving. "I suppose a part of me believes if I am feeling guilty, then I'm not a bad person for abandoning him," she confessed to me.

Often we use guilt for just this purpose—to punish ourselves for our breakthroughs, because they have caused pain to others. It was as if my friend had unconsciously sentenced herself to six months of guilt as a punishment for ending her marriage. Sure enough, once she served her sentence, she stopped feeling guilty, and went on to remarry and live a happy life. And by the way, so did her husband.

My friend was lucky—she got off with only a six-month self-imposed sentence of guilt. If we are not careful, our own guilt and self-reproach can imprison us for years on end, keeping us locked in regret for a past that we cannot change and deprived of a future whose call we hear, but cannot heed.

One way to break out of this pattern is to understand the difference between guilt and remorse:

Guilt makes us feel bad about ourselves.
Remorse helps us learn what we might do differently in the future.

Guilt berates us for our failures.
Remorse gathers wisdom from our mistakes so we can become more successful.

Guilt beats us up and holds us back.
Remorse frees us and guides us forward.

Guilt suffocates us with blame.
Remorse showers us with compassion.

Mourning the past will always include remorse. We can take these important lessons with us, but we must love ourselves enough to leave the guilt behind. We must be cautious about getting stuck looking backward. It is, after all, in the unexplored and unfolding present that we will find new levels of fulfillment and freedom.

Letting Go

You can clutch the past so tightly to your chest
that it leaves your arms too full to embrace the present.
—Jan Glidewell

And so to go forward, finally, we just need to let go—of our guilt, our anger, our illusions, our visible and invisible losses, our outgrown roles and identities and ultimately even our grief.

We need to let go of the past to create a vacancy for the future to take up residence.

We need to let go of our attachment to the roads we thought we always would be traveling and to open ourselves to discover new paths that will lead us to even more beautiful landscapes.

We need to let go and embrace the terrifying emptiness that follows letting go, knowing that when we do, that emptiness will soon begin to fill with new wisdom and awakening beyond anything we can imagine.

I know—even as I write this, I know—that letting go is very difficult to do. We are a society of collectors. We like to accumulate, not discard; to collect, not release. We cling to the familiar and mistrust the unknown. We are not very good with endings.

We experience this habit of stubbornly holding onto things even in the most mundane ways. Each of us has possessions in our life we have a difficult time getting rid of even though we know we should. It could be books, back issues of magazines, photos, souvenirs, CDs, childhood mementos, catalogues or any number of things. For me, it is clothing. I have way too many clothes, stuffed into every closet in my house, and the explanation is simple—once I buy something, I have a very hard time giving it away.

I understand all too well the psychological source of my reluctance—we lived very modestly when I was growing up, and I didn't have money to buy nice clothes like those my friends had. I was always extremely self-conscious about how I looked—my thick, ugly glasses didn't help—and wished I could afford the beautiful outfits worn by the other girls. When I grew up and eventually became successful, one of my greatest pleasures became shopping. To this day, it remains my only true addiction.

Of course, I know I need to purge my closet of all the items that no longer fit or have long gone out of style, and periodically I set this task for myself. Each time, I go through the same excruciating procedure—I make a pile of the clothes I should give away, and then, one by one, I look at each blouse, or skirt, or suit, and recall the memories associated with it:

"Oh, I remember wearing this outfit the first time I appeared on Geraldo.*"*

"Look, the blouse I bought at that little store in Sante Fe."

"I love this dress! I wore it to my friend Debbie's wedding—I still have those pictures."

"How can I give these shoes away? They were such a bargain!"

Most of these items don't fit me anymore. Some are ten years old or even more. Many are so out of style that if I wore them in public, I would end up on the "don't" page of women's magazines. Yet there I am, sighing, reminiscing, resisting letting them go. They are pieces of my past and, therefore, pieces of me. Eventually, of course, I give them away, but not without these long good-byes.

I am sure you get my point. If it is difficult for us to let go of material things to which we are attached, then it is all the more challenging to release the emotional roles with which we've identified. If we feel a twinge of sadness thinking about giving away our favorite old torn raincoat or a comfortable dilapidated chair, then it is no surprise that we would experience grief as we relinquish roles that once fit just fine, but that we have now outgrown. If we cling to photographs of old lovers we haven't seen in years, no wonder we mourn as we let go of people who have been part of our recent life, even when we know they are not good for us.

> **To willingly give up something that we once longed for can feel like a failure, a mistake, a defeat, even when holding onto it is holding us back.**

My friend brings her two-year-old daughter, Danielle, over to my house, and as we talk, we watch Danielle play with a big box of costume jewelry that I'd pulled from my closet. Danielle is transfixed by the sparkling colors and shiny trinkets. She begins to sort carefully through the box, picking out the ones she likes the best. She holds the first chosen bauble in her left hand, and with the other hand finds her next prize, adding that to the stash in her left hand. This continues for a while, until Danielle's little hand is full. I can see Danielle's mind trying to figure out her next move. Then she goes into action, awkwardly using her right hand to scoop up more jewelry, until it, too, is full.

Now Danielle faces a dilemma. She wants to pick up more jewelry, but doesn't want to let go of what she worked so hard to collect and is holding tightly in her overflowing hands. So there she is, sitting on the floor with her little fingers clenched around her treasures, staring at the remaining jewelry, which she still covets, with no clue as to what she should do.

Suddenly the strain becomes too much for Danielle, and she bursts into frustrated tears. As my friend gathers her daughter in her arms to soothe her with kisses, I can't help smiling to myself. We are all like Danielle: **We have a difficult time letting go of what we have acquired, but as long as our hands are full, we have no room for anything else.**

From Letting Go to Liberation

To live fully is to let go and die with each passing moment,
and to be reborn in each new one.
—Jack Kornfield

We spend our time on earth dying and being reborn, over and over again. Many of these passages go by unobserved. In the few seconds that it took you to read the last sentence, for instance, a part of you has died—two million cells in your body die each second. Every few years, all of the cells in your body are totally replaced. You are literally not the same person you were before. Your body has died and been reborn, and you didn't even notice.

Then there are the little deaths that happen imperceptibly over time—old childhood dreams are discarded; early friendships fade; schools and teachers are left behind; ideas, obsessions and interests are tossed out; people we once knew are forgotten; parts of us we battled are conquered; problems that once consumed us vanish. We sense these departures, but do not stop even to wave good-bye.

When we feel the time has come to let go of the past and step into the future, we need to find our own way of saying good-bye, one that honors the significant passage we are making, and frees us to proceed forward with renewed hope and optimism.

I have a dear friend who is a monk in the Hindu tradition. After many years of spiritual study, she chose to make a profound change in her life: to take on the role of a renunciate, giving up all of her worldly responsibilities and relationships and dedicating herself only to the search for God and service to others. The formal ceremony during which she was initiated into the monastic order is called *sannyasa*. The Sanskrit word *sannyas* means *laying or setting aside, abandoning,* or *giving up*. This ancient ritual of giving up one way of life for another has been practiced in India for thousands of years. Early in the morning on the chosen auspicious day, the candidate prostrates him- or herself before his guru. After many blessings, the candidate's head is shaved. Then, divested of all possessions, having given up all things belonging to his past, he conducts his own ritual funeral rites, symbolizing the relinquishing of his entire life up until that point, the death of his former self and his rebirth as a spiritual being.

Now he places the remnants of his personal identity—his hair, his clothing and his name—into a ritual fire, and pronounces his vows of renunciation. He walks around the fire and returns to kneel at his teacher's feet. His old self is dead. Finally, he goes to bathe in a nearby river, and when he emerges, his guru gives him his new robes and a new name.

I remember listening in awe to my friend as she shared the details of this powerful ritual.

"What was that like," I asked, "to perform your own funeral rites? Did it feel strange?"

"No, it didn't feel strange at all," she replied. "It made the transformation I was undergoing real, and filled me with an enormous sense of peace and bliss. I was dying and being reborn while I was alive, and the power of that experience humbled me deeply. I was overwhelmed with love for God. I felt free."

We may never experience anything as radically transformative as this formal ritual. Yet in our own way, as we attempt to renew our lives, we must offer up what no longer serves us into a sacrificial fire that we build within the temple of our own heart. Into this fire we place all that we want to relinquish: our pain, our disappointments, our attachment to those things that cause us suffering, our broken dreams of how we hoped things would be, the parts of ourselves we need to release, the roles that no longer fit, old grief, old guilt, old anger. We make our own vows renouncing our unhappiness, and ask to be freed from everything that interferes with our ability to feel joy.

Offer that which you are ready to let go of to the sacred fire. This fire of grace, this fire of truth will take what you offer it and transmute all that is old into what is new—new life, new love, new freedom.

· · ·

Endings are an inevitable and essential part of growth.
Without them, there can be no new beginnings.
Remembering this, we find the courage to unclench our fists and
    let go.
And when we do, when we finally release what we have been
    mourning, we discover a part of us has been changed forever.
We have been marked by our pain, and sculpted by our losses.

*Somehow, our grief itself has carved us into a beautiful shape,
    and we emerge like a gem
        that has been painstakingly cut and faceted,
Now to reveal the exquisite, mysterious light
that had always been trapped inside.*

❧ 9 ❧

Proceeding Without a Map:
Turning Dead Ends
into Doorways

There will be a time when you believe everything is finished.
That will be the beginning.
—Louis L'Amour

There is a famous scene in the now-classic book *Harry Potter and the Sorcerer's Stone* by J.K. Rowling in which young Harry Potter is on his way to the *Hogwarts School of Witchcraft and Wizardry* to receive his official training as a wizard. He has been told to catch the train from Platform Nine and Three Quarters, but when he arrives at the train station, he cannot find any such number—there's Platform Nine and Platform Ten, but no Platform Nine and Three Quarters. Harry turns to his fellow wizards in training and asks them where he can find Platform Nine and Three Quarters. "Through there," one responds, pointing to a solid cement wall.

Harry is bewildered. He cannot see any doorway—just a thick wall. Then, to his amazement, his more experienced classmates run, one at a time, full speed into the solid wall, and magically disappear! And of course, when Harry follows them, he, too, miraculously passes through the wall to find himself standing on Platform Nine and Three Quarters looking at the wondrous train that will take him and his companions to Hogwarts School, where he will study the secrets of magic. Harry is already beginning to understand one of the essential lessons he must learn in order to become a great wizard: *Things are not always as they appear to be.*

When we go through times of challenge, transition and transformation, we may find ourselves, like Harry Potter, facing what appears at first glance to be an impenetrable wall, a dead end. We stare at the obstacle before us, and in spite of our longing to get beyond it, we cannot see any doorway that will lead us through, nor any other paths nearby that will take us around it:

- Our intimate relationship comes to an end or feels perpetually stuck.

- Our job or career feels unsatisfying, or like it's going nowhere.

- A project in which we've invested a lot of time and energy doesn't work out.

- The funding we were counting on to finance an idea or plan falls through.

- Our dream to do, be or achieve something doesn't seem to be coming true.

- Tragic events occur in our life from which we can't imagine recovering.

How are we supposed to go forward in such difficult times? How can we pass through what seem to be impossible roadblocks on our way to happiness?

We begin by remembering: things are not always as they appear to be.

What appear to be dead ends in our relationships may be powerful opportunities for deeper intimacy, or new love beyond what we can imagine.

What appear to be dead ends in our work or career may be powerful opportunities for new avenues of creativity and new realms of success.

What appear to be dead ends in our happiness may be powerful opportunities for new experiences of rediscovery and regeneration.

What appear to be dead ends in our faith and hope may be powerful opportunities for new levels of wisdom and awakening.

In Harry Potter's magical world, he runs straight into the cement in order to pass through it. In our less enchanted reality, we probably shouldn't fling ourselves at what appear to be stone walls blocking our path. Instead, we may want to consider this:

The obstacles in our path are not blocking us—they are redirecting us. Their purpose is not to interfere with our happiness; it is to point us toward new routes to our happiness, new possibilities, new doorways.

I remember playing an intriguing game as a child in which we would divide up into two teams. One person on each team would be blindfolded, and the other team members would try to give instructions to lead the blindfolded person through an obstacle course until he reached the end. The first team to get their representative to the goal would win a prize.

Of course, part of what was so challenging, and therefore exciting to us, were our attempts at preventing our teammate from getting hurt by crashing into trees and bushes, tripping over rocks or falling into holes. We would all stand together and shout out the directions meant to serve both as protection from harm and enthusiastic help: "Take two steps to the left . . . now go forward . . . keep going . . . slowly, or you'll bump into a tree . . . NO! STOP! . . . Okay, now turn to your right . . . keep turning . . . NO, that's too much, turn back. . . . Okay, now walk five paces straight ahead . . . You're going too fast—TAKE SMALLER PACES! . . . You're almost there . . . Now, get down on your hands and knees because you are going to have to crawl under that hedge . . . PUT YOUR HEAD DOWN! . . . Oops, too late . . ."

What if Universal Intelligence is trying to lead each of us through an obstacle course to destinations we cannot even imagine? How would it communicate with us? How would it get us to turn around from the direction we think we should take, to redirect us to travel in a different direction that will lead us to where we truly need to go? If there is no one to shout out our instructions in words, then how are we guided toward our goals?

The answer seems clear: a roadblock is put in our path so that we cannot go farther on that highway. A door is shut so that we cannot continue through it. An opportunity vanishes so that we cannot pursue it. These are messages, communications from cosmic intelligence, if you will—we are being guided on a mysterious journey and steered toward a goal even if it feels as if we are blindfolded and cannot yet see where we are or to which new destination we are being redirected.

. . .

When one door closes another door opens;
but we often look so long and so regretfully
upon the closed door,
that we do not see the ones which open for us.
—Alexander Graham Bell

My dog Bijou, along with his sister Shanti, is the light of life. Bijou is a bichon frise, and is loving, flirtatious, soulful and devoted. He also has an amazing ability to focus on what he wants, exhibiting astonishing degrees of determination.

One of the things that never fails to make me laugh is how Bijou gets me to give him treats. Bijou knows the door that leads into the pantry where the dog goodies are stored. He will stand there and stare at that door as if his gaze alone will melt the wood and gain him entryway into treat heaven. When it's time for a snack, I will go into the pantry and come out with a handful of biscuits for Bijou and his sister. Often he is so intent on staring at that door that he doesn't even notice I have put the treats down somewhere else. He just continues to stare at the closed door. "Bijou! Look!" I say, pointing to the treats in the other room. Bijou doesn't move a muscle. He remains in intense yogic concentration, willing the door to open.

Eventually, of course, Bijou does find his treats. Even when I move the stash of treats to another cupboard that is not in the pantry, he still remembers that they used to be behind that particular door. If Bijou ever suddenly disappears from a room, I know where he is going—to keep his vigil staring at that closed pantry door.

Often this is how it is for us as well. A door has closed in your life—the door to a relationship, an opportunity, a job, a dream. You know you should move on. You know it is time to redirect yourself to find new doorways, new paths, new possibilities. But you, like Bijou, keep staring longingly at the closed door, remembering what used to be behind it.

"We used to be so in love years ago."
"That would have been such a fantastic business if only it had gotten off the ground."
"I had such high hopes for that project."
"Nothing will ever be the same now that my mother has passed away."
"It was so great when the kids were little and we all took vacations together."
"I was so happy back then."

Here is the problem: **you are facing the wrong direction.** The solution is simply to turn around.

Turn around and turn away from where you've been and can no longer reside.

Turn around and turn away from what has ended.

Turn around and face what lies in front of you: the new path, the new destinations, the new doors waiting to be opened.

Until you turn around, you won't see anything but the past with all of its disappointments. All you will see is what is no longer possible, no longer available. And this can make you feel despondent, defeated and, worst of all, powerless.

Powerlessness is not being able to see any options.
When you keep gazing at the past,
you will not be able to see the future
that is waiting for you.
You will not see the possibilities that are available.
You need to turn around and face forward.

Even when you are at what appears to be a dead end, there are always options, always new possibilities. We get ourselves stuck when we stand there and stare at the one thing that is no longer possible, and don't look at everything else that is now available.

What Am I Free to Do Now?

Joel has come to me because he can't seem to recover from the news that his wife, Eileen, wants a divorce. It has been months since she told him she no longer wants to be married, something that he should have seen coming, but didn't. Eileen is waiting for Joel to move out, but he keeps telling himself that maybe she will change her mind, even though she makes it clear to him that this isn't going to happen. In spite of these facts, Joel can't seem to get himself to do anything. He feels miserable and stuck.

I listen to Joel and know I am seeing a man stunned at the devastation of his old life. He is standing in a road staring at the pile of rubble that used to be his marriage and family life. He knows he should move forward, but he can't see any new roads. He is so preoccupied with gazing backward at his past that he doesn't realize the road continues beyond where he is. He needs to turn around.

"I just want my wife and my home back," Joel says morosely.

"That door is closed. You can't walk through it anymore. But there are many other possibilities available to you. What other doors can you see?"

"I don't see any other possibilities," he complains. "The only thing I want is what I had."

"Of course there are other possibilities—you just aren't looking at them," I explain. "Just sit quietly, ask yourself this question and see what answers come up."

"What am I free to do now?"

Joel is silent for a few minutes. Then, slowly, he begins:

> I'm free to live in a different house, maybe one that is closer to town, and on a street where the kids could play instead of being so isolated as they are in our present house.
>
> I'm free to decorate my house in the style I like, since my wife and I had very different tastes.
>
> I'm free to spend time doing more of the activities I enjoy like hiking and camping, since she didn't like doing outdoor kinds of things.
>
> I'm free to spend more time with my friends, since I won't be with the kids every single weekend.
>
> I'm free to do more traveling.
>
> I'm free to have more quiet time to myself to read and recharge my batteries.
>
> I'm free to meet new people.
>
> I'm free to spend time with my kids by myself and introduce them to things my wife didn't enjoy doing.
>
> I'm free to get a dog, since my wife was allergic and I couldn't have one.

It is remarkable to watch Joel's face transform and light up as he recites this list. These are all things he hadn't thought about as he stood facing the doors that have closed to him. This is a list of his new doors, each one waiting to be opened, each one leading to experiences and insights Joel cannot see, and could not even imagine until he turned around.

Several months pass and Joel calls me to give me an update. He sounds like a different man. "I found the most wonderful house!" Joel reports enthusiastically. "It is just a few minutes away from the old house, but much closer to town in a great neighborhood for kids, with a beautiful backyard. You won't believe this, but it's been used for years as a holistic health clinic—it's literally a healing house! I knew you'd like that part! I've been decorating it with all of my old stuff that was in storage, and bought some furniture that I love. The kids are crazy about the new place. And I must admit, I'm pretty excited about my new life."

Joel continues: "I have to tell you what happened last week. Eileen and I took the kids out to eat—we still do things as a family sometimes, and it's pretty harmonious. At dinner, Cassie, my oldest girl, who just turned nine, said: 'I've been thinking—now that you guys are getting divorced, you both can get married again, right? That means, I can be in the weddings, right? Two weddings! That means I can have two dresses! I didn't get to come to your first wedding so I can come to these. Hurray!'"

"Cassie and her little sister Carly both started cheering and giggling. In that moment," Joel says to me, "I knew the kids were going to be okay. I think it was Cassie's way of trying to tell me to relax and know that everything was all right, even though it was different. *Cassie is seeing doors I haven't quite spotted yet, but I'm going to do my best to find them.*"

. . .

Though no one can go back and make a brand new start,
anyone can start now and make a brand new ending.
—Carl Bard

Once, in the midst of a very turbulent time, I called my dear friend Amanda, who lives in Australia, since the middle of the night in California is afternoon in Sydney because of the time difference, and Amanda was there to talk to me. Amanda is also a therapist, so we get to take turns being the wise one for the other. On this particular occasion, I was upset and overwhelmed, trying to make sense of several stressful situations in my life. After talking with Amanda for about an hour, I concluded by saying:

"I haven't figured it out yet, but I have figured out that I need to figure it out!"

Sometimes that is our first step—admitting to ourselves: "I am at a dead end. I need to turn around and find a new doorway."

One of the most important lessons I have learned in my spiritual travels is that the state of not knowing is a powerful state, filled with seeds of awakening. Knowing we need to figure something out is the beginning of figuring it out. Remember what I wrote in the first chapter of this book:

"How did I get here?" has a "here" in it.
We are not lost— we are simply in a place that is more fluid than fixed, more shifting than static.

And it is from this place that we begin to look for the new doorways waiting to be opened.

With No Map in Hand

Just because we cannot see clearly the end of the road,
that is no reason for not setting out on the essential journey.
—John F. Kennedy

With great courage, we have put the old maps aside. With great surrender, we have let go of where we hoped we would be and have determined that finally we are ready to move forward. Suddenly it dawns on us that something is missing—*a map to guide us on this next part of our journey.*

We wait for this new map to reveal itself, hoping to discover a step-by-step plan for this new phase of our life. Nothing happens. We desperately look around, sure that there must be a new map somewhere, but try as we might, we can't seem to find it. We see old maps that can chart a course to places others have gone, or where we have gone before—the lives our parents led, conventional destinies society would choose for us, professional and personal paths that are clearly marked. But for those of us in the midst of a powerful emotional and spiritual rebirth, there is often no map to guide us, just a daunting expanse ahead of us that is unknown and uncharted.

We are used to maps, schedules, plans and timelines. They create the illusion that we are going in the right direction, even if we are not. They comfort us that we are not traveling far off-course, even if we are. Finding ourselves without a map in hand, we may feel confused, disoriented and afraid that if we proceed, we will end up lost.

And so we wait, afraid to make new decisions, chart a new course or try a new direction until we receive our itinerary. "I know I am supposed to move through this period," we tell ourselves. "I know I am supposed to take steps to get to a new place. I just wish someone would give me the list of what the steps were so I could begin. I feel restless. *I feel I am supposed to move, but I don't know what to do next.*"

Here is the problem:

We often get stuck in our insistence on needing to see the whole path before we are willing to move forward, rather than just seeing the next step.

This is especially difficult for those of us who don't like feeling out of control. We are uncomfortable not knowing what lies ahead, and so we stay where we are, too insecure to make any kind of move or decision for fear of making a mistake.

In the midst of my own powerful rebirth, I recall saying to a friend:

I used to be able to see so far in front of me—years at a time. It was as if there were enormous searchlights illuminating the whole length of the road ahead, and everything was clear. Now I feel like I have just enough light to see one tiny step in front of me.

When we have been used to certainty and stability, finding ourselves with just enough light for one step can be terrifying. But it is this fear itself that we must put aside, as we gently remind ourselves that *we don't need to see the whole path to begin—we just have to see one step in front of us.*

Learning to proceed without a map means taking one step at a time, even though we can't see a clear path to our destination, or even what that destination may be.

This is the formula for moving forward without a map: *Just begin by taking one step or doing one thing.* Maybe this first step in front of you is all you can see. Even so, take it—soon after you do, the next step will be clear, and after you take that one, the next step will reveal itself, and the next and the next.

There is always a scene in classic spy films in which the hero or heroine is told to go to a certain location—a street corner, a cafe or a phone booth—and wait for further instructions. He follows the directions, arriving at a new destination. And he waits. Finally he receives another message—now he must go to this next location and again, wait for directions. This pattern continues until eventually he finds whatever it is he was looking for.

Proceeding without a map while we transform ourselves is very much like this—**we take one step, the only one we can figure out to take, and then we wait.** From within us, some clarity will come, guiding us to the next step. There, again, we wait. Perhaps at this point something or someone in our life will help us discover what our next step is. We continue to move forward intuitively like this, moment by moment, step by step, and with each step, the next direction is revealed. The map becomes a living, breathing work in progress, rather than a rigid, formulaic blueprint that we mindlessly follow.

．　　．　　．

I may not have gone where I intended to go,
but I think I have ended up where I intended to be.
—Douglas Adams, *The Hitchhiker's Guide to the Galaxy*

Here is something else I have learned in my own quest as a seeker: the Universe isn't very responsive to those of us who insist on receiving a detailed itinerary before we're willing to take action. "I'll wait until I get a sign before moving forward," we tell ourselves. But consider this: What if the Universe is waiting for you? What if those beneficent forces that mysteriously guide us all on our journey are on hold until you indicate your intention?

You can't learn anything by doing nothing.
You can't discover your future by remaining,
unmoving, where you are.
Make a choice.
Decide.
Act.
Then the Universe will correct your course
and point you in the right direction.

You can't get any help from Universal Intelligence when you are standing still, afraid to make a move. It can't correct your direction if you aren't willing to choose one. It can't help steer you toward your destiny if you won't leave the seemingly safe harbor of inaction.

To become aware of new doors that are opening up before us, we have to pay attention and look for possible openings, often where we least expect them to be. At first these may appear to be leading us in directions that make no sense, or even look like detours. But they may very well be "appointments with destiny"— seemingly chance meetings or unplanned encounters that radically transform our lives.

Here are some true stories about appointments with destiny.

. . .

Sharon's good friend becomes ill and calls to offer her his ticket for a concert that evening. She's had an exhausting week, but decides she could use some entertainment and decides to go to the concert. She's hardly gone anywhere since her breakup with her boyfriend six months before, and promised herself she would force herself to get out of the house even if she didn't feel like it.

As Sharon arrives at the theater and makes her way down the aisle to her seat, she is a bit anxious. She doesn't like going to social events alone, and she hopes she's not seated next to anyone strange. Sharon finds her seat and discovers a very cute guy sitting in the seat next to hers. He, it turns out, has also come to the concert alone. As soon as they begin to talk, sparks fly between them, and at the end of the concert, they go to a restaurant and talk for hours. It seems crazy to Sharon, but she is sure she is falling in love. And they are. One year later, Sharon and this man are married.

. . .

Gloria's last appointment of the day runs late, and she misses her train home. She is stuck in the station for another hour until the next train arrives. Annoyed at herself for lingering too long with her last client, Gloria contemplates what to do for an hour. She considers going back out on the street and doing some shopping, but decides to have some tea and just sit for a change, hoping to calm down from her day and the traumatic events of the last few weeks.

In the café, Gloria strikes up a conversation with a woman

who's also waiting for her train and discovers that she is a physician specializing in cancer research. Gloria tells the woman that her younger sister was just diagnosed with a rare form of terminal cancer. The doctor is amazed, explaining that this is the exact type of cancer she has been researching for ten years. She happens to be starting a trial for a new drug in three weeks and is in the process of choosing candidates. Gloria gets the doctor's phone number and arranges for her sister to be part of the trial, which even her own physician didn't know about. Four months later, thanks to the experimental drugs, her sister's cancer is in total remission, and it never returns again.

. . .

Patrick is having a horrible day. He's been trying to get an audition with the casting director of a new film for weeks, but has been unsuccessful. He's sure that he's perfect for a part in an upcoming movie, but can't figure out how to get in to see this very busy man. Today, again, he went to the casting director's office and was turned away by the very unfriendly secretary. His next appointment isn't until six o'clock, and he hasn't gone to the gym yet that day, something he rarely misses. For some reason, he decides instead to go to the nearby New Age book store, a place he normally would never visit, thinking that perhaps finding an inspiring book will lift his spirits.

Patrick finds himself drawn to the section of the store with books on yoga and meditation. Suddenly he is astonished to see the casting director he's been chasing down standing a few feet away. Patrick walks over and introduces himself, confessing his whole story about trying to get an audition, and shares his amazement at bumping into this man in this store. The two of them talk for about ten minutes, and then the casting director invites Patrick to see him the next morning for an audition. Patrick gets the part in the film, which launches him as a new star.

. . .

Each of these people had an appointment with destiny—something good was waiting for them in a place they didn't expect to find it. In every case, they felt things in their life were heading in the wrong direction. With no map to guide them toward finding what they are looking for—a relationship, a medical miracle, a career break—they felt lost and disheartened. Then, in the space of one moment, each of them was guided to an encounter that would change their lives. *By going where they did not intend to go, they ended up where they intended to be.*

**The gift of dead ends is that there is nowhere else
to go but somewhere else.
The blessing of not having a map is that
you are forced to go places you would not go
if your path were predetermined and well marked.**

Proceeding without a map is a new paradigm for us to understand and put into practice. It means allowing life to design us, rather than our trying to design it. The less we try to control the new direction our life is taking, the better. We are invited to put aside our wish list, our goals, and be open to experiencing our life fully in each moment, listening to each moment, responding to each moment.

In doing this, we leave room for the magical, and for the unveiling of the surprises the universe has in store for us. When we are traveling our path with no destination that is certain, we can stop somewhere we wouldn't have noticed if we were in a hurry to arrive at a particular place. We can change our minds. We can go back and start again. We can do anything we want. We are not bound by a rigid goal we set. We are free.

John Schaar, Professor Emeritus of Political Philosophy at the University of California at Santa Cruz, helps us with this new understanding of our future as something that is not mapped out, but that we are creating in each and every moment:

The future is not a result of choices among alternative paths offered by the present, but a place that is created—created first in the mind and will, created next in activity. The future is not some place we are going to, but one we are creating. The paths are not to be found but made, and the activity of making them changes both the maker and the destination.

The Courage to Be Nothing and Nobody for Awhile

The body first, and the spirit later; and the birth and growth of the spirit, in those who are attentive to their own inner life, are slow and exceedingly painful. Our mothers are racked with the pains of our physical birth; we ourselves suffer the longer pains of our spiritual growth.
—Mary Antin

Rebirthing ourselves takes time. Like our own physical birth process, it cannot be rushed. That means we must have the understanding and the willingness to endure the labor pains we experience as we traverse the gap between who we were and who we are becoming:

Navigating the unexpected in one's life requires great emotional courage— the courage to be nothing and nobody for a while as you question who you have been and who you want to be.

The most difficult decisions I have made in my own process of renewal during the past seven years have not been decisions to *do* something, but rather decisions to *not* do things: not to host a TV show; not to write another book immediately after I'd finished the previous one; not to commit myself to so many speaking engagements; not to follow my old maps automatically, even though they had led me to great success. It meant relinquishing many things to which I had become attached, creating a profound sense of emptiness in my life.

I knew that I was emptying out so I could be filled again—with new vision, new inspiration, new purpose, new love. But being willing to feel the ache of that emptiness and holding myself back from the compulsion to instantly fill it up was, at times, more than I could bear. "I've gone through enough!" I would announce in my prayers to whatever cosmic powers I hoped were listening. "I've learned so many lessons, and grown in profound ways. Isn't it time to stop now? I'm sure I'm 'done,' and ready to be filled back up again."

Like a child on a long car ride who keeps asking her parents, *"Are we there yet?"* I felt impatient to quickly get to the end of my journey of awakening, to move rapidly through this gap between who I had been and whoever I was turning out to be, to rush through the thick forest of questions and confusion that filled my head to the place that held the answers. I grew tired of feeling unsure, of not knowing. I yearned to feel certain and secure, to once again see all the way down the road, and not just the tiny step in front of me.

Slowly, a searing and astonishing revelation dawned on me: **I had spent my whole life in a hurry to do everything**—to complete the smallest task, to talk, to read, to achieve, to be intimate, to fall in love, to become enlightened. It was as if I were racing against an invisible clock that only I could see. Why was I in such a rush? What drove me to be this way?

Suddenly I knew the answer. I had been in an eternal battle with emptiness. I was trying to fill up the empty space, afraid that if I did not, it would remain empty forever. And so I would hurry to fill any void I encountered, whether it was unoccupied space in a conversation, unoccupied time in my schedule, unoccupied space on my wall, my desk, my shelves, my closet or anywhere else in my home, and especially, and most difficult to admit, unoccupied space in my heart.

No wonder I had always created a new romantic life so soon after the end of the previous one. No wonder I would always start working on a new book as soon as I finished writing the last one. And no wonder I was now terrified as I chose to become more of a nothing and a nobody than I'd ever been before.

I collapsed into this void, and let it become my very breath, my very awareness, the very beat of my heart. This is what I had been running from all of my life. Now it filled my days and nights with its unmistakable and demanding presence. And now, somehow, I surrendered to it, perhaps knowing that this is what all of my digging deep had finally brought me to.

In that letting go, to my great astonishment, I discovered more light than I knew existed, and embraced a transformation I had long awaited. It is out of that awakening that this book and the wisdom it contains have emerged.

When we are in the process of redesigning ourselves, we miss clarity. We miss certainty. We do not like when things are murky. But try as we might, we cannot and should not rush to a new understanding. We cannot force our awakening to happen any faster than it already is. We must be patient.

Consider this wisdom from the *Tao Te Ching,* written in China roughly 2,500 years ago by the Chinese Taoist philosopher Lao Tzu:

> Do you have the patience to wait
> until your mud settles and the water is clear?
> Can you remain unmoving
> until the right action arises by itself?

We make our move, and then we wait for the Universe to make its move, and for awakening to dawn. It always will.

· · ·

When things seem to be taking longer than you think they should, when you feel your new doors aren't revealing themselves quickly enough, you may be growing and unfolding in beautiful ways you can't yet see. Here is a parable of unknown origin.

A man found a cocoon of an emperor moth. Fascinated by the mysterious and rare specimen, he took it home so that he could watch the moth come out of the cocoon.

The next day a small opening appeared. He sat and watched the moth for several hours as it struggled to force the body through that little hole. Then it seemed to stop making any progress. It appeared as if it had gone as far as it could through the hole, and had gotten stuck. It stopped moving completely.

The man felt horrible for the little moth. In his kindness, he decided to help it get free. He took a pair of scissors and snipped off the remaining bit of the cocoon. The moth then emerged easily. But the man noticed that its body was swollen, and its wings were small and shriveled.

The man continued to watch the moth because he expected that at any moment the wings would enlarge and expand to be able to support the body, which would contract in time. But neither happened. In fact, the little moth spent the rest of its life crawling around with a swollen body and shriveled wings. It never was able to fly.

What the man in his compassion and haste did not understand was that the restrictive cocoon and the struggle required for the moth to get through the tiny opening was Nature's way of forcing fluid from the body of the moth into its wings. This would help the wings fully develop, so that once the moth achieved its freedom from the cocoon, it would be ready for flight.

For the moth, freedom and flight could only come after its struggle. But the man hadn't known this. By depriving the moth of a struggle and trying to rush it out of the cocoon, he unintentionally crippled it, preventing the moth from becoming everything it was supposed to be.

I have shared my own very personal experiences with you so that as you undergo your own rebirth, you, too, can find the strength and the wisdom not to rush through or misinterpret your own voids, your own emptinesses. They are the cocoon that will enable your wings to grow. With love, patience and pride, we must watch ourselves begin to move forward out of our awakenings, one step at a time, just as a parent watches their child slowly take his first step, and then another, and another.

We need to know the difference between when we are stuck and when we are simply still in our cocoon. We need to give our new self time to emerge so that when it does, we will know how to fly . . .

Discovering New Doorways

When you follow your bliss . . . doors will open
where you would not have thought there would be doors;
and where there wouldn't be a door for anyone else.
—Joseph Campbell

The new doorways are there. Perhaps we can't yet see them, but they are waiting just the same. So how do we locate them?

Proceeding without a map does not mean that nothing is there to guide us. It simply means that the old ways we use to move forward may not work in times of challenge and rebirth. **It is the intuitive wisdom of the heart that can help us on our journey to discovering new doorways.**

The heart is always speaking to us in small, gentle whispers, so quiet that they often go unnoticed. We experience a fleeting sensation; we have a fragment of a thought; we encounter a sudden, unexplained emotion. Often we discount these, if we are aware of them at all. In doing so, we are ignoring our own inner voice that is trying to communicate with us—to steer us away from danger, to point us in a new direction, to lead us to new waiting doorways.

The intuitive wisdom of the heart does not always make sense. It may not always seem logical, practical or even reasonable. That is because it is not linear, taking us from Point A to Point B in a straight line. Instead, it moves us forward with steps that are in tune to cosmic rhythms and designs. Only when we arrive at our new destination will we begin to understand the mysterious route we have taken to get there.

There are many names for the wisdom that speaks through the heart. Some call it the "Higher Mind" as opposed to the conventional mind. Others call it Cosmic Intelligence or Spirit. To many, it is simply the voice of God.

Whatever its name, how do we learn to listen to the voice of the heart and follow its guidance? We need to stop asking ourselves: "What should I do now?" "What is my new list of goals?" or "What action steps should I take?" Instead, we must begin contemplating what I call *"the questions within the questions."* These questions are not designed to give us informative answers. Their purpose is to by-pass the mind and open us to the wisdom of our own heart. They cannot be answered honestly by using our intellect—we must *feel the answers*, rather than *thinking about the answers*.

There are many ways to work with these questions. You can take one at a time and write about what it brings up for you. You can contemplate the questions in meditation. You can discuss each question with your partner, a friend or a therapist. You can have the intention of delving deeply into one question each week. These questions are not part of an intellectual exercise. They are very powerful guides that will help you travel deep within yourself. Pay close attention to the answers you receive. And as the saying goes, "When your heart speaks, take good notes."

Here are some "questions within the questions" for you to work with:

Am I living as the person I want to be?

How much of the time do others see me as I really am?

What authentic parts of myself have I been hiding from people who know me?

Am I happy with what I've been doing with my life?

Do my everyday activities and interactions bring me joy?

What parts of myself have I been ignoring, neglecting or denying?

What do I need to do or let go of to finally grow up?

What do I need to do or let go of to finally be free?

If my life was over tomorrow, would I feel fulfilled with how I have lived and what I have accomplished?

What would my life be like if I weren't judging it against expectations I've had, or comparing it to the life others have?

If I weren't worried about what other people might think or how they might react, what changes or decisions would I make in my life?

If I had one year left to live, what changes or decisions would I make in my life?

If I listened to what my heart has been trying to tell me, what would I do, change or decide?

. . .

If we can see the path laid out for us, there is a
good chance it is not our path: it is probably
someone else's we have substituted for our own.
Our own path must be deciphered every step of the way.
—David Whyte

As we strive to listen to the wisdom of our heart, we must remind ourselves that it is our wisdom, our vision, our awakenings, and no one else's, that will take us to our new doorways. We can be inspired by mentors, teachers, pastors, priests, therapists, authors, friends and well-meaning loved ones. Ultimately, for our journey to be authentic, we must decipher our own path.

You are the only one who will be given the clarity to see your new doorways.

One of my favorite Chinese proverbs reminds us: *"The person who says it cannot be done should not interrupt the person doing it."* If someone cannot see what you see, they will not understand why you are doing what you are doing. Do not let this hold you back. You have been given your vision for a reason. You must follow it.

Several years ago, after I'd finished writing and promoting my latest book, it was time for me to start writing a new one. That's what writers are supposed to do—decide on their next project and begin again. I had many clever ideas for books that would be easy to write and fun to promote, but that is not the way I have ever participated in my craft as an author. *My books come through me, rather than from me.* They choose me—I don't choose them. That means I must wait until the wisdom decides it's ready to emerge and that I'm ready to receive it, and only then can I finally begin. At that time in my life, nothing was coming.

As I waited longer than I ever had for the topic of my next book to materialize in my awareness, some people in my life became increasingly nervous and began to make suggestions:

"Why don't you write another book about sex? That will be a bestseller for sure, and it will be easy to get you on talk shows." Or, "Write a sequel to one of your most popular books. You don't have to come up with a new idea every time—other authors don't." Or, "Write something short and easy to read—no one wants to think that much about themselves anyway."

These are the doorways others may have wanted me to walk through. They were familiar, even logical, and they made financial sense, but they were not the doorway I could feel waiting for me. As one of my spiritual mentors reminded me when I told her I was turning down these very commercially sound ideas, "Barbara, you have never worked for money. You have always worked for God." And she was right. This fact has not always made me a clever businesswoman, but it has defined me as a committed seeker and servant of Truth.

Of course you already know what happened—*How Did I Get Here?* finally began to reveal itself, and I was finally ready to write it. After so long in the dark, I saw the doorway I had been longing to discover.

**Being true to your vision means fitting your life
into your dreams rather than
trying to fit your dreams into your life.**

As you wait for your new doorways to reveal themselves, hold fast to your unfolding vision. It does not matter if anyone else approves of the path you are traveling, or appreciates where you are trying to go. All that matters is that you being true to the wisdom in your own heart, a voice only you can hear that whispers: *"Go that way!"*

Again, we hear from the writer Katharine Hathaway:

> Oh, lucky beyond most human beings is the . . . person who is bold and crazy enough to defy the almost overwhelming chorus of complacency and inertia and other peo-

ple's ideas and to follow the single, fresh, living voice of his own destiny, which at the crucial moment speaks aloud to him and tells him to come on.

The Unpaved Road to Paradise

Not knowing when the dawn will come, I open every door.
—Emily Dickinson

On the magical Hawaiian island of Kauai, there is a beautiful road that is a popular drive for tourists visiting this part of the world. This road parallels the ocean and is lined with palm trees, perfectly landscaped lawns, fragrant flowering trees and luxurious resorts. Driving along the well-paved two-lane highway, you can see the sun-drenched mountains in the distance and miles and miles of lush, tropical splendor.

Suddenly, at one of its most picturesque points, the paved road just stops, coming to a dead end into a narrow, pothole-lined, rock-filled dirt lane surrounded on both sides by unruly, overgrown bushes rising eight feet in the air. There are no signs that warn the driver that the road is ending or indicate that there is anything beyond this place. The dirt path looks treacherous and uninviting and doesn't appear to lead anywhere but into a neglected field.

Most visitors who find themselves at this unexpected dead end in their sightseeing tour stop, back up and turn their cars around, returning the way they came. *"There's nothing down that road worth risking getting stuck in a pothole, or getting a flat tire,"* they reassure themselves. After all, if there was something really wonderful there, wouldn't it be on the map? Wouldn't there be a sign pointing the way?

The dangerous-looking dirt road is very difficult to drive on. You have to go very, very slowly, navigating the car carefully around the deep holes, avoiding the sharp rocks, peering through the huge cloud of dust stirred up by the tires as you brace yourself for the next jolt. It takes tremendous patience—driving too quickly will land you in a ditch. After twenty minutes of this, with no end in sight, you begin to have doubts about your decision to come down the road at all and wonder if you've made a terrible mistake. And then, something happens that you didn't think was possible—the road gets even worse, so narrow and chopped-up that you suspect it isn't even a road anymore, and you are certain that you are done for.

If, in spite of all this, you don't give up and keep on going, in just a few moments you will arrive at a small clearing in which you can park your car. And when you walk down the rocky path at the end of the clearing, you will suddenly find yourself on the most exotic, exquisite coastline imaginable. There before you is the turquoise sea crashing up against intricately carved rock formations, secluded sandy beaches, hidden coves and cliffside trails that take you on a magical hike where every vista takes your breath away. You gaze around you at all of this unfathomable beauty, and you are sure you've arrived in Heaven.

Each time my partner and I have made the pilgrimage to this sacred spot, I am filled with gratitude that it exists, and feel so blessed to be able to experience it. And each time we drive back out and arrive at the place where the paved road begins, we see cars filled with visitors making U-turns, certain that they've avoided disaster by not traveling down that unmarked road. *"If they only knew what lies at the end of this impossible dirt lane!"* we always say to each other with a smile.

. . .

I once heard someone say that God hides things by putting them all around us. I believe this to be true.

Blessings are disguised as loss and disappointment.

Wisdom and revelation are disguised as emptiness and despair.

Doorways to paradise are disguised as dirt roads and dead ends.

Things are not as they appear to be.

This, then, is how we proceed forward on our journey, remembering this mysterious cosmic game of hide-and-seek, look-

ing for the new pathways that may be right before our eyes—
unmarked, unmapped, challenging, always where we least expect
them to be, but there to lead us to joy, wonder and glorious awakening.

Not knowing when the dawn will come,
but beginning to believe that it will,
we open every door.

PART THREE

Roads to Awakening

❧ 10 ❧

Finding Your Way
Back to Passion

We do not have to die to enter the kingdom of Heaven.
In fact, we have to be fully alive.
—Thich Nhat Hanh

There is a power in our heart far greater than anything we can imagine. This power is our passion—the life force that pulsates within us, bringing energy, vitality and meaning to everything it touches. When that passion flows into our relationship, it brings intimacy and deep connection. When that passion flows into our work, it brings creativity and vision. When that passion flows into our quest for Truth, it brings wisdom. When that passion flows into our spiritual journey, it brings awakening.

No matter how battered we are by love or life, no matter what we endure, we never really lose our passion. Perhaps we leave it for a while, but it never leaves us.

When what you held dear has been lost or taken from you, you still have your passion.
When love seems to have abandoned you, and your heart and your body ache for union, you still have your passion.
When you are disappointed and disillusioned, you still have your passion.
When you are balancing precariously between the past and the future in an uncertain and shifting present, you still have your passion.

*When you are weary of traveling a new and unmarked road to a
destination that has not yet come into clear view, you still have
your passion.*

Just as a fire whose flames have died down hides its heat in the
glowing coals, so your passion still smolders within you, waiting
for the moment when you will call on it to rise again and burn
brightly. It is from this fire of passion that all of your new beginnings will emerge.

As you travel life's difficult roads and meet unexpected challenges, it is your passion that becomes your saving grace. It keeps
you going forward even when you feel like giving up. It keeps you
searching for love even when you are afraid you will never find it. It
keeps you awake. It keeps you truly alive.

If you have read this far, if you have been digging deep, if you
have been inviting truth into your awareness, then you have already been reclaiming your passion. Can you feel it waking up inside
of you?

Right Here, Right Now, There Is Passion

*The aim of life is to live, and to live means to be aware,
joyously, drunkenly, serenely, divinely aware.*
—Henry Miller

Today is the day to be fully alive. Today is the day to reach out
and embrace the joys available in each moment. Today is the
day for passion.

Passion is not something we are only supposed to experience
on a romantic vacation or while visiting an exciting destination. It
is not something to be rationed out in reasonable doses or saved for
special occasions. It is not only available to people with unlimited
funds and free time.

**Passion is not found in escaping from
our usual life in a search for
some high-charged experience.
We rediscover our passion when we
open ourselves fully to every
experience, and learn to see the
world with passionate eyes.**

How do we do this? It is simpler than we realize.

We learn to be aware, to pay attention to the ordinary, everyday miracles that are all around us: the sound of tree branches dancing in the wind; the delicacy of a cloud; the tender kiss from a young child; the enthusiastic greeting of your animal companions when you arrive home; the sweet juiciness of a piece of ripe fruit; the soothing hot water of your bath or shower; the songs birds sing as they wake up the dawn.

We take these and so many other natural gifts for granted. In the midst of our overscheduled and stressful days, we often fail even to notice, let alone rejoice in the abundance of the marvelous and the amazing that surrounds us.

Imagine for a moment that the night sky was always devoid of all light—no moon, no stars, no planets, no galaxies—utterly black. Then imagine that suddenly one evening a veil was lifted and all of these shining, celestial bodies were made visible. All over the world, the people of the earth would stare weeping up into the heavens, certain that the Divine had finally revealed itself.

Are the stars any less awe-inspiring because we can see them every night? Is the love of our mate, our children, our best friend any less precious because we assume they will be there the next day, and the next? Are our body and our brain any less magical because they continue to function the way we expect them to? Is our existence any less miraculous because we are blessed with so many days of it in a lifetime?

**Living a passionate and awakened life means
looking at the stars each night as if it were your
first time and as if it were your
last time. It means embracing your
loved ones as if this were the only
embrace you will ever be granted.
It means living each day with reverence
and wonder as if it were the only
day you will be given to live.**

. . .

Last year, one of my dear friends had emergency triple bypass surgery on his heart. Samuel is only sixty years old and always
thought he was in excellent health, so his heart failure came as a total shock and, needless to say, a very dramatic wake-up call. Samuel
has a very successful career as an actor. Like many of us, he gets
caught up in the pressures and demands of his work. Before his illness, he never seemed to take time to relax or even enjoy the full and
prosperous life he'd created for himself. Now all of that has changed.

When I told Samuel I was writing this book, I asked him to describe what he learned from his brush with death, and to articulate
how his life is different. He described it this way:

Now, I consciously evaluate my life on a daily basis,
judging it by how the day was, and not what new movie I
was cast in, or how my investments are doing, or what
awards I've been nominated for. I keep asking myself,
"Would I want this to be my last day?" This keeps me focused on what is important—my relationship with my wife,
my kids, enjoying very simple pleasures. I am so acutely
aware of how limited our time on earth is, my time, and
how at any moment it could all be over. Knowing that, I
don't want to miss anything.

Samuel is more alive now than he ever was before his life-
threatening heart failure, not because he is in better physical

health, but because he has committed himself to living each day with awareness and gratitude. He has stopped postponing his joy and started actively searching for things to be passionate about. For the first time in his life he is at peace.

The Courage to Live Passionately

I've been absolutely terrified every moment of my life—
and I've never let it keep me from doing a single thing
I wanted to do.
—Georgia O'Keeffe

It takes courage to live passionately. The choice to live with passion is the choice to open yourself fully to each moment and to each situation. You give everything. You hold nothing back.

Living with passion means sometimes living on the edge of our comfort zone. We are awake. We are alive. We are feeling—everything. We meet the circumstances and challenges of our life boldly. *It's not that we don't feel doubt or fear—it's that we learn to make our passion for growth and truth stronger than our fear.*

This kind of courage isn't the same as physical bravery. It is *emotional courage.* Emotional courage allows you to participate 100 percent in whatever you are doing and wherever you are going. It allows you to see beyond that which is the way of your dreams, your desires, your destiny, and to go forward with enthusiasm. You aren't saving some of your passion for a time in the future when you will be absolutely certain about how things will turn out. You are offering all of who you are to life right now.

Mark Twain wrote:

"Twenty years from now you will be more disappointed by the things you didn't do than by the ones you did do."

Emotional courage helps you venture out of your safe harbors into open and exciting seas, to do the things you want to do so you do not end your life with regret.

Opening up to passion means becoming open to the mysterious, the unexpected, the subtle, and allowing that which is out of the ordinary to reveal itself. This means being willing to let go of control, and adventure into new pathways of feeling, of perception, of experience, pathways that will lead you to more joy and wonder than you knew was possible.

. . .

One certain way to kill your experience of passion is to care too much about what others think. This will cut you off from your intuitive wisdom. *The more careful, calculated and analytical we are, the more difficult it will be to be passionate about anything.*

**The only person's opinion that is going to matter
to you at the end of this lifetime is yours.
To reclaim your passion, you must push past
your fear of what others think of you
and do what makes you think well of yourself.**

Someone recently sent me this beautiful poem by writer and teacher Dawna Markova, who when faced with a life-threatening illness retreated to a cabin in the mountains where she contemplated how she could reclaim her true passion. She writes:

> I will not die an unlived life
> I will not live in fear
> of falling or catching fire,
> I choose to inhabit my days,
> to allow my living to open me,
> to make me less afraid,
> more accessible,
> to loosen my heart
> until it becomes a wing,
> a torch, a promise

I choose to risk my significance;
to live so that which came to me as a
seed goes to the next blossom
and that which came to me as a blossom,
goes on as fruit.

Reclaiming our passion means choosing to fully inhabit our days, living our lives so that no moment goes unlived, no delight goes unnoticed, no sweetness goes untasted. Right now, all around you, there are a thousand things for you to be passionate about.

Living a Turned-on Life

There is a land of the living and a land of the dead,
and the bridge is love,
the only survival, the only meaning.
—Thornton Wilder

When we wake up from the sleep of numbness and denial and reconnect with our own inner passion, then, and only then, can we infuse that passion into our emotional and sexual life.

To reawaken the erotic intimacy in a relationship, we must first rediscover and reignite our own secret fire. Then our passion will not be dependent upon being stimulated from the outside. Rather it will emerge from our own consciousness, our own vibrant aliveness, our own willingness to feel fully and deeply.

Often people ask me: "How can I put the passion back into my relationship?" This is how I respond:

Are you passionate about your everyday life?
Are you passionate about your work?
Are you passionate about yourself?
Are you passionate about loving your partner deeply?
Are you passionate about being alive?

If you cannot answer each of these questions with an emphatic "yes," then there is no way you can put the passion back into your relationship. The passion has to be alive in you before you can experience it in something else."

When you are not turned on inside yourself, your partner will have a difficult time doing it for you.

If you are the one who has been the ghost lover in a relationship, if you are the one who has been turned off and shut down, you must first embody yourself again in love and passion. Then, and only then, can you offer that new self humbly to your beloved, hoping she or he will receive it. You will need to be patient as your partner learns to trust that you have indeed come back from the emotional dead. With luck, you can resurrect your relationship and create the magical connection in body, mind and soul for which you have always longed.

Sometimes it does not work out this way. You find your way back to your own passion only to arrive and discover that your efforts are too late. Your partner has grown weary of waiting for you to feel again and has closed the door to his or her heart. Instead of facing what you hoped would be a wonderful new beginning, you face a painful good-bye. "What horrible timing," you proclaim in despair. "Finally, when I am ready to love again, my mate no longer wants me."

If this is the case for you, remember: things are not what they appear to be. What looks like a dead end will soon reveal itself to be a doorway.

Your awakened heart, your rediscovered passion will not be wasted. They are being saved for someone else whose name and face you do not know yet, but who is praying to find you. When this

person does, he or she will be grateful for all of the courageous work you did to melt the ice around your heart. He will honor you for every hard-earned moment of revelation and growth. And he will joyfully drink every drop of love you have been saving up.

The course of love is mysterious and unfathomable. Some intimate relationships endure for a lifetime. And sometimes we are destined only to share our journey with a mate for a while and then we separate, either by choice or by fate.

> No matter what the outcome of our connection
> with another person,
> when love enters our lives,
> it never leaves without transforming us to the
> very depth of our being.
> We may lose the relationship, but we never lose the love.

Look for the Daffodil

> *Every now and again take a good look at something*
> *not made with hands—*
> *a mountain, a star, the turn of a stream.*
> *There will come to you wisdom and patience*
> *and solace and, above all,*
> *the assurance that you are not alone in the world.*
> —Sidney Lovett

On a frigid February day several years ago, I was in upstate New York, staring out the window at more than two feet of snow covering the ground. This was definitely *not* California—it was an uncivilized 9 degrees outside, 12 below zero with the windchill. *"How did I get here?"* I said to myself, more out of amazement than a sincere inquiry. Because, of course, I knew the answer: the true love of a remarkable man. What else could prompt me to regularly leave the warmth, the ocean and the delight of Santa Barbara for weeks at a time? Still, it is not always easy to be so far from home, especially when it is brutally cold and I hadn't seen the sun in what seemed like decades.

I bundled up in my enormous coat, thick scarf and heavy boots to make a trip to the supermarket, hoping to finish my shopping before the next blizzard arrived. My car slipped and slid along the icy roads, and by the time I arrived, my hands were stiff from gripping the wheel so tightly. As I waddled as quickly as possible through the parking lot into the store, I caught a glimpse of myself in a mirror—I looked like a walking sleeping bag! I noticed to my amazement that many of the other customers—obviously native upstaters—were just wearing light jackets, in spite of the frigid temperatures. I smiled apologetically as I passed them in my arctic attire, as if to say: "Have pity on me: I wasn't born here!"

As I wheeled my cart toward the produce section, I spotted a display of live plants and fresh flowers across the store. "JUST IN TIME FOR SPRING," the sign optimistically read. My California soul, thirsty for green, took over and I found myself practically racing toward the foliage. Then I noticed it, there in the middle of the aisle—a potted yellow daffodil just beginning to bloom.

My first reaction when I saw the daffodil was a bittersweet rush of sadness. It reminded me of home in California, where everything is always in bloom, and where my garden was overflowing with a colorful variety of lovely flowers. Even though I chose to be here and not there, I still missed it terribly. Suddenly I knew that I must buy this little daffodil as a defiant act against the interminable bitterness of winter. It would be my piece of sunshine against the backdrop of gray. It would be my own little secret garden.

When I arrived back at the house, I placed the potted daffodil on my desk where I do my writing. Outside the window, I could see the snow once again beginning to fall, until soon there was nothing but white. Another storm had arrived. But my daffodil and I were safely inside.

I cared for my daffodil tenderly, and it rewarded me by blossoming in golden abundance. Each day I delighted in its refusal to acknowledge winter, and its persistence in blooming despite the icy, sunless times. Its tender yellow petals glistened with the promise of regeneration. When it seemed the world had come to a frozen standstill, my daffodil's bold burst of color sang out with triumph and passion: "Spring is coming!"

Something is always blooming in cold, dark times. Even in the midst of challenge and difficulty, we must look for signs of beauty and delight. Even in the midst of turmoil, there are miracles. Even in the midst of desolation, there are moments of passion.

Look for the daffodil.

Measuring Your Life in Love and Miracles

When it's over, I want to say:
all my life I was a bride married to amazement.
I was the bridegroom taking the world into my arms.
—Mary Oliver

This year a dear friend of mine passed away from leukemia at the untimely age of fifty-two. Kathy was everything that is good about this world. She was brave, wise, loving and passionate. Kathy did not want to die. She underwent two excruciating bone marrow transplants, fighting for every extra day of life she could grab. It was impossible for me to imagine that someone who possessed as much energy and vitality as Kathy could be worn down by cancer, but in the end, even she realized it was time for her to go. When her spirit left her battered body, Kathy was in a state of peace and grace, knowing that she had died with as much courage, consciousness and dignity as she had lived.

When Kathy's family asked me to perform her memorial service, I felt humbled and honored. I prayed that I would find the right words to give some comfort to her mother, her siblings, her friends and especially her son and only child, Gregory, who was just about to graduate from college. Kathy had been a single mother and had done a remarkable job raising Greg to be a sensitive young man with a beautiful heart. The two of them had always been very close, and I knew that losing his mother when he was still so young was going to be difficult for Greg to bear.

Before everyone arrived for the service, I went into the chapel to spend some time alone meditating, praying and preparing myself for whatever wanted to come through me when I spoke. There in the front of the room was Kathy's body laid out in the open coffin. I was surprised at how strangely distant I felt seeing it. *"That is no longer Kathy,"* I thought to myself. Kathy's spirit had ascended to another realm, leaving her old body behind, a cast-off shell that had once housed her soul, and no more.

In that moment, I was struck once again with a truth I have always known and try each day to remember: **We are here on this earth for such a short while.** I have always been amazed when I witness people living as if they do not understand this—squandering time, hiding from love, getting caught up in things that do not matter, and never attending to what does.

Kathy understood. She had been completely and radiantly alive. She had always thrown herself into everything she did as if she had no time to spare, and it turned out, sadly for those of us who will miss her, that she was right. In her dying, as in her living, Kathy gave the people she loved a priceless gift—*the reminder to live and love with joy, determination and passion, so that at the end of our days, we will have no regrets.*

I think about Kathy every day. I started out as her teacher and mentor, but in the end, she became my teacher and my inspiration. I know she would be pleased that I am writing about her so that even in death, she can help make a difference. Her goodness continues to touch and open hearts, even from the unseen places beyond this physical world.

. . .

A joyful heart is the inevitable result of a heart burning with love.
—Mother Teresa

How do we measure a life? In dollars earned? In awards won? In how many material things we possessed? In how perfectly we did everything? In what other people thought of us? In how old we lived to be? In his remarkable Broadway musical *Rent,* the late Jonathan Larson, who tragically passed away just weeks before his show opened, suggests that we measure in love.

When I measure my life in love, I find myself rich beyond imagining. I have loved deeply. I have loved often. I have loved passionately. Somehow I have emerged from my own recent challenges and awakenings able to feel even more, give even more, love even more.

We do not need to be in a relationship to love. We do not need to have money to love. We do not need to have conquered our fears to love. We do not need to know where the road is taking us to love. All we need to do to love is find the passion and sweetness in the center of our heart. All we need to do to love is to feel the love that is already burning inside us, a fire whose spark cannot be extinguished. All we need to do to love is . . . just love.

.   .   .

There are only two ways to live your life. One is as though nothing is a miracle. The other is as though everything is a miracle.
—Albert Einstein

Recently I was walking my dogs in one of our favorite Santa Barbara parks. It was a glorious afternoon with warm temperatures and a cloudless azure sky. Ahead of us down the path, I noticed a strange-looking man sitting on a bench. He was oddly dressed and had an air about him that told me he was a few degrees shy of normal.

As we got closer, I saw that this fellow was trying to speak to everyone who passed, although they were all ignoring him. He pointed a finger up into the air and emphatically repeated a phrase that I couldn't quite hear. "Maybe he's drunk or disturbed," I thought to myself, wondering if I should avoid walking in his direction.

Just then one of my dogs began pulling me directly toward the bench where the man sat. When he noticed me approaching, he smiled tenderly, and with wide eyes full of wonder and with passionate reverence in his voice, he pointed to the sky and announced:

"The sun is awake! The sun is awake! The sun is awake!"

It took me a moment to comprehend what the man was saying, and why he was so excited by it. Then I got it: *The sun is awake. Once again, it has showed up to bless us with light and warmth. The darkness has vanished. Another day of life is here. What a miracle!*

I looked into the man's eyes and nodded: "Yes," I said to him gently, "you are right—the sun *is* awake!"

His face broke out into a wide grin. He had delivered his message, and I'd received it into the very depth of my being. What could be more cause for celebration than the fact that the sun is, indeed, awake? Why wasn't I getting up each day and, upon looking out of my window and seeing the earth bathed with light, rejoicing in the sun's faithful and benevolent presence? What could be more of a miracle?

Perhaps some would say this man was developmentally challenged. I prefer to think of him as a special being with an innocent heart, capable of seeing things most of us don't normally see, of feeling things most of us can't normally feel. Maybe he was an angelic messenger sent to remind anyone who would listen of the truth we often forget. Maybe he was sent just for me. All I know is that ever since that remarkable encounter in the park, not a morning goes by when I do not rise from my bed and smile as I greet the day, thinking with gratitude: "The sun is awake!"

. . .

What is this precious love and laughter
Budding in our hearts?
It is the glorious sound
Of a soul waking up!
—Hafiz (tr. Daniel Ladinsky)

What is not a miracle? This body that houses our spirit? This consciousness that tells us "I exist"? These eyes that perceive an unending parade of wonders? This heart that feels love, longing, aching, everything? This life, this ecstatic, maddening life? It is, all of it, utterly miraculous.

In the end, it is the celebration of this miracle of our own self that will fill our hearts with the most independent and lasting joy, and the most unabashed passion. Like the unlikely prophet I met in the park, we announce our delightful discovery.

"I am alive! I am alive! I am alive!"

❧ 11 ❧

Coming into Your
Wisdom Time

*We don't receive wisdom; we must discover it for ourselves
after a journey that no one can take for us or spare us.*
—Marcel Proust

There is a wisdom born of having seen so much, experienced so much, felt so much, lost so much, faced so much, found so much. This wisdom cannot be gained by staying comfortably in the same place, nor can it be won by fleeing from that which is frightening or unpleasant. It is unearthed from the depths of our being as we travel the precarious path of our own personal transformation and rebirth.

This is one of the most astonishing truths about navigating through unexpected and challenging times: *When we finally pass through them, we discover that somewhere along the way, we became much wiser than we were when we began.* Like a sailor arriving home from a long and dangerous journey, we look back on the rough seas we've just crossed, happy to be—for the moment— on solid ground. Suddenly we notice a bundle in our belongings that we don't recognize. Upon closer inspection, we are amazed to discover that we have carried home great riches. *"Where did this come from?"* we ask ourselves. *"I don't remember receiving it."* And although we cannot identify the moment in which we were handed this treasure, it is indeed ours, the reward for our bravery and hard work.

We, too, will discover our own mysterious bundle of riches in the form of new wisdom, understanding and clarity once we have given birth to ourselves again. At first, emerging from the darkness, we can't see clearly. Our eyes are still unaccustomed to such light after so much time spent in thick shadows. We need to adjust to the brightness. Gradually, as we gaze around at new, intriguing landscapes of consciousness, astonished at the vistas we see with transformed vision, we realize that we have indeed arrived at our time of wisdom.

We have been on a journey to a new, unknown place. This journey has tested our courage, our inner strength, our sense of trust, our very spiritual core. **Now we need to take time to savor our newfound wisdom before we rush forward. If we are not careful, we will miss our own victories of the heart and triumphs of the spirit.** We will glimpse the next challenge in the distance and hurry toward it, anxious to have that, too, behind us. Instead, we must stop for a moment and simply arrive.

It has taken so much courage for us to even ask the question *"How did I get here?"* let alone answer it. We remind ourselves of this, and know that more than anything else we work to accomplish, this is and will be one of our most significant achievements.

· · ·

The turning point in the process of growing up is when you discover the core of strength within you that survives all hurt.
—Max Lerner

Someone I love just underwent serious medical surgery. The procedure was necessary but risky, and he was naturally quite nervous about the operation. Luckily, everything went well, and as soon as the surgery was over, his wife called to tell me that he had made it through just fine. "The strangest part," she added, "is that when I saw him in the recovery room, he didn't think he'd had the surgery yet, and kept asking me when the doctors were going to come and get him. I told him it was all over—that the results were great and he had nothing to worry about—but he kept insisting that he would certainly know if he had been operated on. Since he didn't remember anything like that happening, he was still horribly anxious about what he thought was his upcoming surgery!" Of course we both knew that her husband's temporary loss of clarity and confusion were due to the anesthesia, and once it wore off, he would indeed realize he could go home and celebrate the positive results of his procedure.

Sometimes when we emerge from our own equivalent of "cosmic surgery," in which we have faced our terrors, we, too, aren't even aware that it is over. At first we may not realize how profoundly we have been transformed. We may not appreciate the enormous hurdles we've overcome. We may not recognize the new wisdom we've gained. It may take someone else to tell us that we've made it through, to be a loving mirror reflecting back the great accomplishment of our transformation.

Slowly we look around and it dawns on us—the fog has lifted, the path before us is clear. We have survived something we cannot even describe, and miraculously we are strong in ways we never could have imagined we would be. This awakened wisdom will reveal itself in many parts of our life: as new creativity in our work; new, more fulfilling ways of relating to our intimate partner; new kinds of cooperation and harmony in our family; or new levels of confidence and optimism with which we face the world. We feel hopeful, renewed and more alive than ever before.

The Magical Alchemy of Transformation

Behold, I show you a mystery; we shall not all sleep,
but we shall all be changed, in a moment,
in the twinkling of an eye.
—Corinthians 15:51–52

Our questioning began with *"How did I get here?"* but a moment comes when we realize that "here" has turned into "there," and we have finally arrived on the other side of the storm. Now, once again, our question changes into a series of new ones:

"How did I make it through to the other side?"

"How has this passage transformed me?"

"What do I know now that I did not know before?"

Just as we have learned the importance of naming and identifying our transitions and turning points, now, too, we must recognize our awakening, honor what we have learned by naming it wisdom, and understand the process by which we have been changed.

What is that process? **It is a certain kind of alchemy, one in which we take the unexpected and attempt to transform it into enlightenment.**

In the ancient art of alchemy, something is transformed from one form to another of greater value—lead into gold, for instance. This transformation occurs through a process of intense purification. A substance is heated, elements are separated, and a new essence is distilled to produce something precious and valuable.

This alchemical process is similar to what we have been examining—how to take something not particularly desirable that occurs in our lives and turn it into something valuable. In our journey of transformational alchemy, we, too, go through the fire of our own difficulties and challenges, and from these distill new meaning and wisdom.

One of the most exquisite examples of the transformational powers of alchemy is seen in the creation of the pearl. I have always loved pearls because of their luminous beauty. What is fascinating is that a pearl is the result of an oyster's defense against an irritant that has been introduced into its body. Either by natural or human means, a tiny piece of sand or shell becomes lodged inside the oyster. This irritates the oyster, which surrounds the foreign object with nacre, the same material used to make an oyster shell.

It can take years for an oyster to produce a pearl, and the bigger and more valuable the pearl, the longer it will take to grow. But here is where the alchemy comes into play. Pearls cannot be made from the irritant alone, nor can they be made just from the oyster. They are created from what the oyster does with the irritant. It is the alchemy of the secretions from the oyster and the piece of sand that produces the valuable pearl.

Like this, the unexpected comes into our lives in the form of struggle, pain and irritating obstacles. We feel its sting. It invades us, wounds us, but slowly a miraculous alchemy takes place. We surround the unexpected with our patience, our perseverance and our courage. And slowly, we make a pearl.

It is not our difficulties or our suffering alone that makes us wise. It is what we add to them— patience, perseverance, compassion, courage, love. From this combination, our priceless pearls of wisdom grow.

Coming into your wisdom means honoring the part you have played in the mysterious alchemy that makes up your revelations, rebirths and awakenings. Why is this so important? Most likely, you will someday again encounter unexpected twists and turns on your journey. At those moments, if you can recall the lessons you have learned, it will help make what you face a lot less confusing and frightening. Digging deep into the wisdom you have gained, you will be able to turn periods of questioning, challenge and transition into new times of growth, mastery and revelation.

Wisdom Born of Tears

There is a sacredness in tears.
They are not the mark of weakness, but of power.
They speak more eloquently than ten thousand tongues.
They are the messengers of overwhelming grief,
of deep contrition, and of unspeakable love.
—Washington Irving

All wisdom springs from some form of alchemy. Sometimes it is the process of being forced to find solutions for what appear to be insoluble problems that transforms us. Sometimes it is the alchemy of love, with all the exasperating ways it tests our heart, that births us into a new way of living. Then there are the times when life unexpectedly plunges us into sorrow and despair, and we are irrevocably changed, and ultimately awakened, through the alchemy of tears.

All of us have experienced times of sadness in our lives, when it is difficult to imagine ever being happy again. We try and reassure ourselves that some important growth and learning will eventually come from these painful experiences, but we don't completely be-lieve it. "How could what's happening to me possibly result in any good?" we wonder, afraid that the idea that everything happens for a reason applies to everyone else's situations, but not to ours.

Perhaps you are going through one of these times now. Perhaps as you read what I write about turning the unexpected into your own enlightenment, you are thinking, "This sounds very positive and uplifting, but my heart still hurts too much for me to see any purpose or meaning, let alone wisdom, in what I've experienced. Barbara doesn't understand how sad I feel."

Oh, dear one, but I do.

Here is what happened to me while I created this book for you.

There is never a good time for the unexpected," I wrote toward the beginning of these pages. I had no idea when I penned these words that soon the unexpected would smash its way into my life, and that as a result all I was telling you, and indeed, all that I knew, would be severely put to the test.

For many years, I have had three precious animal companions who are like children to me—my two bichon frise dogs, Bijou and Shanti, and my Himalayan cat, Luna. They are my family members, and have been my most devoted loved ones over the past fourteen years. The hardest part about traveling is not seeing them for weeks at a time. They hate when I leave, and invariably climb into my suitcases and lie there looking up at me with sad eyes, making me feel even more guilty than I already do. Of course, once I am actually gone, they get to be with my assistant, Alison, and her husband, Andres, whom they adore, and soon settle into a happy routine. Still, each time I say good-bye to them, my heart hurts.

It was very early one Saturday morning when the phone rang, waking me from a deep sleep. I had just arrived in New York the day before, and was in the middle of writing my section of the book on wake-up calls. I'd been working quite late the previous night, so I was very disoriented when I heard Alison's trembling voice on the other end of the line.

"Barbara, it's Luna," she said. "She's gone. She suddenly went into severe respiratory failure and stopped breathing. We rushed her to the hospital, but there was nothing they could do."

"This isn't real," I thought to myself as I began to shake uncontrollably. "I must be dreaming." But I wasn't. My Luna had died.

"I don't understand," I wept to Alison. "She was fine when I left just yesterday. What happened?"

"We don't know yet," she replied. "The vet couldn't tell us any more right now."

My heart filled with a sick, sinking sensation. For several weeks before this, I had been plagued by the inexplicable and bizarre thought: "Luna is dying." I knew this was impossible—she'd just been to the vet for a checkup and everything was normal. "I'm worried about Luna," I told the people close to me. "I have this awful feeling that something is really wrong." They assured me that Luna was in good health, assuming that I was just being over-protective. I reminded myself that I was under tremendous pressure writing the book, and that they were probably correct, Still, I hadn't been able to stop thinking that something terrible was happening, and the night before I left California, I was so agitated that I couldn't sleep.

Now, as I hung up the phone after hearing the worst, I knew I had been right. In some mysterious wordless way, Luna had been trying to tell me that she was leaving, and in that same mysterious way, I knew, but didn't trust my knowing.

I was overwhelmed with grief, and for days all I could do was weep. I had always expected Luna would be with me until the end, that my puppies would pass on first as dogs often do, and that

Luna would outlive them. "One day," I would think to myself sadly, "it will be just me and Luna." But she had been the first to leave. What had gone wrong? I had taken such perfect care of her, and she was still so young—just ten years old. How could I forgive myself for not having been there with her when she passed? Why was this happening now, of all times when I needed to be wise and strong to write this book?

Luna had always been the one to keep the night vigil with me when I was unable to sleep, or working late on a manuscript, or nursing a troubled heart. She would jump onto my desk when I was writing and sit on the papers as I tried to finish each chapter of a new book. She would come running up to the bathroom each evening when she heard the bathwater run and would perch gracefully on the edge of the tub and stare at me lovingly while I took my bath. She would sleep next to my head at night when I was alone, and kiss my hands to wake me up or just to say, "I love you." And during hard or lonely times, when I would cry in the dark, Luna would lick the tears off my face with her little pink tongue.

Luna was selfless—she demanded very little, generously allowing most of my worries and attention to be focused on my little dogs and their health issues, needs and concerns. She took care of me, and she took care of them, too, grooming her sister Shanti with her tongue as if she were one of her kittens, chasing my oldest dog, Bijou, around to keep him young and frisky, amusing them when I was busy and they were bored.

Anyone who met Luna knows how exceptional she was. She often sat upright against a wall or couch just like a furry white Buddha as she listened to our conversations. She would come running into a room to be part of whatever was happening. She would curl herself up next to the dogs for a nap. She would stare at you for minutes on end with her mysterious blue eyes as if to impart her wisdom.

How was I going to live without such a delightful source of joy and unconditional love by my side?

Several weeks after she died, we discovered that Luna had a very aggressive form of cancer that had presented no obvious physical symptoms, but had progressed to her lungs and brought Luna to the moment where she stopped breathing. She had been so brave, bearing her discomfort silently. I began to see that Luna had left just as she lived: *selflessly, thinking of how to make things easier for others, with strong intention, with dignity, with grace.*

Luna leapt into the Light with no hesitation or confusion. It was just her time to leave.

. . .

I called for help and there came to me a spirit of wisdom.
—the Wisdom of Solomon

Weeks passed, and as I mourned the loss of Luna, I struggled with my deep sadness about not having had a chance to say good-bye. "I wish I could see you one last time," I prayed to Luna's spirit. "I wish I could understand what I am supposed to learn from this."

One night Luna came to me in a very vivid dream. In the dream Luna was soaring and leaping in and out of my field of vision, as happy as I'd ever seen her. Luna would land in front of me, and then bounce back up into the air, far, far away. I noticed that she was wearing a thin rope lead like the one we used to put on her so she could wander around the garden or sit on the patio—except in the dream, the lead was so long that when she flew away, she could go on forever.

"Luna—you've come back to see me!" I cried with delight. "I'm sorry I never got to say good-bye to you." Luna's response to this was to once again land at my feet and then soar playfully back up into the heavens.

As I stood there in the dream, I realized what Luna was trying to tell me: she was still connected to me as she had always been, but now the leash was infinitely long, passing through time and space so that she could run free in another dimension. But where was the other end of the leash, I wondered? I began looking for it. Suddenly I realized the reason I couldn't see it: *it was tied inside my own heart.*

Once more Luna flew down, and this time I picked her up and embraced her, burying my face in her long, soft fur as I always used to love to do, hearing her loud, blissful purr rumble in my ear like a soothing mantra. And then she vanished out of my arms and was gone.

When I woke up, I felt a sense of peace I hadn't experienced since Luna had died. I knew Luna's soul body had come to comfort me, reminding me that our connection, though now invisible to the eye, transcended the physical and would always exist. And I knew that she had left me many gifts that, over time, I would discover. *"Trust,"* I seemed to hear her spirit whispering to me. *"Trust yourself. Trust what you hear and feel inside you. Trust what you know. Trust that love cannot be lost."*

My heart still aches in that place where Luna's physical presence used to be. I still weep for her. And there is a grief that has not left me, and perhaps never will, in the way grief becomes a form of our love for those no longer with us. But day by day, something else has happened: *I have discovered an unexpected deepening of my capacity to feel, an unexpected and heightened appreciation for each moment I share with my partner, my dogs and all those I love, and an unexpected new richness to the experience of being alive.* Luna's leaving cracked me wide open, and I know that this book would not have emerged as it has if I had not been forced, in the midst of writing it, to dig so deeply and feel so much.

It was important to me that I share this story with you. So often, when we are tested by sad, unanticipated times, we can't imagine how our sorrow will ever have meaning, let alone contribute to our wisdom. But I am more certain than ever that these tears, like everything else we have encountered on our journey, are part of what changes us with an incomprehensible alchemy. We feel the tears flood up from our broken heart, and we sink into them, fearing we will drown. Instead they become a sacred stream, carrying us out of our grief and our loss, carrying those we have lost home to the light—tears of remembrance, tears of blessing, tears of love.

My beautiful Angel Luna, may I always make my leaps as courageously and gracefully as you made yours.

Trusting Your Wisdom and Passing It On

Neither fire nor wind, birth nor death
can erase our good deeds.
—Buddha

I magine a world in which people were paid enormous sums of money not for how good they were at a sport, or how beautiful and thin they were, or how well they played an instrument or sold shares of stock, but for how wise they were . . .

Imagine a world in which we respected those who bravely faced their tests and turning points, and honored those who had been shattered awake, instead of judging them . . .

Imagine a world in which we recognized natural rites of passage as powerful, sacred times of radical rebirth . . .

Imagine a world in which our success was defined by how much wisdom we had accumulated, how much transformation we had undergone, how much inner awakening we had experienced . . .

As you emerge from your own Vision Quest, it is important that you honor it for what it has been—an initiation, a sacred journey into the mysteries of your own being. Welcome yourself into your new time of wisdom. Know that your journey of questioning and awakening has made you a truly successful human being, transforming you in ways you will continue to discover day by day.

. . .

We are all teachers, It does not matter if we want to teach or not—we still teach. Teachers are not just those of us who write books or give lectures, not just those of us who have students assigned to sit in our classes, not just those of us who have initials after our names indicating that we have an advanced degree. Each of us teaches others every day: our children, our lovers, our family members, our friends, our colleagues, everyone with whom we have contact in even small ways. We teach hope or cynicism, kindness or insensitivity, generosity or selfishness, trust or suspicion, love or apathy.

Andrew Harvey is one of the world's leading writers on mystical and spiritual traditions, and one of my favorite inspirational teachers. I heard him interviewed at Grace Cathedral in San Francisco, and one idea he expressed struck me deeply. *"Our job as teachers is to be in flame ourselves,"* he said, *"but also to help people, to encourage people to allow the flame to come and light them up."*

As you come into your time of wisdom, you must find ways to pass that flame of wisdom on to others. How do you do this? **Look for opportunities to share what you have with someone who needs it.** If your time of challenge has passed, then your task is to recall your moments of feeling lost, isolated, frightened of what was to come. Look around—you are sure to find someone who is experiencing that despair or confusion now. Share your strength and courage with that person. Have the willingness to offer your love, your service, your support, and opportunities will present themselves. You won't have to go looking for them—they will find you.

You do not have to be perfect to share your wisdom. Even if you are in the middle of your own challenges, you still have something to offer. Someone behind you needs your hand to help them take their next step. Perhaps you don't yet know how to climb up the step in front of you, but you know enough to help that person behind you up to their next step, upon which you are already standing.

Once you have gone through your own challenges and difficulties and come out the other side, you have something priceless to share. When you offer what you know to others when they need it, you solidify and recognize your new wisdom.

· · ·

Last week as I stood in a long line at the bank, I struck up a conversation with a young man behind me. We didn't discuss anything significant—just the usual polite chitchat one would make with a stranger—and our whole interaction lasted only one or two minutes. When it was my turn to go to the next teller, I said to the young man: "Have a nice day." He smiled sweetly and replied: "I'll do my best. **The hard part about living is leaving the world a better place than the day before."**

It is overwhelming to contemplate the task of trying to make a dent in the enormous amount of suffering, hatred and anger that exists in this world. When I watch the news, I feel heartbroken at the sheer ignorance and cruelty that are all too common on this planet. Still, this does not excuse me from doing my part to alleviate a small piece of that suffering.

I may not be able to do something for everyone, but I can do something for someone. In some small way, I can leave the world a better place than the day before.

Here is a true story:

In the middle of a busy and stressful week, I decided to go to a home furnishings store and buy some things I needed for my kitchen. As I wheeled my cart up and down the crowded aisles, I began to berate myself for even being there in the first place. "You have too much to do to be shopping," my inner critic scolded. "Think of all the projects you should be working on. Instead, you're here looking at omelet pans."

I didn't even have a response in my own defense. I was in one of those moods when nothing seemed right and everything annoyed me. Lately I had been very frustrated with the lack of support I was feeling from people I thought I could count on. I felt overburdened, as if the Universe was telling me I was going to have to do everything alone with no help from anyone.

As I made my way to the cashier, I realized that I'd forgotten my 20-percent-off coupon that I'd been saving to use with these purchases. "Shoot!" I exclaimed, angry with myself for being so spaced out that I'd left the coupon on the counter. My mood had now officially gone from bad to worse.

Just then I saw a woman walk in the front door of the store, glance up and down at the people in line, and start to walk toward me. "Oh boy," I thought cynically, "Probably someone who wants to get in line in front of me."

"Excuse me," the woman said to me as she held out a folded-up piece of paper, "But I wondered if you could use this discount coupon? I was passing the store when I realized I had it in my purse, and since I don't need anything now and it expires in a few days, I thought maybe someone else could use it."

I was stunned. I thanked her profusely and explained that I'd forgotten my own coupon and had just been wishing I had one when she walked in.

"Yep, well, like I said, I thought you might need it," she explained with a smile. "Bye-bye now." And with that, she turned and walked out the door.

That day I got more than my coupon, which I thought I needed. I got what I *really* needed—a reminder that I am always being supported, whether I know it or not. It was as if a cosmic messenger arrived with a telegram from God that said, "By the way, in case you think I've forgotten you, here's your coupon."

Several weeks passed, and I had to travel to Toronto to speak at a woman's conference. In my presentation, I talked about many of the ideas in this book, and shared the story of the coupon. At the end of my speech, a woman came up and pressed a folded note into my hand. "I know you're busy signing autographs," she said, "but when you read this, you'll understand how grateful I am that you came to Toronto at this exact time in my life when I needed to hear everything you had to say."

That night in my hotel room, I opened the note. It read:

You gave me my coupon! Thank you. Love, Julie

My eyes filled with tears as I read Julie's words. I felt deeply gratified knowing that she had received whatever she needed from my talk that day. That good-hearted woman who had given me the coupon would be amazed to know that her random act of kindness had inspired a slogan of sorts. I will always be grateful to her for showing up at the right moment. I will always be grateful to Julie for coming up with this phrase that embodies what it means to look for simple ways to serve others. And, of course, I hope I've given you at least one of your coupons in these pages.

**Find ways to share your love, your caring
and your wisdom.
Someone needs what you know.**

The Triumph of Wisdom

*Suddenly there was a great burst of light through the Darkness.
The light spread out and where it touched the Darkness,
the Darkness disappeared. The light spread until the
patch of Dark Thing had vanished, and there was only a
gentle shining, and through the shining came the stars,
clear and pure. A glimpse of the cosmic battle between
light and darkness, and the triumph of light.*
—Madeleine L'Engle, *A Wrinkle in Time*

Right here, right now, you are wise beyond your own imagining. There is an abundance of wisdom within you. It is wisdom carefully collected by your heart and by your soul from both joys and sorrows, wisdom retrieved from the wreckage of defeated dreams, wisdom faithfully salvaged from broken love affairs, wisdom painstakingly gathered from among the ruins of idealistic plans, wisdom sanctified by tears. It is the wisdom you have earned from being a parent, a friend, a husband, a wife, a brother, a sister, a grandmother or a grandfather. It is the incomparable wisdom that is the result of loving deeply and often, whether that love is for your partner, your family or your precious animal companions.

This wisdom—your wisdom—is a light brighter than any darkness you have encountered, and its power is more formidable than any adversity you have battled, It is a glorious medal won in your own secret wars, a symbol of your courage, your tenacity and your triumphant spirit.

This wisdom is the fruit of all your struggles.
   Do not let it go untasted.
You have earned this moment.

Arriving at the Placeless Place

You are that mystery which you are seeking to know.
—Joseph Campbell

You have been on a path since the moment you were born into this world.
No matter where your journey has taken you,
No matter where you believed you were going,
your path was always leading you to only one place—
Back to the wholeness of your own Self.

The road that leads you home to your Self is not a straight line from point A to point B. In fact, it is not a line at all. Rather, it is a spiral, swirling around through time and space, but never really going anywhere.

This is the mysterious paradox of our life journey: *We seem to be traveling somewhere, but we have actually been moving in circles, spiraling more and more deeply inward as we discover who and what we are.* Everything we experience, everything we love, everything we lose and everything we gain all ultimately serve to reveal more and more of our Self to us.

If we look around at the physical world, we can't help but notice that the sacred geometry of the circle is universally present in creation. It can be found everywhere, from the cells in our body to the electromagnetic fields around subatomic particles to the structure of snowflakes to the spinning planets in our solar system. Our own life began in the microcosmic circle of a fertilized egg, and our first home was in the safety of our mother's circular womb. Even the movement of time is circular—the changing of the seasons, the rising and setting of the sun and the moon, the flow of the tides.

The archetype of the spiral has existed since the beginning of civilization throughout all of the world's cultures—as an art form, a religious symbol, and a sacred vehicle for meditation. Spirals have been found on Neolithic rock carvings, indicating that the earliest human inhabitants of our planet considered them an important part of their cosmological understanding. Many ancient peoples and indigenous and Eastern religions depicted our life journey using sacred circular symbols—the Native American medicine wheel, the Aztec calendar, the Mandala of Hinduism and Buddhism, the circles in the Celtic cross, the interlocking halves of the Chinese yin and yang, and the mystical labyrinth.

These are physical representations of the great circle of existence and the interior journey of the soul. Each of them focuses our eye on a point within the symbol, as if gathering the outside energies and drawing them inward. In this way, they are designed as mystical and powerful forms of spiritual contemplation, inviting the seeker to travel within and discover the divine.

Here is the truth we begin to understand:

Reality is not linear at all—it is circular.
Life does not move forward in a straight line,
but swirls around in a mysterious cosmic dance

This radically transforms our vision of what the path toward happiness and wholeness should look like. Instead of imagining it as a superhighway leading us into the future, we begin to see it as a circle, spiraling us around and around, each revolution sending us deeper into the mystery and wonder that is our Self.

Native American wisdom teaches us that the life path of a soul is like the sacred hoop. Each individual travels on a circular path toward his or her own wholeness. A life is seen as complete when one has finished his own circle of lessons and learning. So, too, we are riding on our own cosmic merry-go-round. Even though we have believed otherwise, we aren't really going anywhere. *Where have we been rushing to, we wonder? What did we expect to find when we got there?*

Happiness, enlightenment, fulfillment—
all the experiences we have been seeking are only
available now, in this moment.
There is nowhere to go
but more deeply into the here and now.

This is the secret of the spiral: it brings us back to what great sages have called "the eternal Now." Reverend Joshua Mason Pawelek, an inspiring Unitarian minister, suggests this point of view:

> Perhaps the promised land is not out there in the future, but is here now. The religious task is not so much to journey to the promised land, but to recognize it in our midst and live it.

. . .

My place is the placeless.
—Rumi

What is at the center of the circle? Where is the sacred spiraling of our journey leading us? What is it that we will discover in the here and now?

In one of his poems, the great mystic Rumi calls it "the placeless place." He writes of inhabiting a realm within himself that transcends all roles, all definition and all limitation. It is only by finding our way to this placeless place within us, says Rumi, that we will truly ever feel free.

All of the world's spiritual traditions allude to this placeless place. In the *Tao Te Ching*, Lao Tzu calls this formless source of all existence the *Tao*, which is both the path and the goal. He writes:

> Look, it cannot be seen—it is beyond form.
> Listen, it cannot be heard—it is beyond sound.
> Grasp, it cannot be held—it is intangible.
> These three are indefinable, they are one.
>
> From above it is not bright;
> From below it is not dark:
> Unbroken thread beyond description.
> It returns to nothingness.
> Form of the formless,
> Image of the imageless,
> It is called indefinable and beyond imagination.
>
> Stand before it—there is no beginning.
> Follow it and there is no end.
> Stay with the Tao, move with the present.

Here, in the center of the circle of our existence, in a place that cannot be seen, that cannot be described, that has no form, we discover the ultimate secret that lies at the core of all mystical paths: **This cosmic source of creation that abides within us is our own divine nature.** The ancient Indian scriptures, the Upanishads, tell us: *"Tat tvam asi,"* "Thou art That." Our true Self is the same as that infinitely intelligent energy that has created all things. Everything we think we are—our mind, our personality, our experiences—are all just expressions of the One source.

We read this and feel awe at the insights of these great saints and seers. But what do these realizations have to do with us? The answer is: everything. They invite us to remember where we are really going, to understand that every achievement, every loss, every relationship, every problem, every lesson—all of these are delivering us to the same destination: that placeless place of truth and meaning within ourselves.

What we are learning, then, is how to recognize the placeless place, how to "stay with the Tao," how to find the still point in the spiral, how to discover the inner sanctuary hidden beneath our difficulties, beneath our pain, beneath our successes, beneath our dramas, beneath even what appear to be obstacles to our joy.

When we touch the center of our being, even for a brief moment, we remind ourselves that the peace and fulfillment we experience there are not something foreign to us, but are the true nature of our Self.

Lessons the Earth Teaches Us

Should you shield the canyons from the windstorms,
you would not see the beauty of their carvings.
—Elizabeth Kubler-Ross

Recently I was flying across the country, and rather than reading or working, I sat for several hours with my face pressed against the window of the plane watching the changing and miraculous landscape. We passed over great mountain ranges, vast deserts and ancient canyons. And from the sky I could see the scars and wounds of our planet.

Our earth has not had an easy time in her 4.6 billion years of existence. She, too, has known her challenges and catastrophes, and she, too, has been transformed by them. Her surface has been attacked by asteroids and meteors, some of which have created cavernous holes miles deep, others that have caused enormous dust storms that killed off most life for millions of years. Volcanic upheavals have pressed her surface upward, distorting her flatness into mountains, ripping her into pieces. The relentless sea has worn down her land, pulverizing it into sand and carving it into coastlines.

We never think about all our earthly home has gone through. The irony is that many of our beautiful planet's treasures in which we take the greatest delight have been born of what we would consider natural disasters. When we travel to national parks to witness deep, majestic canyons or gaze upon beautiful sparkling lakes, we are actually visiting spots where the earth has been assaulted by objects that have smashed into her from outer space. When we go to the seashore and walk on the beach, we are enjoying places that have been battered and broken by the angry ocean. When we go skiing or hiking, or when we gaze up at spectacular mountain ranges, we are enjoying the result of violent continental collisions that created the breathtaking peaks.

This is what we learn from truly scrutinizing our planet—her existence has not been stable, uneventful or free from calamity. She has been tested over and over again, crushed, cracked, eroded and shattered. *And yet the effects of these very difficulties have created some of her most exquisite gifts and breathtaking magic that fill our hearts with wonder and awe and bring joy to our everyday lives.*

We can learn so much from the earth. We, too, feel irrevocably marked by the events we have gone through. Our heart has its own canyons carved by grief. The shapes of our hopes and dreams have been battered by stormy tides of fate until they are often unrecognizable, even to us. We have been rocked by emotional earthquakes to our very core.

It is tempting to look at your life and allow these scars and wounds of your battles to define you. **Inhabiting the placeless place means reminding yourself that you are more than the events of your outer journey.** This is a delicate balancing act—to tenderly embrace your pain, losses and disappointments, to feel them, to honor them, but not to identify with them. It is saying: *"I see this, but I am not this."*

As I have come into my wisdom, I have learned not to define myself by what has happened to me on the outside, but rather by the metamorphosis that has occurred on the inside:

I do not define myself by how many roadblocks have appeared in my path. I define myself by the courage I've found to forge new roads.

I do not define myself by how many disappointments I've faced. I define myself by the forgiveness and the faith I have found to begin again.

I do not define myself by how long a relationship lasted. I define myself by how much I have loved, and been willing to love again.

I do not define myself by how many times I have been knocked down. I define myself by how many times I have struggled to my feet.

I am not my pain.

I am not my past.

I am that which has emerged from the fire.

Do not define yourself or allow others to define you by what has happened to you or what you've been through. Do not define yourself by your pain or even your triumphs. You are more than that.

You may have been divorced, but you are not a divorcee.

You may have a disease, but you are not sick.

You may have been fired from your job, but you are not without usefulness or purpose.

You may have lost someone or something, but you are not a loser.

You may have failed at something, but you are not a failure.

Your wounds are the sacred temple in which you have been transformed. They are the signs of your redemption; they are not your weakness. They are the road you have traveled; they are not who you are. Do not hide them, apologize for them or judge them. Embrace your scars. Honor them. When others notice them, proudly say:

"These tell the remarkable story of how I was made brave and wise."

Beyond your challenges, beyond your successes, beyond the events with which life has molded your spirit, there is a placeless place within you. It is a place of peace. It is a place of freedom. It is the place where the Self you have been seeking resides.

A Time for Blooming

From wonder into wonder, existence opens.
—Lao Tzu

When I first moved to Santa Barbara several years ago, I bought a beautiful cymbidium orchid plant. I have always loved orchids, and this particular one was large and full of exotic blooms. For almost two months the orchid thrived, but finally, one by one, the blooms died, until the orchid went dormant.

I knew that orchids are very delicate and difficult to grow, and I'd heard that if I cared for it properly, there was a chance that it would bloom again. With my busy traveling schedule, I didn't have time to repot the orchid during its dormant cycle as suggested, or move it from light to dark, and one temperature to another. All I did was put the pot outside in my garden and water it along with my other plants and flowers.

Six months passed, then a year, and the cymbidium still didn't bloom. "If it hasn't bloomed yet, it probably won't," a friend told me. "You may have damaged it by letting it get too hot or too cold." I knew she was right, but I couldn't bear just to throw the orchid plant away. So when it was time for me to move to a new home, I packed the orchid into the truck with my other healthy plants and put it in my new garden.

Another six months passed. By this time I had stopped checking to see if my orchid was going to bloom, and just accepted that it would never again be anything but a pot of limp green stalks. Still, I watered it faithfully, always remembering what it had once looked like.

That winter, it rained more than usual, and I didn't have to water my garden, because Nature did it for me. One sunny day, as I sat outside on my patio for the first time in many weeks, something unusual caught my eye. As I got up to see what it was, I was astonished to discover that it was my orchid, covered with beautiful pink buds that promised gorgeous blossoms! Where had they come from? Why hadn't I noticed the beginnings of their sproutings? I shook my head in amazement—it had taken the orchid almost three years to rebloom, but it finally did.

My orchid plant had surprised me. Deep within, in a placeless place I could not see, it *was* growing, it *was* renewing itself. It was waiting for its own time to blossom again. I smiled as I realized that I, too, had been a part of the orchid's resurrection. I had given up all of my expectations, I wasn't impatient and I had no timetable for any outcome. I had just kept caring for the orchid as best as I could. And when it was ready, it bloomed.

Inhabiting the placeless place in your life often requires nurturing your dreams, your visions and your self without any idea of what is going to happen.

It means relinquishing the timetable that would make you so much more comfortable.

It means trusting that there is life, hope and renewal even when it appears there is none.

It means holding onto your vision of what can be, even when nothing seems to be presenting itself to you.

It means remembering that there is a time for blossoming that is mysterious, nonlinear and beyond our comprehension, but that it cannot happen if you do not allow yourself to linger in the placeless place.

Years ago I taped a little piece of paper onto the edge of my computer screen. It contains a verse by Kabir, another great poet-saint of India. It is there to remind me about patience, trust and surrender:

> Wait for the opportune moment, oh my heart.
> Everything happens in its own time.
> The gardener may flood the orchard with water,
> But the trees don't bear fruit out of season.

Catching the Winds of Grace

The winds of grace are always blowing,
It is you that must raise your sails.
—Rabindranath Tagore

I stand outside tonight and watch the moon rise. From her throne in the sky, the moon reveals her dance of love. Some evenings, she boldly seduces us by displaying a beautiful piece of herself. On other nights, she withdraws her favor and teases us with the smallest, hardly noticeable sliver of silver. Sometimes she will hide herself from us so completely that it is as if she has disappeared.

On a full moon night like tonight, the moon offers herself to us in all her glory. She holds nothing back, spilling the perfect fullness of her radiance upon us. It is easy to admire the moon when it appears that she is bestowing more of her light. The truth is that the moon is always there, and her beauty is equally abundant even when we can't see it reflected by the Sun.

This is the nature of grace—the life-bestowing power of Universal Consciousness that mysteriously guides us toward more goodness, more wisdom, more freedom. Its presence is always there in our life, even when we can only see a sliver. Its support is always abundant, even when it appears that we are being offered less than what we think we need. And like the full moon, when the moment is right, the power of grace reveals itself to us completely, illuminating what had been a dark corridor of our journey, helping us to find our way forward.

As I watch the moon night after night, I learn to understand the mystery of grace. I learn to surrender to each phase of my journey, the times of darkness as well as the times of clarity. I learn to see that just as the moon never really vanishes, grace is equally there for me in every moment, even when I can't see it.

Perhaps this is what Tagore means when he reminds us that the winds of grace are always blowing, and that to catch the winds, we must raise our sails. How do we do this? *We invite grace into our life by our willingness to see the truth, to let go of what no longer serves us and to move out of our old, familiar harbors, traveling—even without a map—in whatever new direction grace takes us.*

This is how it often works. Grace waits for you to make the first move.

In this moment, your future is waiting—
not to be discovered, but to be created.
It is a work already in progress.
Each forward step you take invites the participation
of cosmic forces and the intervention
of unexpected miracles into your life.

Listen: The future is whispering to you.
Not from in front of you,
    but from within you.

. . .

Our task must be to free ourselves from this prison
by widening our circle of compassion to embrace all living
creatures and the whole of nature in its beauty.
—Albert Einstein

We live in difficult and troubling times. The twenty-first century has been marked by unexpected terrors and unimaginable challenges. It is easy to despair. It is easy to retreat. And it is tempting to tune out and turn away. My heart hurts when I consider that in my lifetime, I may never know a world that is free from war, from harshness, from hatred and from unnecessary suffering. I grieve that our children and their children may never get to live on a peaceful planet.

Whenever I become angry and frustrated at the inhumanity of humankind, I recall the late Carl Sagan's eye-opening model of the universe in the form of a "cosmic calendar," a model that is now taught in basic astronomy and science courses all over the world. Consider this:

Astrophysicists estimate that the universe is approximately fifteen billion years old. When they compress the age of the universe to the equivalent of a calendar year, the creation of the universe begins on January 1. The Milky Way forms on May 1, and our solar system doesn't come into existence until September 9. The first plants don't show up until November 28, and the first primates come into being on the equivalent of December 30. *Homo sapiens* arrive just minutes before midnight on December 31, and all of human history as we know it begins at 11:59:39. At 11:59:45, writing was invented. At one second before midnight, Columbus discovered America. **What we consider recent history is contained in a fraction of the last second of the year.**

In the scheme of things, we human beings have just gotten here. We are still so young. We have so much to learn.

Remembering this does not make living in challenging times easier, but it does give us the opportunity to practice compassion, for others, for the earth and for ourselves.

**Even when we don't know what else to do,
even when it seems that nothing we do can make a
difference, we can offer our love and compassion
to the pain we witness around us.**

The unexpected *will* continue to invite itself back into our lives and our world. Again and again, we will be required to navigate through adversity, obstacles, confusion and loss. Things will keep changing, in both welcome and unwelcome ways. Remembering this, even anticipating this, we stay anchored to that placeless place within ourselves and, from that refuge, share as much goodness and light as we can, wherever we can, whenever we can.

My friend and colleague Clarissa Pinkola Estes says:

> *Ours is not the task of fixing the entire world all at once, but of stretching out to mend the part of the world that is within our reach.*

Walking Around the Sacred Fire

> *In every soul, there is an "abyss of mystery."*
> *Each person has his abyss of which he is not aware,*
> *which he cannot know.*
> *When hidden things shall have been revealed to us,*
> *according to the Promise,*
> *there will be unimaginable surprises.*
> —Leon Bloy

So how should we travel the circular path? We walk in a circle, and hold our awareness not in front of us, but on that place deep in the center.

One summer several years ago, while participating in a meditation retreat, I was privileged to witness a formal three-day *yagna,* or sacred fire ceremony, performed by Brahmin priests who had come from India. Yagnas have been performed for thousands of years in the Vedic culture as a means of purification and alignment with the Divine. Yagna is a Sanskrit word that translates as "sacrifice." As Brahmin priests recite mantras and make offerings into a specially prepared fire, those witnessing the yagna are invited to enter into their own act of inner offering and sacrifice, letting go of whatever it is they wish to release. The sacred fire is said to transmute all that is not whole and perfect, so that we can experience the Divine within ourselves.

For several days, I sat with dozens of other spiritual seekers, watching with awe and fascination as the renowned Brahmin priests performed the very formal and intricate ritual building of the circular fire pit, which is as large as a small house. Then, chanting sacred Vedic mantras, they made offerings of clarified butter, seeds and grains into the fire. As the flames rose high into the air and the rhythmic sound of the chanting filled my head, I was deeply moved. I thought about all the things in my own life I wished to offer to the fire. *"Purify my heart of all that is not love,"* I silently prayed.

On the evening of the third day, the yagna came to an end. Now we were invited to make a sacred circular walk around the enormous fire, which was still blazing. This practice, called *pradakshina,* means to circumnavigate, or walk around clockwise. It is a traditional way to gain the benefit from the sacred rituals that have been performed, to take it inside you. We could walk around just once or as many times as we wished.

As I stood up to begin my *pradakshina,* my heart was beating rapidly. I knew this ancient practice was very powerful, and I could feel the energy that had built up over three days pulsating in the intoxicating atmosphere that filled the hall in which we had been sitting. Now, except for the crackling of the flames, there was only silence as many of us began slowly to walk around the outer edge of the round fire pit. There was no light except that of the orange flames, leaping high into the darkness, as if to welcome us on our sacred walk.

I had decided to walk around the fire 108 times, since that is a sacred number in India, suggesting completeness or wholeness. There are 108 beads on the Hindu and Buddhist rosary, or *mala,* for instance. I knew this many trips around the fire would take me several hours, but I sensed that something profound was going to happen, and I was ready. Besides, I had a lot I wanted to let go of.

As I began walking, I concentrated on quieting my breathing and calming myself. Soon I felt soothed by the warm of the fire and the stillness of the room. At first as I walked, I simply watched the firelight changing shapes and counted how many circles I'd completed. After a while, I started thinking about all of the things I wanted to release into the flames—my past, my limitations, my worries, my fears. I could almost feel the power of the fire pulling these out of my heart.

Some time passed, and I began to experience a loving energy emanating from the fire in the center out toward me. The heat of the flames was caressing me, soothing me, healing me. Now, as I walked, my eyes filled with tears of gratitude as I realized how much grace I had in my life, how many blessings had always been there, even when I'd felt utterly miserable and alone. I could almost hear a divine voice speaking to me from the fire, filling me with its wordless wisdom.

"This is the true meaning of the word 'yoga,' " I thought to myself, *"Reunion. I am reunitting with the essence of my Self. I am walking back to myself."*

Now there was nothing but me and the fire—no hall, no world outside the hall. There was just this circle of yoga, reunion. I felt myself spiraling deeper and deeper inward, until soon I was no longer aware of walking or of even having a body. All I could feel was the presence of the fire. I was one with the fire. I had disappeared into it.

And then the fire itself disappeared. There was no me. No fire. Just a silent throb of blissful awareness. *I had arrived at the placeless place.*

. . .

As I contemplated this rare and profoundly moving experience over the next few days, I recalled another of my favorite Rumi verses, translated by Shahram Shiva. I had read this poem many times, but had never fully understood it until my walk around the sacred circle.

> From the dust of the Earth to a human being
> there are a thousand steps
> I have been with you through these steps,
> I have held your hand and walked by your side.
> You may think that I have left you
> on the side of the road.
> Don't complain,
> don't become mad,
> and don't open the lid of the pot.
> Boil happily and be patient.
> Remember what you are being prepared for.

This is how I had felt, as if I had been heated by the fire, boiled by the flames, purified of everything and prepared for awakening. My walk around the sacred circle was a metaphor for the journey I'd been on my whole life. And now I knew I had never been alone. I had always been walking with grace.

This is our journey—to walk around the sacred fire of all that happens to us in life. Sometimes this walk will be joyful. Sometimes it will be hard. Sometimes we may only see the flames. We may feel burdened by the troubles and hurts we carry in our heavy hearts. But as we keep walking, focused not only on where we are going, but also on the placeless place in the center, a profound and unshakable peace will dawn from deep within us.

. . .

No tears in the writer, no tears in the reader.
No surprise in the writer, no surprise in the reader.
—Robert Frost

I found this intriguing quote by the poet Robert Frost when I first began doing research for this book. I liked the quote but put it aside, thinking that it seemed a bit dramatic. I had no idea at that time how many tears and surprises of my own I would encounter writing *How Did I Get Here?* and now that I am almost finished, the quote has indeed found its place in the book. I am amazed that somehow back then a part of me sensed what was to come.

For all the words I have shared with you, I cannot seem to find any to describe how important and life-changing this experience has been for me. If what I have written on these pages gives you even a fraction of what I have gained from its writing, then you will know from inside yourself what I have no words to say.

Right now, you and I are meeting in the placeless place. We are in two different locations, in two different times. I am writing this at one moment, and you are reading it later. But somehow, in this mysterious now, we meet, and our own alchemy takes place.

The mystical poet Hafiz writes:

"Between your eye and this page, I am standing."

Can you feel me?
I can feel you.

Everyday Nirvana

The life of one day is enough to rejoice.
—Zen master Dogen

Last week someone sent me an e-mail containing this humorous takeoff on a popular spiritual saying:

> Be here now.
> Be someplace else later.
> Is that so complicated?

Of course, the answer is: "No, it isn't complicated, but it is also not so easy." Fully inhabiting the present moment without being haunted by the past or worrying about the future is not a simple task. And yet that is exactly what we must do—strive to connect ourselves to a steadiness that will remain unmoving no matter what storms come. This is the placeless place, which can only be found in the moment we are in.

The Sanskrit meaning of the word "Buddha" is "awakened." The Buddha was enlightened because he was fully awake. **This is a new understanding of what it means to be wise—not to know, but simply to be aware; not to be certain, but simply to be awake.**

The great American spiritual teacher Ram Dass, who first introduced the phrase "Be here now" back in the 1960s, was recently interviewed after having suffered a severe stroke. When asked about his purpose in life, he replied:

> First I thought my life's work was psychology. And then I thought my life's work was psychedelics. Then I thought my life's work was bringing eastern philosophy to the West. . . . Whatever I'm doing now is my life's work, even if it's sitting by the window.

Perhaps this is the greatest tribute to a well-lived life, to be able to say: *"I was awake!"*

> To experience everyday Nirvana, everyday bliss,
> allow whatever you are doing in the moment
> to be your purpose.
> To do this, you do not have to be living a perfect life.
> To do this, you do not have to have things
> turn out the way you expected them to,
> or hoped they would.
> To do this, all you need to do is
> to just be awake.

. . .

> *Yes, there is Nirvana. It is in leading your sheep*
> *to a green pasture, and in putting your*
> *child to sleep, and in writing the*
> *last line of your poem.*
> —Kahlil Gibran

Once some years back, I had a near-death experience. I remember so clearly the grief I felt at the thought that my life was over. It was not regret that I wouldn't get to accomplish more successes in my career, or travel to any more fascinating places, or enjoy any of the things I owned. It was the fear that I would no longer be able to hold my dogs and cat in my arms, or look into the eyes of the man I loved, or hear the sound of the ocean, or feel the sun on my skin. It was grief for the loss of all the things I had not always remembered to cherish.

Everyday Nirvana is not flashy. I have had extraordinary peak experiences in my life. But if I had to pinpoint the occasions on which I felt my truest peace and my deepest contentment, they would not be these. They would be simple moments of sweetness and delight. They would be quiet moment of subtle miracles.

Every day that you are alive,
you are being showered by an abundance of
extraordinary gifts and priceless blessings.

Anytime you forget this,
talk to someone who has just a few days left to live.
He or she will tell you that each day you are alive
is reason enough for rejoicing.

Already Home

Once you realize that the road is the goal
and that you are always on the road,
not to reach a goal, but to enjoy its beauty and its wisdom,
life ceases to be a task and becomes natural
and simple, in itself an ecstasy.
—Sri Nisargadatta Maharaj

Where is the place in which you feel your love?
Where is the place from which your dreams are born?
Where is the place you go to pray for those who suffer?
Where is the place in which you hear God speak?
Where is the place from which you understand these words?

It is that placeless place within you,
    beyond all limits of this physical plane,
    beyond time, distance, logic, and reason,
    beyond all that comes and goes,
    beyond change.

In that place, nothing can harm you,
    and nothing can be taken from you.
In that place, you are whole.
In that place, you are free.

Find the placeless place within yourself.
Meet yourself there.
　You are already at your destination
　You are already home.

It has been my privilege to offer these pages to you.
　May the words I've shared open doors, kindle lights and help gently guide your way.
　May you travel knowing you are not alone, with Love and Grace as your ever-present companions.
　May abundant blessings always surround you, and fill your heart with peace.

Be brave. Be joyful. Be free.

Acknowledgments

The names of those who have loved me, guided me, supported me, inspired me, sustained me, protected me, healed me and nurtured me while I wrote this book are forever etched on the most sacred place in my heart.

I honor them here with my deepest love and gratitude.

My spiritual teachers and guides, divine and human, visible and invisible, in this world and beyond, especially Maharishi Mahesh Yogi, Gurumayi Chidvilasananda, Baba Muktananda, Swami Kripananda, and Chalanda Sai Mai Lakshmi Devi: for mystical initiations, oceans of grace and longed-for awakening.

My incomparable assistant, Alison Betts: for courageously leaping hand in hand with me off enormous cliffs, for loyally following me down unmapped and unfamiliar roads, for learning from me and helping me learn from you, for your impeccable integrity and strength of character that makes me feel safe leaning on you, for the private tears we shed together, and especially for sharing in my secret triumphs that no one else will even know to celebrate.

My mother, Phyllis Garshman, for teaching me the true meaning of devotion and for being a constant source of unconditional love; and Dan Garshman, for adoring my mother so unabashedly and for being proud of me through all my ups and downs.

Mariarosa Ortega de Muller and Walter Muller, for holding me up with loving arms, caring for me like a daughter and helping me achieve what once seemed impossible.

Harvey Klinger, my brilliant literary agent, for two decades of invaluable support, counsel, friendship, comic relief and so much more.

Everyone at St. Martin's Press: My publisher, Sally Richardson, for giving me the opportunity to share the message and wisdom of this book with so many people; my editor, Diane Reverand, for taking me under your protective wing, for generously sharing your abundant experience and expertise and for your compassionate patience as I waited for this book to emerge; John Murphy, Matthew Baldacci, James Di Miero, Steve Snider, Regina Scarpa, David Rotstein, Gregg Sullivan, Michelle McMillian, Mark Steven Long and all the rest of the team who have worked so hard to support this book.

Tom Campbell, for being the most wonderful of neighbors, and inspiring me with your steadiness, focus and courage; and Target, for always visiting just when I need a dose of kitty love.

Gail Schlachter, for this magical sanctuary high up on the hill that has nourished my soul and given me the most lovely womb from which to birth this book.

My fabulous girls from University of California at Santa Barbara: Helena Lor, Lindsay Watson and Jennifer Terry, for taking such good care of me and the "kids" when I was locked in my room writing all year.

Ruth Cruz, for all the ways in which you are part of my family.

Lorin Roche, for always and only seeing who I really am and reminding me of it with such loyalty and gentleness for the past thirty years.

Amanda Kamsler, my Australian angel, for being my sister, my confidante, my companion on the path and my own personal late-night advice hotline.

Bobbee Kellner, for the priceless gift of your friendship and for miraculously being there in Santa Barbara to welcome me into my new life.

Marilyn Tam, for being such a wise and dear friend whose

serene presence and generous spirit inspire me to always see the highest.

Daisy White, for a bond whose gift amazes us both.

Judith Light, for oneness that transcends time.

Marisa Morin, for keeping my awareness focused on the Light and for delivering cosmic messages with so much love.

Karin Chesley, for profound healing and a perfectly timed re-union.

Dr. Sat Kaur Khalsa for pointing the way home.

All my other dear ones whose love feeds my heart whether we are together or apart: Norman and Lyn Lear, Jack and Inga Canfield, Eric Dahl and Barbara Holdrege, Robyn Todd and David Steinberg, Gay and Kathlyn Hendricks, Pam Kear, Sandra Crowe, Michael De Angelis, Stella Der, Debra Poneman, and Sandy Jolley.

Special thanks to Robbie Gass, Jim Brickman, Chris Spheeris, Josh Groban, Gary Malkin, Michael Stillwater, Deuter, Riley Lee, Kathy Landry, Yanni, Peter Kater, R. Carlos Nakai, Stephen Halpern, Erik Berglund, Gerald Jay Markoe, Suzanne Cianni and Secret Garden, whose beautiful music I played day and night while I wrote. Your exquisite compositions became the emotional soundtrack that kept my heart open, allowing it to receive the wisdom that poured through me onto these pages.

My adorable blessings, Bijou and Shanti, now more than ever: for love so pure and precious that I am certain you are angels disguised as little white dogs, here to remind me of what heaven must be like.

And most of all, for my beloved Paul: without you, there would be no book, nor the courage it took to write it, nor any of the lessons it contains, nor the unimaginable happiness I have discovered by your side. There are no words on this earth to describe love that is this divine.

More About
Barbara De Angelis

Seminars, Online University and Professional Training

Barbara De Angelis offers workshops and seminars throughout North America as well as via the Internet. Her Online University and live tele-seminars are a convenient way you can work with Barbara to gain more wisdom and create powerful personal transformations, as well as train to become a certified coach in the Barbara De Angelis methods.

Personal Consultations

For those people who wish to work personally with her, Barbara De Angelis offers Transformational Consultations. These consultations are conducted by phone and are designed to assist you in gaining deeper understanding of your life challenges and issues, as well as to offer practical tools for making significant breakthroughs.

Speaking Engagements

Over the past twenty years, Barbara De Angelis has been a highly sought-after motivational speaker, giving hundreds of trainings and presentations to groups including AT&T, Proctor & Gamble and Crystal Cruise Lines, as well as major corporations, universities and health-care facilities throughout North America. Barbara is available for lectures, conferences and speaking engagements anywhere in the world.

Share Your "How Did I Get Here?" Story

Barbara would love to hear about the impact *How Did I Get Here?* has had in your life. Please send your stories to Barbara@BarbaraDeAngelis.com.

Contact Information

If you would like to receive a schedule of Barbara's seminars, wish to book her for an event or a consultation, or find out about a *How Did I Get Here?* Support Group in your area, please go to her Web site:

www.BarbaraDeAngelis.com

or contact her office at:

Barbara De Angelis
12021 Wilshire Boulevard Suite 607
Los Angeles, CA 90025
Phone: (310) 535-0988
E-mail: Info@BarbaraDeAngelis.com

A Special Invitation from Barbara De Angelis

SPREAD THE LOVE AND MAKE A DIFFERENCE

Dear Reader,

I hope that *How Did I Get Here?* has inspired you to honor your own wisdom and life lessons, and motivated you to make even more of a difference in the world. Remember: *You may not be able to do something for everyone, but you can do something for someone. Each day, in some small way, you can leave the world a better place than the day before.*

One immediate way you can do this is to share *How Did I Get Here?* with as many people as possible. Someone you know needs this book right now, and I need your help getting it to that person.

I've created an easy and immediate way that you can spread the love and make a difference. **If you know someone who could benefit from the information in this book, or if you would like to send a copy of *How Did I Get Here?* as a gift to someone special, please go to this Web address:**

www.BarbaraDeAngelis.com/spreadthelove

You will be able to order this book and have it sent as a gift, along with a special message from you, to the people you care about. *You can order as many books as you wish and personalize each message to your friends and family—and I will autograph each copy you order before we ship them for you.*

You will also be able to *e-mail a free excerpt* from *How Did I Get Here?* to as many friends as you wish without ordering anything. **To thank you for your help, we'll give you a year's free subscription to my monthly e-newsletter.**

Please take a moment to think of all the people whose lives you can touch by sharing the information in *How Did I Get Here?* Thank you for joining me as we make a difference in the world.

Spread the Love.

With deep gratitude,
Barbara